1–3 John

1–3 John

Worship by Loving God and
One Another to Live Eternally

John Paul Heil

CASCADE *Books* • Eugene, Oregon

1–3 JOHN
Worship by Loving God and One Another to Live Eternally

Copyright © 2015 John Paul Heil. All rights reserved. Except for brief quotations in critical publications or reviews, no part of this book may be reproduced in any manner without prior written permission from the publisher. Write: Permissions. Wipf and Stock Publishers, 199 W. 8th Ave., Suite 3, Eugene, OR 97401.

Cascade Books
An Imprint of Wipf and Stock Publishers
199 W. 8th Ave., Suite 3
Eugene, OR 97401

www.wipfandstock.com

ISBN 13: 978-1-4982-0160-5

Cataloguing-in-Publication Data

Heil, John Paul

 1–3 John : worship by loving god and one another to live eternally / John Paul Heil

 p. ; cm. —Includes bibliographical references and index(es).

 ISBN 13: 978-1-4982-0160-5

 1. Bible. Epistles of John—Commentaries. 2. Worship. I. Title.

BS2805.3 H43 2015

Manufactured in the U.S.A.   01/19/2015

Contents

Abbreviations | vii

1 Introduction | 1
2 3 John: The Elder to Gaius | 31
3 2 John: The Elder to an Elect Lady | 45
4 1 John 1:1–10: He Will Cleanse Us from All Unrighteousness | 57
5 1 John 2:1–14: If We Keep His Commandments the Love of God Has Been Perfected | 71
6 1 John 2:15–17: Do Not Love the Things in the World | 89
7 1 John 2:18–27: The One Confessing the Son Also Has the Father | 93
8 1 John 2:28–3:6: You Know Whoever Does Righteousness Has Been Begotten from Him | 105
9 1 John 3:7–12: We Should Love One Another | 114
10 1 John 3:13–17: We Ought To Lay Down Our Lives for the Brothers | 123
11 1 John 3:18–24: Believe in the Name of His Son Jesus Christ and Love One Another | 130
12 1 John 4:1–6: In This You Know the Spirit of God | 139
13 1 John 4:7–12: God Has Sent His Son so that We Might Live through Him | 149
14 1 John 4:13—5:2: Just as That One Is so We Are in This World | 157

15 1 John 5:3–12: This Is the Love of God that We Keep His Commandments | 172

16 1 John 5:13–21: All Unrighteousness Is Sin | 186

17 Summary and Conclusion | 200

Bibliography | 207
Scripture Index | 211
Author Index | 221

Abbreviations

AB	Anchor Bible
AUSS	*Andrews University Seminary Studies*
BDAG	Danker, Frederick W., Walter Bauer, William F. Arndt, and F. Wilbur Gingrich. *Greek-English Lexicon of the New Testament and Other Early Christian Literature.* 3rd ed. Chicago: Univeristy of Chicago Press, 2000
BDF	Blass, Friedrich, Albert Debrunner, and Robert W. Funk. *A Greek Grammar of the New Testament and Other Early Christian Literature.* Chicago: Univeristy of Chicago Press, 1961
BECNT	Baker Exegetical Commentary on the New Testament
Bib	*Biblica*
BIS	Biblical Interpretation Series
BNTC	Black's New Testament Commentaries
BSac	*Bibliotheca Sacra*
BT	*Bible Translator*
CBET	Contributions to Biblical Exegesis and Theology
CBQ	*Catholic Biblical Quarterly*
CBQMS	Catholic Biblical Quarterly Monograph Series
EDNT	*Exegetical Dictionary of the New Testament*
EvQ	*Evangelical Quarterly*

JBL	*Journal of Biblical Literature*
JETS	*Journal of the Evangelical Theological Society*
JSNT	*Journal for the Study of the New Testament*
JSNTSup	Journal for the Study of the New Testament: Supplement Series
LNTS	Library of New Testament Studies
NAC	New American Commentary
Neot	*Neotestamentica*
NICNT	New International Commentary on the New Testament
NovT	*Novum Testamentum*
NTL	New Testament Library
NTS	*New Testament Studies*
RevScRel	*Revue des Sciences Religieuses*
SBLECL	Society of Biblical Literature Early Christianity and Its Literature
SNTSMS	Society for New Testament Studies Monograph Series
SP	Sacra Pagina
THKNT	Theologischer Handkommentar zum Neuen Testament
WBC	Word Biblical Commentary
ZECNT	Zondervan Exegetical Commentary on the New Testament
ZNW	*Zeitschrift für die neutestamentliche Wissenschaft und die Kunde der älteren Kirche*

1

Introduction

FOLLOWING THE PLAUSIBLE VIEWS of a few others, I will treat the three letters of John as a unified epistolary package.[1] Accordingly, I will consider 3 John as a letter recommending Demetrius as well as Gaius to the audience of 1–3 John, a sister church to the church of the implied author, "the elder" (3 John 1:1; 2 John 1:1, 13). As an introductory cover letter for 1 John, 2 John places 1 John in an epistolary context. Originally written to be orally performed as a hortatory sermon for the church led by the elder at Ephesus, 1 John, together with 2 and 3 John, was possibly delivered by Demetrius to an outlying sister church.[2] Although the order in which they were authored was most likely 1-2-3 John, the order in which they were to be listened to by the sister church in the context of a communal worship service was most likely 3-2-1 John.[3] The close affinities between

---

1. "The three letters were probably sent at the same time to the same destination, for it would be difficult to account for the preservation of letters as unassuming as 2 and 3 John were they not the companions of a more significant writing. . . . The Johannine letters thus make most sense when viewed as parts of the same epistolary package" (Johnson, *Writings*, 497–98). See also Yarbrough, *1–3 John*, 329; Schuchard, *1–3 John*, 19–35; Jobes, *1, 2, & 3 John*, 28–29.

2. Trebilco, *Early Christians*, 263–70.

3. On the characteristics of 1 John, Edwards (*Johannine Epistles*, 45) notes: "The memorable, rhythmic, antithetical style and frequent repetitions suggest the inclusion of material designed for oral delivery and perhaps memorization." On 1 John as a sermon to be read during a worship service, see Hengel, *Johannine Question*, 48. For a recent discussion of the oral dimension of biblical texts, see Horsley, *Text and Tradition*.

the letters and the Gospel of John suggest that the elder authored all four documents. At any rate, the elder seems to presuppose that most of the members of the audience of 1–3 John were familiar with the content in the Gospel of John.[4]

In what follows I will propose two new contributions to the study of 1–3 John. First, I will present new comprehensive chiastic structures for each of the three letters of John based on concrete linguistic evidence in the text.[5] These chiastic structures will serve as the guide for my audience-oriented exegesis of these letters.[6] Secondly, I will treat these letters from the point of view of their worship context and themes. Not only were 1–3 John intended to be performed orally as part of liturgical worship, but together these three letters exhort their audience to a distinctive ethical worship. In accord with the subtitle of this book, I will propose that the three letters of John are concerned with giving their audience an experience of living eternally by the worship that consists of loving God and one another.

The Structures of 1–3 John

The Structure of 3 John

*The Brothers Have Testified to
Your Love before the Church (1:1–8)*

A ¹The elder to Gaius the beloved [ἀγαπητῷ], whom I love [ἀγαπῶ] in truth. ²Beloved [Ἀγαπητέ], concerning all things I pray that you are prospering and are in good health, just as your soul is prospering. ³ªFor I rejoiced greatly at brothers [ἀδελφῶν]

---

4. "It is clear then that the most significant 'influence' on the Johannine Letters is John's Gospel, or the traditions that came to be written in that Gospel" (Trebilco, *Early Christians*, 603).

5. For past discussions regarding the structure of 1 John, see Jensen, "Structure," 54–73; Jensen, *Affirming the Resurrection*, 196–97; Yarbrough, *1–3 John*, 21–24; Lieu, *Commentary*, 14–17; Kruse, *Letters*, 31–32; Marshall, *Epistles*, 22–27; Schnackenburg, *Epistles*, 11–13; von Wahlde, *Letters*, 19–20; Brown, *Epistles*, 116–29; Bigalke, "Unravelling the Structure of First John," 1–10; Bigalke, "First John Structure Resolved," 1–7; Thomas, "Literary Structure of 1 John," 269–81. On the structure of 3 John, see Clark, "Discourse," 109–15.

6. For the chiastic structures of other NT letters, see Heil, "Philemon," 178–206; Heil, *Ephesians*; Heil, *Colossians*; Heil, *Philippians*; Heil, *Hebrews*; Heil, *James*; Heil, *1 Peter, 2 Peter, and Jude*; Heil, *Book of Revelation*.

coming and testifying [μαρτυρούντων] to your truth [τῇ ἀληθείᾳ],

B ³ᵇjust as you in truth are walking [περιπατεῖς].

C ⁴ᵃGreater joy than these things I do not have,

B' ⁴ᵇthat I hear that my children in the truth are walking [περιπατοῦντα].

A' ⁵Beloved [Ἀγαπητέ], a faithful thing you are doing in whatever you accomplish for the brothers [ἀδελφούς] and this even for strangers, ⁶who have testified [ἐμαρτύρησάν] to your love [ἀγάπῃ] before the church, whom you will do well to send forth in a manner worthy of God. ⁷For on behalf of the name they have gone out, receiving nothing from the pagans. ⁸We then ought to support such as these, so that we may become co-workers to the truth [τῇ ἀληθείᾳ].⁷

An A-B-C-B'-A' chiastic pattern establishes the integrity and distinctness of this first unit (1:1–8). Several linguistic occurrences constitute the parallelism between the A (1:1–3a) and A' (1:5–8) elements of this chiasm. First of all, these elements contain the only occurrences in this unit of expressions for love—"beloved" (ἀγαπητῷ) and "I love" (ἀγαπῶ) in 1:1, "beloved" (Ἀγαπητέ) in 1:2, 5, and "love" (ἀγάπῃ) in 1:6. These elements also contain the only occurrences in this unit of the term "brothers"—ἀδελφῶν in 1:3a and ἀδελφούς in 1:5, as well as of the verb "testify"—μαρτυρούντων in 1:3a and ἐμαρτύρησάν in 1:6. And in 1:3a, 8 these elements contain the only occurrences in 3 John of "the truth" (τῇ ἀληθείᾳ) in the dative case with the article but without a preceding preposition (cf. 1:3b, 4).⁸

The only occurrences in 3 John of the verb "walk"—"you are walking" (περιπατεῖς) in 1:3b and "they are walking" (περιπατοῦντα) in 1:4b—determine the parallelism between the B (1:3b) and B' (1:4b) elements. Finally, the unparalleled central and pivotal C element (1:4a) contains the only occurrence in 3 John of the noun "joy"—"greater joy [χαράν] than these things I do not have."

---

7. All translations are my own. The aim is to present a strictly literal translation that attempts, as far as possible, to follow the Greek word order and to render the same Greek words with the same English equivalents.

8. Some of these chiastic elements form chiastic sub-units in themselves, which will be illustrated in the subsequent exegetical chapters of this study.

Diotrephes Does Not Acknowledge the Brothers But Demetrius Is Testified by All (1:9-15)

A ⁹I have written [Ἔγραψά] something to the church, but that one who likes to be first [φιλοπρωτεύων] among them, Diotrephes, does not acknowledge us [ἡμᾶς]. ¹⁰Therefore, if I come, I will draw attention to his works which he is doing, with evil words disparaging us [ἡμᾶς], and not being content with these things, he himself does not acknowledge the brothers and those wishing to do so he hinders and expels from the church.

B ¹¹ᵃBeloved, do not imitate the bad [κακόν]

C ¹¹ᵇbut the good [ἀγαθόν].

C' ¹¹ᶜThe one doing good [ἀγαθοποιῶν] is from God;

B' ¹¹ᵈthe one doing bad [κακοποιῶν] has not seen God.

A' ¹²Demetrius is testified by all and by the truth itself, and we [ἡμεῖς] also testify, and you know that our [ἡμῶν] testimony is true. ¹³Many things I have to write [γράψαι] to you, but I do not want through ink and pen to write [γράφειν] to you. ¹⁴I hope instead soon to see you, and we will speak face to face. ¹⁵Peace to you. The friends [φίλοι] (here) salute you. Salute the friends [φίλους] (there) by name.

An A-B-C-C'-B'-A' chiastic pattern establishes the integrity and distinctness of this second unit (1:9-15). Several linguistic occurrences constitute the parallelism between the A (1:9-10) and A' (1:12-15) elements of this chiasm. First of all, these elements contain the only occurrences in 3 John of the verb "write"—"I have written" (Ἔγραψά) in 1:9 and "to write" (γράψαι) as well as "to write" (γράφειν) in 1:13. These elements also contain the only occurrences in this unit of the first person plural pronoun—"us" (ἡμᾶς) in 1:9, 10 and "we" (ἡμεῖς) as well as "our" (ἡμῶν) in 1:12. And these elements contain the only occurrences in 3 John of words beginning with the Greek root φιλο—"likes to be first" (φιλοπρωτεύων) in 1:9 and "friends" (φίλοι) as well as "friends" (φίλους) in 1:15.

The only occurrences of expressions for "bad" in 3 John—"bad" (κακόν) in 1:11a and "doing bad" (κακοποιῶν) in 1:11d—determine the parallelism between the B (1:11a) and B' (1:11d) elements. Finally, the only occurrences of expressions for "good" in 3 John—"good" (ἀγαθόν) in 1:11b and "doing good" (ἀγαθοποιῶν) in 1:11c form the parallelism between the pivotal C (1:11b) and C' (1:11c) elements at the center of this chiastic unit.

The Structure of 2 John

I Ask that We Love One Another (1:1–13)

A ¹The elder to an elect [ἐκλεκτῇ] lady and her children [τέκνοις], whom I love in truth, and not I only but also all who know the truth, ²because of the truth that remains in us and with us will be forever. ³Grace, mercy, and peace will be with us from God the Father and from Jesus Christ the Son of the Father in truth and love. ⁴I rejoiced [Ἐχάρην] greatly because I have found some of your children [τέκνων] walking in truth, just as we received [ἐλάβομεν] a commandment from the Father. ⁵But now I ask you, lady, not as one writing [γράφων] a new commandment to you but that which we have had from the beginning, that we should love one another. ⁶And this is the love, that we walk according to his commandments. This is the commandment, just as you heard from the beginning, that in it you should walk. ⁷For many [πολλοί] deceivers have gone out into the world, those not confessing Jesus Christ as coming [ἐρχόμενον] in flesh. This is the deceiver and the antichrist. ⁸Watch yourselves, that you do not lose what we worked [εἰργασάμεθα] for but may obtain a full [πλήρη] reward.

   B ⁹ᵃEveryone going ahead and not remaining in the teaching [μένων ἐν τῇ διδαχῇ] of the Christ does not have [ἔχει] God.

   B' ⁹ᵇThe one remaining in the teaching [μένων ἐν τῇ διδαχῇ], this one has [ἔχει] both the Father and the Son.

A' ¹⁰If anyone comes [ἔρχεται] to you and does not bring this teaching, do not receive [λαμβάνετε] him into a house and do not utter a greeting [χαίρειν] to him. ¹¹For the one uttering a greeting [χαίρειν] to him shares in his evil works [ἔργοις]. ¹²Many things [Πολλά] having to write [γράφειν] to you, I do not wish to do so through paper and ink, but I hope to be with you and to speak face to face, so that our joy [χαρά] may be fulfilled [πεπληρωμένη]. ¹³The children [τέκνα] of your elect [ἐκλεκτῆς] sister salute you.

An A-B-B'-A' chiastic pattern establishes the structure of 2 John. Several linguistic occurrences constitute the parallelism between the A (1:1–8) and A' (1:10–13) elements of this chiasm: the only occurrences in 2 John of the adjective "elect"—ἐκλεκτῇ in 1:1 and ἐκλεκτῆς in 1:13; of "children"—τέκνοις in 1:1 as well as τέκνων in 1:4 and τέκνα in 1:13; of the verb "rejoice" or "greet" and the noun "joy"—"I rejoiced" (Ἐχάρην) in 1:4, "greeting" (χαίρειν) in 1:10, 11, and "joy" (χαρά) in 1:12; of the verb "receive"—ἐλάβομεν in 1:4 and λαμβάνετε in 1:10; of the verb "write"—γράφων in 1:5 and γράφειν in 1:12; of the adjective "many"—πολλοί in 1:7 and Πολλά in 1:12; of the verb "come"—ἐρχόμενον in 1:7 and ἔρχεται in 1:10; of expressions for "work"—"we worked" (εἰργασάμεθα) in 1:8 and "works" (ἔργοις) in 1:11; and of expressions for "full"—"a full [πλήρη] reward" in 1:8 and "may be fulfilled" (πεπληρωμένη) in 1:12.

Finally, the only occurrences in 2 John of "remaining in the teaching" (μένων ἐν τῇ διδαχῇ) and of the third person singular verb "has" (ἔχει) in 1:9a, 9b determine the parallelism of the pivotal B (1:9a) and B' (1:9b) elements at the center of the chiasm.

The Thirteen Microchiastic Units of 1 John

In what follows I will first demonstrate how the text of 1 John naturally divides itself into thirteen distinct literary units based upon their microchiastic structures as determined by very precise linguistic parallels found in the text. Where applicable I will point out how other lexical and grammatical features often confirm the integrity of these units. Second, I will demonstrate how these thirteen units form a macrochiastic pattern based upon very precise linguistic parallels found in the text of the parallel chiastic units. Third, I will point out the various transitional words that connect a unit to the immediately preceding unit. These various transitional words, which occur at the conclusion of one unit and at the beginning of the following unit, indicate that the chiastic units are heard as a cohesive sequence. These various transitional words are italicized in the translation of the units below.

INTRODUCTION

1. He Will Cleanse Us from All Unrighteousness (1:1–10)

IF IN THE LIGHT WE ARE WALKING, WE HAVE FELLOWSHIP WITH ONE ANOTHER[9]

A   ^{1:1}What was from the beginning, what we have heard, what we have seen with our eyes, what we observed and our hands touched concerning the word [λόγου] of the life—²indeed the life was manifested and we have seen and testify and declare to you the life eternal which was with the Father and manifested to us—³what we have seen and heard, we declare also to you, so that you also may have fellowship with us. And the fellowship that is ours is with the Father and with his Son Jesus [τοῦ υἱοῦ αὐτοῦ Ἰησοῦ] Christ. ⁴And these things indeed we are writing, so that our joy may be fulfilled. ⁵ᵃAnd this is the message which we have heard from him and announce to you,

    B   ^{5b}that God is light [φῶς] and there is no darkness in him at all. ⁶ᵃIf we say that fellowship we have [κοινωνίαν ἔχομεν] with him yet in the darkness are walking [περιπατῶμεν],

        C   ^{6b}we are lying and not doing the truth.

    B'   ^{7a}But if in the light [φωτί] we are walking [περιπατῶμεν] as he is in the light [φωτί], fellowship we have [κοινωνίαν ἔχομεν] with one another

A'   ^{7b}and the blood of Jesus his Son [Ἰησοῦ τοῦ υἱοῦ αὐτοῦ] cleanses us from all sin. ⁸If we say that sin we do not have, we are deceiving ourselves and the truth is not in us. ⁹If we confess our sins, he is faithful and righteous, so that he will forgive us the sins and cleanse us from all unrighteousness. ¹⁰If we say that we have not *sinned*, we make him a liar and his word [λόγος] is not in us.

An A-B-C-B'-A' chiastic pattern establishes the integrity and distinctness of this first unit (1:1–10). The only occurrences in this unit of the term "word"—λόγου in 1:1 and λόγος in 1:10—and of references to Jesus as God's Son—"his Son Jesus" (τοῦ υἱοῦ αὐτοῦ Ἰησοῦ) in 1:3 and "Jesus his Son" (Ἰησοῦ τοῦ υἱοῦ αὐτοῦ) in 1:7b—constitute the parallelism

---

9. The main heading of each unit is intended to summarize the unit as it relates to its parallel unit within the overall macrochiastic structure of 1 John, while the subheading of each unit is intended to summarize or characterize the microchiastic dimension of each unit.

between the A (1:1–5a) and A' (1:7b–10) elements of this chiasm. The only occurrences in this unit of "light," φῶς in 1:5b and φωτί twice in 1:7a, of "we are walking" (περιπατῶμεν) in 1:6a, 7a, and of "fellowship we have" (κοινωνίαν ἔχομεν) in 1:6a, 7a determine the parallelism between the B (1:5b–6a) and the B' (1:7a) elements. Finally, the unparalleled central and pivotal C element (1:6b) contains the only occurrence in 1 John of the verb "we are lying" (ψευδόμεθα).

2. If We Keep His Commandments the Love of God Has Been Perfected (2:1–14)

You have known the one who is from the beginning

A   ²:¹My little children [τεκνία], these things I am writing to you so that you may not *sin*. But if anyone sins, we have an advocate with the Father, Jesus Christ the righteous one. ²And he himself is the expiation for our sins [ἁμαρτιῶν], not for ours only but also for the whole world. ³And in this we know [γινώσκομεν] that we have known [ἐγνώκαμεν] him, if we keep his commandments. ⁴The one saying, "I have known [ἔγνωκα] him," but not keeping his commandments, is a liar and the truth is not in this one. ⁵But whoever keeps his word, truly in this one the love of God has been perfected. In this we know [γινώσκομεν] that we are in him.

  B   ⁶The one saying that he remains in him ought, just as that one walked [περιεπάτησεν], he himself thus to walk [περιπατεῖν].

    C   ⁷ᵃBeloved, not a new commandment am I writing to you [ἐντολὴν καινὴν γράφω ὑμῖν] but an old commandment which you have had from the beginning. The old commandment

      D   ⁷ᵇis the word which you heard.

    C'   ⁸ᵃOn the other hand, a new commandment I am writing to you [ἐντολὴν καινὴν γράφω ὑμῖν], which is true in him and in you,

  B'   ⁸ᵇbecause the darkness is passing away and the true light already is shining. ⁹The one saying that he is in the light but hating his brother is still in the darkness. ¹⁰The one loving his brother remains in the light and there is no fault in him. ¹¹But the one hating his brother is in the darkness and in the darkness is walking [περιπατεῖ] and does not know where he is going, because the darkness has blinded his eyes.

A' ¹²I am writing to you, little children [τεκνία], because the sins [ἁμαρτίαι] have been forgiven for you on account of his name. ¹³I am writing to you, fathers, because you have known [ἐγνώκατε] the one who is from the beginning. I am writing to you, young men, because you have conquered the evil one. ¹⁴I have written to you, young children, because you have known [ἐγνώκατε] the *Father*. I have written to you, fathers, because you have known [ἐγνώκατε] the one who is from the beginning. I have written to you, young men, because you are strong and the word of God in you remains and you have conquered the evil one.

"So that you may not sin [ἁμάρτητε]" at the beginning of this unit in 2:1 recalls "if we say that we have not sinned [ἡμαρτήκαμεν]" at the conclusion of the preceding unit in 1:10. These first two occurrences in 1 John of the verb "sin" thus serve as the transitional terms linking the first unit (1:1–10) to the second unit (2:1–14).

An A-B-C-D-C'-B'-A' chiastic pattern secures the integrity and distinctness of this second unit (2:1–14). Several linguistic occurrences constitute the parallelism between the A (2:1–5) and the A' (2:12–14) elements of this chiasm: the only occurrences in this unit of "little children" (τεκνία) in 2:1, 12; of the noun "sins"—ἁμαρτιῶν in 2:1 and ἁμαρτίαι in 2:12; and of the verb "know"—γινώσκομεν in 2:3, 5; ἐγνώκαμεν in 2:3; ἔγνωκα in 2:4; and ἐγνώκατε in 2:13, 14 (2x). The only occurrences in this unit of the verb "walk"—περιεπάτησεν as well as περιπατεῖν in 2:6, and περιπατεῖ in 2:11—determine the parallelism between the B (2:6) and the B' (2:8b–11) elements. The only occurrences in 1 John of "a new commandment am I writing to you" (ἐντολὴν καινὴν γράφω ὑμῖν) in 2:7a, 8a establish the parallelism between the C (2:7a) and the C' (2:8a) elements. Finally, the unparalleled central and pivotal D (2:7b) element contains the only occurrence in 1 John of the expression "the word which you heard" (ὁ λόγος ὃν ἠκούσατε).

3. Do Not Love the Things in the World (2:15-17)

THE ONE DOING THE WILL OF GOD REMAINS FOREVER

A ¹⁵Do not love the world [τὸν κόσμον] or the things in the world [τῷ κόσμῳ]. If anyone loves the world [τὸν κόσμον], the love of the *Father* [τοῦ πατρός] is not [οὐκ ἔστιν] in him, ¹⁶ᵃbecause all that is in the world [τῷ κόσμῳ]—the desire [ἡ ἐπιθυμία] of the flesh and the desire [ἡ ἐπιθυμία] of the eyes

B ¹⁶ᵇand the arrogance concerning the livelihood,

A' ¹⁶ᶜis not [οὐκ ἔστιν] from the Father [τοῦ πατρός] but is from the world [τοῦ κόσμου]. ¹⁷Yet the world [ὁ κόσμος] is passing away and the desire [ἡ ἐπιθυμία] concerning it, but the one doing the will of God *remains* forever.

"The love of the Father [τοῦ πατρός]" at the beginning of this unit in 2:15 recalls "because you have known the Father [τὸν πατέρα]" toward the conclusion of the preceding unit in 2:14. These successive references to God as the Father serve as the transitional terms linking the second unit (2:1-14) to the third unit (2:15-17).

An A-B-A' chiastic pattern establishes the integrity and distinctness of this third unit (2:15-17). Several linguistic occurrences constitute the parallelism between the A (2:15-16a) and the A' (2:16c-17) elements of this chiasm: the only occurrences in this unit of "the world"—τὸν κόσμον twice in 2:15, τῷ κόσμῳ in 2:15, 16a, τοῦ κόσμου in 2:16c, and ὁ κόσμος in 2:17; of "the Father" (τοῦ πατρός) and of "is not" (οὐκ ἔστιν) in 2:15, 16c; and in 1 John of "the desire" (ἡ ἐπιθυμία) in 2:16a (2x), 17. The unparalleled central and pivotal B (2:16b) element contains the only occurrence in 1 John of the expression "the arrogance concerning the livelihood" (ἡ ἀλαζονεία τοῦ βίου).

4. The One Confessing the Son Also Has the Father (2:18-27)

REMAIN IN HIM WHO PROMISED US LIFE ETERNAL

A ¹⁸Young children, it is the last hour, and just as you heard [ἠκούσατε] that the antichrist is coming, so now many antichrists have appeared. Thus we know that it is the last hour. [19]From us they have gone out but they were not from us. For if they were from us, they would have *remained* [μεμενήκεισαν] with us, but rather so that they may be manifested that they all are not from us. [20]But you have an anointing [χρῖσμα] from the holy one and all of you know. [21]I have written to you [ἔγραψα ὑμῖν] not because you do not know the truth [ἀλήθειαν], but because you know it, and because every lie [ψεῦδος] is not from the truth [ἀληθείας].

B   [22a]Who is the liar but the one who denies [ἀρνούμενος], saying, "Jesus is not the Christ [οὐκ ἔστιν ὁ Χριστός]?"

B'   [22b]This is the antichrist [ἐστιν ὁ ἀντίχριστος], the one who denies [ἀρνούμενος] the Father and the Son. [23]Everyone who denies [ἀρνούμενος] the Son does not have the Father. The one confessing the Son also has the Father.

A'   [24]As for you, what you heard [ἠκούσατε] from the beginning, in you let it remain [μενέτω]. If in you remains [μείνῃ] what from the beginning you heard [ἠκούσατε], you also will remain [μενεῖτε] in the Son and in the Father. [25]And this is the promise that he himself promised to us—the life eternal. [26]These things I have written to you [ἔγραψα ὑμῖν] concerning those deceiving you. [27]And as for you, the anointing [χρῖσμα] that you received from him remains [μένει] in you and you do not have need that anyone teach you. But as his anointing [χρῖσμα] teaches you concerning all things, indeed it is true [ἀληθές] and is not a lie [ψεῦδος], and just as it has taught you, *remain* [μένετε] *in him*.

"They would have remained [μεμενήκεισαν] with us" near the beginning of this unit in 2:19 recalls "but the one doing the will of God remains [μένει] forever" at the conclusion of the preceding unit in 2:17. These successive occurrences of the verb "remain" serve as the transitional terms linking the third unit (2:15–17) to the fourth unit (2:18–27).

An A-B-B'-A' chiastic pattern secures the integrity and distinctness of this fourth unit (2:18–27). Several linguistic occurrences constitute the parallelism between the A (2:18–21) and the A' (2:24–27) elements of this chiasm: the only occurrences in this unit of "you heard" (ἠκούσατε) in 2:18 and twice in 2:24; of the verb "remain"—μεμενήκεισαν in 2:19, μενέτω, μείνῃ, and μενεῖτε in 2:24, μένει and μένετε in 2:27; in 1 John of "anointing" (χρῖσμα) in 2:20, 27; in this unit of "I have written to you" (ἔγραψα ὑμῖν) in 2:21, 26; of "truth/true"—ἀλήθειαν as well as ἀληθείας in 2:21and ἀληθές in 2:27; and in 1 John of "lie" (ψεῦδος) in 2:21, 27. The only occurrences in 1 John of "denies" (ἀρνούμενος) in 2:22a, 22b, 23 and of the antithetical statements "is not the Christ" (οὐκ ἔστιν ὁ Χριστός) in 2:22a and "is the antichrist" (ἐστιν ὁ ἀντίχριστος) in 2:22b establish the parallelism between the B (2:22a) and the B' (2:22b–23) elements at the pivotal center of this chiastic unit.

5. You Know Whoever Does Righteousness Has Been Begotten from Him (2:28–3:6)

EVERYONE WHO SINS HAS NEITHER SEEN HIM NOR KNOWN HIM

A [28]And now, little children, *remain in him* [μένετε ἐν αὐτῷ], so that when he is manifested [φανερωθῇ] we may have confidence and not be shamed away from him at his coming. [29]If you know [εἰδῆτε] that he is righteous, you know [γινώσκετε] that also everyone who does [πᾶς ὁ ποιῶν] righteousness from him has been begotten. [3:1]See [ἴδετε] what sort of love the Father has given us, that we may be called children of God, and indeed we are. For this reason the world does not know [γινώσκει] us, because it did not know [ἔγνω] him. [2]Beloved, now we are children of God, but it has not yet been manifested [ἐφανερώθη] what we will be. We know [οἴδαμεν] that when it is manifested [φανερωθῇ], we will be like him, because we will see [ὀψόμεθα] him just as he is.

B [3a]And everyone who has this hope in him purifies [ἁγνίζει] himself,

B' [3b]just as that one is pure [ἁγνός].

A' [4]Everyone who *does* [Πᾶς ὁ ποιῶν] *sin* also does lawlessness, indeed sin is lawlessness. [5]And you know [οἴδατε] that that one was manifested [ἐφανερώθη], so that he might take away sins, but sin is not in him. [6]Everyone who in him remains [ὁ ἐν αὐτῷ μένων] does not sin. Everyone who sins has neither seen [ἑώρακεν] him nor known [ἔγνωκεν] him.

"Remain in him" (μένετε ἐν αὐτῷ) at the beginning of this unit in 2:28 repeats "remain in him" (μένετε ἐν αὐτῷ) at the conclusion of the preceding unit in 2:27. These identical exhortations to remain in the

Son of the Father serve as the transitional terms linking the fourth unit (2:18–27) to the fifth unit (2:28–3:6).

An A-B-B'-A' chiastic pattern secures the integrity and distinctness of this fifth unit (2:28–3:6). Several linguistic occurrences constitute the parallelism between the A (2:28–3:2) and the A' (3:4–6) elements of this chiasm: the only occurrences in this unit of expressions for "remaining in him"—"remain in him" (μένετε ἐν αὐτῷ) in 2:28 and "who in him remains" (ὁ ἐν αὐτῷ μένων) in 3:6; of the verb "manifest"—φανερωθῇ in 2:28 and 3:2 as well as ἐφανερώθη in 3:2, 4; of the verb "know"—εἰδῆτε and γινώσκετε in 2:29, γινώσκει and ἔγνω in 3:1, οἴδαμεν in 3:2, οἴδατε in 3:5, and ἔγνωκεν in 3:6; of "everyone who does" (πᾶς ὁ ποιῶν) in 2:29 and 3:4; and of the verb "see"—ἴδετε in 3:1, ὀψόμεθα in 3:2, and ἑώρακεν in 3:6. The only expressions in 1 John of "purify/pure"—ἁγνίζει in 3:3a and ἁγνός in 3:3b—determine the parallelism between the B (3:3a) and the B' (3:3b) elements at the pivotal center of this chiastic unit.

6. We Should Love One Another (3:7–12)

The one not loving his brother is not from God

A ⁷Little children, let no one deceive you. The one doing righteousness [ποιῶν τὴν δικαιοσύνην] is righteous [δίκαιός], just as that one is righteous [δίκαιός]. ⁸The one *doing sin* is from the devil, for from the beginning [ἀπ' ἀρχῆς] the devil has been sinning. For this the Son of God was manifested, so that he might destroy the works [τὰ ἔργα] of the devil. ⁹Everyone [πᾶς] who has been begotten from God [ἐκ τοῦ θεοῦ] does not do sin, because his seed remains in him, and thus he is not able to sin, because from God [ἐκ τοῦ θεοῦ] he has been begotten.

B ¹⁰ᵃIn this is manifest the children [τὰ τέκνα] of God

B' ¹⁰ᵇand the children [τὰ τέκνα] of the devil.

A' ¹⁰ᶜEveryone [πᾶς] who does not do righteousness [ποιῶν δικαιοσύνην] is not from God [ἐκ τοῦ θεοῦ], that is, the one not loving his brother. ¹¹For this is the message which you heard from the beginning [ἀπ' ἀρχῆς], that we should love one another, ¹²not like Cain. He was from the evil one and slaughtered his brother. And why did he slaughter him? Because his works [τὰ ἔργα] were evil but those of his *brother* righteous [δίκαια].

"The one doing sin" (ὁ ποιῶν τὴν ἁμαρτίαν) near the beginning of this unit in 3:8 recalls "everyone who does sin [ὁ ποιῶν τὴν ἁμαρτίαν]" near the conclusion of the preceding unit in 3:4. These identical references to one who does sin serve as the transitional terms linking the fifth unit (2:28–3:6) to the sixth unit (3:7–12).

An A-B-B'-A' chiastic pattern secures the integrity and distinctness of this sixth unit (3:7–12). Several linguistic occurrences constitute the parallelism between the A (3:7–9) and the A' (3:10c–12) elements of this chiasm: the only occurrences in this unit of "doing righteousness"—ποιῶν τὴν δικαιοσύνην in 3:7 and ποιῶν δικαιοσύνην in 3:10c; of "righteous"—δίκαιός twice in 3:7 and δίκαια in 3:12; of "from the beginning" (ἀπ' ἀρχῆς) in 3:8, 11; of "the works" (τὰ ἔργα) in 3:8, 12; of "everyone"—"everyone [πᾶς] who has been begotten" in 3:9 and "everyone [πᾶς] who does not do righteousness" in 3:10c; and of "from God" (ἐκ τοῦ θεοῦ) in 3:9 (2x), 10c. The only occurrences in this unit of "the children" (τὰ τέκνα) in 3:10a, 10b determine the parallelism between the B (3:10a) and the B' (3:10b) elements at the pivotal center of this chiastic unit.

7. *We Ought to Lay Down Our Lives for the Brothers (3:13–17)*

WHOEVER HATES HIS BROTHER DOES NOT HAVE
LIFE ETERNAL REMAINING IN HIM

A   ¹³And do not be amazed, *brothers*, if the world [κόσμος] hates you. ¹⁴We know that we have moved from death to life, because we love the brothers. The one not loving remains in death. ¹⁵Everyone who hates his brother is a murderer, and you know that every murderer does not have [ἔχει] life eternal in him remaining [ἐν αὐτῷ μένουσαν].

    B   ^{16a}In this we have known love, that that one for [ὑπέρ] us his life [ψυχήν] laid down [ἔθηκεν];

    B'   ^{16b}so we ourselves ought for [ὑπέρ] the brothers our lives [ψυχάς] to lay down [θεῖναι].

A'   ¹⁷But whoever has [ἔχῃ] the livelihood of the world [κόσμου] and observes his brother having [ἔχοντα] a need and shuts off his compassion from him, how does the *love* of God remain in him [μένει ἐν αὐτῷ]?

The address "brothers" (ἀδελφοί) at the beginning of this unit in 3:13 recalls the reference to the "brother" (ἀδελφοῦ) of Cain at the conclusion of the preceding unit in 3:12. These successive occurrences of the word for "brother" serve as the transitional terms linking the sixth unit (3:7–12) to the seventh unit (3:13–17).

An A-B-B'-A' chiastic pattern secures the integrity and distinctness of this seventh unit (3:13–17). Several linguistic occurrences constitute the parallelism between the A (3:13–15) and the A' (3:17) elements of this chiasm: the only occurrences in this unit of the word "world"—κόσμος in 3:13 and κόσμου in 3:17; of the verb "have"—ἔχει in 3:15 and ἔχῃ as well as ἔχοντα in 3:17; of the expression "remain in him"—ἐν αὐτῷ μένουσαν in 3:15 and μένει ἐν αὐτῷ in 3:17. The only occurrences in 1 John of the expression "to lay down one's life for someone"—"for [ὑπέρ] us his life [ψυχήν] laid down [ἔθηκεν]" in 3:16a and "for [ὑπέρ] the brothers our lives [ψυχάς] to lay down [θεῖναι]" in 3:16b—determine the parallelism between the B (3:16a) and the B' (3:16b) elements at the pivotal center of this chiastic unit.

8. Believe in the Name of His Son Jesus Christ and Love One Another (3:18–24)

IF OUR HEART DOES NOT CONDEMN, WE HAVE CONFIDENCE WITH GOD

A   ¹⁸Little children, let us not *love* [ἀγαπῶμεν] with word or with the tongue but in work and truth. ^{19a}And in this we will know [ἐν τούτῳ γνωσόμεθα] that we are from the truth,

    B   ^{19b}and before him [ἔμπροσθεν αὐτοῦ] we will assure our heart [καρδίαν ἡμῶν], ^{20a}that if our heart [ἡμῶν ἡ καρδία] condemns [καταγινώσκῃ], that God [θεός] is greater than our heart [καρδίας ἡμῶν]

        C   ^{20b}and knows all things.

    B'   ²¹Beloved, if our heart [καρδία ἡμῶν] does not condemn [καταγινώσκῃ], we have confidence with God [θεόν] ²²and whatever we ask we receive from him, because we keep

> his commandments and do the things pleasing before him [ἐνώπιον αὐτοῦ].

A' > ²³And this is his commandment, that we should believe in the name of his Son Jesus Christ and we should love [ἀγαπῶμεν] one another, just as he gave the commandment to us. ²⁴And the one keeping his commandments in him remains and he in him. And in this we know [ἐν τούτῳ γινώσκομεν] that he remains in us, from the *Spirit* which to us he gave.

The verb for love in the exhortation "let us not love [ἀγαπῶμεν] with word or with the tongue" at the beginning of this unit in 3:18 recalls the noun for love in the question of "how does the love [ἀγάπη] of God remain in him" at the conclusion of the preceding unit in 3:17. These successive references to love serve as the transitional terms linking the seventh unit (3:13–17) to the eighth unit (3:18–24).

An A-B-C-B'-A' chiastic pattern secures the integrity and distinctness of this eighth unit (3:18–24). Several linguistic occurrences constitute the parallelism between the A (3:18–19a) and the A' (3:23–24) elements of this chiasm: the only occurrences in this unit of the verb for love—ἀγαπῶμεν in 3:18, 23, as well as of the similar expressions "in this we will know" (ἐν τούτῳ γνωσόμεθα) in 3:19a and "in this we know" (ἐν τούτῳ γινώσκομεν) in 3:24. The only occurrences in 1 John of the prepositional phrase "before him"—ἔμπροσθεν αὐτοῦ in 3:19b and ἐνώπιον αὐτοῦ in 3:22, of "our heart"—καρδίαν ἡμῶν in 3:19b, ἡμῶν ἡ καρδία as well as καρδίας ἡμῶν in 3:20a, and καρδία ἡμῶν in 3:21, of the verb "condemn"—καταγινώσκῃ in 3:20a, 21, and in this unit of the term "God"—θεός in 3:20a and θεόν in 3:21—determine the parallelism between the B (3:19b–20a) and B' (3:21–22) elements of this chiasm. Finally, the unparalleled central and pivotal C (3:20b) element contains the only occurrence in 1 John of the expression "knows all things" (γινώσκει πάντα).

9. *In This You Know the Spirit of God (4:1–6)*

THE ONE KNOWING GOD HEARS US

A > ⁴:¹Beloved, do not believe every *spirit* [πνεύματι] but test whether the spirits [πνεύματα] are from God [ἐκ τοῦ θεοῦ], because many false prophets have gone out into the world. ²In this [τούτῳ] you know [γινώσκετε] the Spirit [πνεῦμα] of God.

Every spirit [πνεῦμα] that confesses Jesus Christ as having come in flesh is from God [ἐκ τοῦ θεοῦ], ³ᵃbut every spirit [πνεῦμα] that does not confess Jesus is not from God [ἐκ τοῦ θεοῦ]. ³ᵇAnd this [τοῦτο] is that of the antichrist, which you have heard [ἀκηκόατε] that he is coming,

B   ³ᶜbut now is already in the world [ἐν τῷ κόσμῳ].

    C   ⁴ᵃYou are from God, little children, and you have conquered them,

B'   ⁴ᵇbecause the one in you is greater than the one in the world [ἐν τῷ κόσμῳ].

A'   ⁵ They are from the world, on account of this [τοῦτο] from the world they speak and the world hears [ἀκούει] them. ⁶We are from God [ἐκ τοῦ θεοῦ], the one knowing [γινώσκων] God hears [ἀκούει] us, whoever is not *from God* [ἐκ τοῦ θεοῦ] does not hear [ἀκούει] us. From this [τούτου] we know [γινώσκομεν] the Spirit [πνεῦμα] of truth and the spirit [πνεῦμα] of deceit.

The command "do not believe every spirit [πνεύματι]" at the beginning of this unit in 4:1 recalls the reference to "the Spirit [πνεύματος] which he gave to us" at the conclusion of the preceding unit in 3:24. These successive occurrences of the word for "spirit" serve as the transitional terms linking the eighth unit (3:18–24) to the ninth unit (4:1–6).

An A-B-C-B'-A' chiastic pattern secures the integrity and distinctness of this ninth unit (4:1–6). Several linguistic occurrences constitute the parallelism between the A (4:1–3a) and the A' (4:5–6) elements of this chiasm: the only occurrences in this unit of the word for "spirit"—πνεύματι and πνεύματα in 4:1, πνεῦμα in 4:2 (2x), 3a, 6 (2x); of the phrase "from God" (ἐκ τοῦ θεοῦ) in 4:1, 2, 3a, 6 (2x); of the demonstrative pronoun "this"—τούτῳ in 4:2, τοῦτό in 4:3b, 5, and τούτου in 4:6; of the verb "know"—γινώσκετε in 4:2, γινώσκων and γινώσκομεν in 4:6; and of the verb "hear"—ἀκηκόατε in 4:3b and ἀκούει in 4:5, 6 (2x). The only occurrences in this unit of the phrase "in the world" (ἐν τῷ κόσμῳ) in 4:3c, 4b determine the parallelism between the B (4:3b) and B' (4:4b) elements of this chiasm. Finally, the unparalleled central and pivotal C (4:4a) element contains the only occurrences in this unit of the noun "little children" (τεκνία) and the verb "you have conquered" (νενικήκατε).

10. God Has Sent His Son so that We Might Live through Him (4:7–12)

IF WE LOVE ONE ANOTHER, GOD REMAINS IN US AND HIS LOVE IS PERFECTED IN US

A   ⁷Beloved [Ἀγαπητοί], let us love one another [ἀγαπῶμεν ἀλλήλους], because love is *from God*, and everyone who loves from God has been begotten and knows God. ⁸The one not loving does not know God, because God is love.

B   ⁹ᵃIn this [ἐν τούτῳ] the love of God was manifested in us, because his Son [υἱὸν αὐτοῦ], the unique one, God has sent [ἀπέσταλκεν] into the world

C   ⁹ᵇso that we might live through him.

B'   ¹⁰ In this [ἐν τούτῳ] is love, not that we have loved God but that he loved us and sent [ἀπέστειλεν] his Son [υἱὸν αὐτοῦ] as expiation for our sins.

A'   ¹¹Beloved [Ἀγαπητοί], if God so loved us, then we ourselves ought to love one another [ἀλλήλους ἀγαπᾶν]. ¹²No one has ever observed God. If we love one another [ἀγαπῶμεν ἀλλήλους], God *remains* in us and his love is perfected in us.

The phrase "from God" (ἐκ τοῦ θεοῦ) at the beginning of this unit in 4:7 recalls the same phrase at the conclusion of the preceding unit in 4:6. These successive occurrences of the identical phrase "from God" serve as the transitional terms linking the ninth unit (4:1–6) to the tenth unit (4:7–12).

An A-B-C-B'-A' chiastic pattern secures the integrity and distinctness of this tenth unit (4:7–12). Several linguistic occurrences constitute the parallelism between the A (4:7–8) and the A' (4:11–12) elements of this chiasm: the only occurrences in this unit of the address "beloved" (Ἀγαπητοί) in 4:7, 11; and of the exhortation to "love one another"—ἀγαπῶμεν ἀλλήλους in 4:7, 12 as well as ἀλλήλους ἀγαπᾶν in 4:11. The only occurrences in this unit of the phrase "in this" (ἐν τούτῳ), of "his Son" (υἱὸν αὐτοῦ) in 4:9a, 10, and of the verb "send"—ἀπέσταλκεν in 4:9a as well as ἀπέστειλεν in 4:10—determine the parallelism between the B (4:9a) and B' (4:10) elements of this chiasm. Finally, the unparalleled central and pivotal C (4:9b) element contains the only occurrence in 1 John of the verb "live"—"so that we might live [ζήσωμεν] through him."

11. Just as That One Is so We Are in This World (4:13–5:2)

The one loving God should love also his brother

A ¹³In this we know [Ἐν τούτῳ γινώσκομεν] that in him we *remain* and he in us, because he has given us from his Spirit. ¹⁴And we ourselves have observed and testify that the Father sent the Son as savior of the world. ¹⁵Whoever confesses that Jesus is the Son of God [θεοῦ], God [θεός] in him remains and he in God [θεῷ]. ¹⁶And we ourselves have known and believed [πεπιστεύκαμεν] the love which God [θεός] has in us. God [θεός] is love, and the one remaining in love in God [θεῷ] remains and God [θεός] in him remains.

    B ¹⁷In this has love been perfected [τετελείωται] with us, so that we may have confidence on the day of the judgment, because just as that one is so we ourselves are in this world. ¹⁸ᵃThere is no fear [φόβος] in love but perfect [τελεία] love drives out fear [φόβον],

    B' ¹⁸ᵇbecause fear [φόβος] has to do with punishment, and one fearing [φοβούμενος] has not been perfected [τετελείωται] in love.

A' ¹⁹We ourselves love, because he first loved us. ²⁰If anyone says, "I love God [θεόν]," but hates his brother, he is a liar. For the one not loving his brother whom he has seen, is not able to love God [θεόν] whom he has not seen. ²¹And this commandment we have from him, that the one loving God [θεόν] should love also his brother. ⁵:¹Everyone who believes [πιστεύων] that Jesus is the Christ, from God [θεοῦ] has been begotten, and everyone who loves the one begetting loves also the one begotten from him. ²In this we know [ἐν τούτῳ γινώσκομεν] that we love the children of God [θεοῦ], whenever we *love God* [θεόν] and do his commandments.

"In him [God] we remain [μένομεν]" at the beginning of this unit in 4:13 recalls "God remains [μένει] in us" at the conclusion of the preceding unit in 4:12. These successive occurrences of the verb "remain" serve as the transitional terms linking the tenth unit (4:7–12) to the eleventh unit (4:13–5:2).

An A-B-B'-A' chiastic pattern secures the integrity and distinctness of this eleventh unit (4:13–5:2). Several linguistic occurrences constitute the parallelism between the A (4:13–16) and the A' (4:19–5:2) elements of this chiasm: the only occurrences in this unit of the expression "in this we know" (ἐν τούτῳ γινώσκομεν) in 4:13 and 5:2; of "God"—θεοῦ in 4:15 and 5:1, θεός in 4:15, 16 (thrice), θεῷ in 4:15, 16, and θεόν in 4:20 (2x), 21 and 5:2; and the verb "believe"—πεπιστεύκαμεν in 4:16 and πιστεύων in 5:1. The only occurrences in this unit of expressions for "perfect"—"in this has love been perfected [τετελείωται]" in 4:17 as well as "perfect [τελεία] love" in 4:18a and "has not been perfected [τετελείωται] in love" in 4:18b—and in 1 John of the noun and verb for fear—φόβος in 4:18a, 18b, φόβον in 4:18a, and φοβούμενος in 4:18b—determine the parallelism between the B (4:17–18a) and the B' (4:18b) elements at the pivotal center of this chiastic unit.

12. *This Is the Love of God that We Keep His Commandments (5:3–12)*

Life eternal God has given to us, and this life is in his Son

A   ³For this [αὕτη] is the *love of God* [θεοῦ], that we keep his commandments, and his commandments are not burdensome, ⁴because everyone begotten from God [θεοῦ] conquers the world. And this [αὕτη] is the conquering power that conquers the world—our faith [πίστις]. ⁵Who is the one conquering the world except the one believing [πιστεύων] that Jesus is the Son [υἱός] of God [θεοῦ]? ⁶ᵃThis is the one who came through water [ὕδατος] and blood [αἵματος], Jesus Christ, not in the water [ὕδατι] only but in the water [ὕδατι] and in the blood [αἵματι].

B   ⁶ᵇAnd the Spirit is [τὸ πνεῦμά ἐστιν] the one who testifies,

B'   ⁶ᶜbecause the Spirit is [τὸ πνεῦμά ἐστιν] the truth.

A'   ⁷For three are they who are testifying, ⁸the Spirit and the water [ὕδωρ] and the blood [αἷμα], and the three are as the one. ⁹If we receive the testimony of human beings, the testimony of God [θεοῦ] is greater, because this [αὕτη] is the testimony of God [θεοῦ] that he has testified concerning his Son [υἱοῦ]. ¹⁰The one believing [πιστεύων] in the Son [υἱόν] of God [θεοῦ] has the testimony in himself, the one not believing [πιστεύων] God [θεῷ] has made him a liar, because he has not believed [πεπίστευκεν] in the testimony which God [θεός] has testified concerning his Son [υἱοῦ]. ¹¹And this [αὕτη] is the testimony, that life eternal God [θεός] has given us, and this [αὕτη] life is in his Son [υἱῷ]. ¹²The one having the Son [υἱόν] has the life. The one not having the Son [υἱόν] of God [θεοῦ] does not have the *life.*

The phrase "love of God" (ἀγάπη τοῦ θεοῦ) at the beginning of this unit in 5:3 recalls "whenever we love God [τὸν θεὸν ἀγαπῶμεν]" at the conclusion of the preceding unit in 5:2. These successive occurrences of expressions for the love of God serve as the transitional terms linking the eleventh unit (4:13–5:2) to the twelfth unit (5:3–12).

An A-B-B'-A' chiastic pattern secures the integrity and distinctness of this twelfth unit (5:3–12). Several linguistic occurrences constitute the parallelism between the A (5:3–6a) and the A' (5:7–12) elements of this chiasm: the only occurrences in this unit of the demonstrative nominative feminine singular pronoun "this" (αὕτη) in 5:3, 4, 9, 11 (2x); of "God"—θεοῦ in 5:3, 4, 5, 9 (2x), 10, 12, θεῷ in 5:10, and θεός in 5:10, 11; of expressions for faith/believing—the noun "faith" (πίστις) in 5:4, the verb "believing" (πιστεύων) in 5:5, 10 (2x), and the verb "believed" (πεπίστευκεν) in 5:10; of "Son"—υἱός in 5:5, υἱοῦ in 5:9, 10, υἱόν in 5:10, 12 (2x), and υἱῷ in 5:11; in 1 John of "water"—ὕδατος in 5:6a, ὕδατι in 5:6a (2x), and ὕδωρ in 5:8; and in this unit of "blood"—αἵματος as well as αἵματι in 5:6a and αἷμα in 5:8. The only occurrences in 1 John of "the Spirit is" (τὸ πνεῦμά ἐστιν) in 5:6b, 6c determine the parallelism between the B (5:6b) and B' (5:6c) elements at the pivotal center of this chiastic unit.

13. *All Unrighteousness Is Sin (5:13–21)*

Guard yourselves from the idols

A ¹³These things I have written to you so that you may know that [εἰδῆτε ὅτι] you have *life* [ζωήν] eternal [αἰώνιον], you who believe in the name of the Son of God [υἱοῦ τοῦ θεοῦ]. ¹⁴And this is the confidence which we have with him that if we ask anything according to his will, he hears us. ¹⁵And if we know that [οἴδαμεν ὅτι] he hears us in regard to whatever we ask, we know that [οἴδαμεν ὅτι] we have the requests which we asked from [ἀπ᾽] him.

B   ¹⁶ᵃᵇᶜIf anyone sees his brother sinning a sin [ἁμαρτίαν] not resulting in death [πρὸς θάνατον], he should ask and he will give to him life, to those sinning not resulting in death [πρὸς θάνατον].

B'   ¹⁶ᵈᵉThere is a sin resulting in death [πρὸς θάνατον]. Not concerning that do I say that he should request. ¹⁷All unrighteousness is sin [ἁμαρτία], but there is a sin [ἁμαρτία] not resulting in death [πρὸς θάνατον].

A'   ¹⁸We know that [Οἴδαμεν ὅτι] everyone who has been begotten from God does not sin, but the one begotten from God, he keeps him, and the evil one does not touch him. ¹⁹We know that [οἴδαμεν ὅτι] we are from God but the whole world lies in the evil one. ²⁰And we know that [οἴδαμεν ὅτι] the Son of God [υἱὸς τοῦ θεοῦ] has come and has given us understanding so that we might know the true one, and we are in the true one, in his Son Jesus Christ. This one is the true God and life eternal [ζωὴ αἰώνιος]. ²¹Little children, guard yourselves from [ἀπό] the idols.

The word "life" in the expression "you have life [ζωήν] eternal" at the beginning of this unit in 5:13 recalls the same word in the expression "does not have the life [ζωήν]" at the conclusion of the preceding unit in 5:12. These successive references to eternal life serve as the transitional terms linking the twelfth unit (5:3–12) to the thirteenth and final unit (5:13–21).

An A-B-B'-A' chiastic pattern secures the integrity and distinctness of this thirteenth unit (5:13–21). Several linguistic occurrences constitute the parallelism between the A (5:13–15) and the A' (5:18–21) elements of this chiasm: the only occurrences in this unit of the expression "know that"—εἰδῆτε ὅτι in 5:13 and οἴδαμεν ὅτι in 5:15, 18, 19, 20; of "eternal life"—ζωήν ... αἰώνιον in 5:13 and ζωὴ αἰώνιος in 5:20; of the "Son of God"—υἱοῦ τοῦ θεοῦ in 5:13 and υἱὸς τοῦ θεοῦ in 5:20; and of the preposition "from" (ἀπό) in 5:15, 21. The only occurrences in this unit of "sin"—ἁμαρτίαν in 5:16a and ἁμαρτία in 5:17 (2x)—and "resulting in death" (πρὸς θάνατον) in 5:16a, 16c 16d, 17—determine the parallelism between the B (5:16abc) and the B' (5:16de–17) elements at the pivotal center of this chiastic unit.

The Macrochiastic Structure of 1 John

Having illustrated the sequence of the various microchiastic structures operative in the thirteen distinct units of 1 John, I will now demonstrate how these thirteen units form an A-B-C-D-E-F-G-F'-E'-D'-C'-B'-A' macrochiastic structure unifying and organizing the entire document.

> A He Will Cleanse Us from *All Unrighteousness* (1:1–10)
>
> A' *All Unrighteousness* Is Sin (5:13–21)

The only occurrences in 1 John of the expression "all unrighteousness" indicate the parallelism between the opening A unit (1:1–10) and the closing A' unit (5:13–21) within the macrochiastic structure of 1 John. The statement that "all unrighteousness [πᾶσα ἀδικία] is sin" (5:17) recalls that if we confess our sins, Jesus "will cleanse us from all unrighteousness [πάσης ἀδικίας]" (1:9).

> B If *We Keep His Commandments the Love of God* Has Been Perfected (2:1–14)
>
> B' This Is *the Love of God* that *We Keep His Commandments* (5:3–12)

The first and last occurrences in 1 John of the expressions "we keep his commandments" and "the love of God" provide the chiastic parallels between the B (2:1–14) and the B' (5:3–12) units. "In this we know that we have known him [Jesus Christ], if we keep his commandments [ἐντολὰς αὐτοῦ τηρῶμεν]" (2:3) as well as "whoever keeps his word, truly in this one the love of God [ἡ ἀγάπη τοῦ θεοῦ] has been perfected" (2:5) occur in the B unit. And "for this is the love of God [ἡ ἀγάπη τοῦ θεοῦ], that we keep his commandments [ἐντολὰς αὐτοῦ τηρῶμεν]" (5:3) occurs in the B' unit.

> C Do Not Love the Things *in the World* (2:15–17)
>
> C' Just as That One Is so We Are *in This World* (4:13–5:2)

The first and last occurrences in 1 John of the phrase "in the/this world" provide the chiastic parallels between the C (2:15–17) and the C' (4:13—5:2) units. "The things in the world [ἐν τῷ κόσμῳ]" (2:15) as well as "because all that is in the world [ἐν τῷ κόσμῳ]" (2:16) occur in the C unit. And "we are in this world [ἐν τῷ κόσμῳ τούτῳ]" (4:17) occurs in the C' unit.

    D   The One Confessing *the Son* Also Has the Father (2:18–27)

    D' God Has Sent *His Son* so that We Might Live through Him (4:7–12)

The first and last occurrences in 1 John of the term "the/his Son" in the accusative case in reference to Jesus as the Son of God provide the chiastic parallels between the D (2:18–27) and the D' (4:7–12) units. The phrase "the Son [τὸν υἱόν]" (2:22, 23 [2x]) occurs in the D unit and "his Son [τὸν υἱὸν αὐτοῦ]" (4:9, 10) in the D' unit.

    E   *You Know* Whoever Does Righteousness Has Been Begotten from Him (2:28–3:6)

    E' In This *You Know* the Spirit of God (4:1–6)

The only occurrences in 1 John of the second person plural indicative active verb "you know" provide the chiastic parallels between the E (2:28–3:6) and the E' (4:1–6) units. "You know [γινώσκετε] that also everyone who does righteousness has been begotten from him" (2:29) occurs in the B unit. And "in this you know [γινώσκετε] the Spirit of God" (4:2) occurs in the B' unit.

    F   *We Should Love One Another* (3:7–12)

    F' We Should Believe and *We Should Love One Another* (3:18–24)

The first two occurrences in 1 John of the exhortation "we should love one another [ἀγαπῶμεν ἀλλήλους]" (3:11, 23) provide the chiastic parallels between the F (3:7–12) and the F' (3:18–24) units.

    G We Ought To Lay Down Our Lives for the Brothers (3:13–17)

The G unit (3:13–17) functions as the unparalleled central and pivotal unit within the macrochiastic structure of 1 John. This unit contains the statements that "we know that we have moved from death to life, because we love the brothers" (3:14) and "in this we have known love, that that one for us laid down his life; so we ourselves ought for the brothers to lay down our lives" (3:16). These unique statements at the center of 1 John provide the pivot from the F (3:7–12) to the F' (3:18–24) units for the exhortations that "we should love one another" (3:11, 23).

Outline of the Macrochiastic Structure of 1 John

A   1:1–10: He Will Cleanse Us from *All Unrighteousness*

   B   2:1–14: If *We Keep His Commandments the Love of God* Has Been Perfected

      C   2:15–17: Do Not Love the Things *in the World*

         D   2:18–27: The One Confessing *the Son* Also Has the Father

            E   2:28–3:6: *You Know* Whoever Does Righteousness Has Been Begotten from Him

               F   3:7–12: *We Should Love One Another*

                  G   3:13–17: We Ought To Lay Down Our Lives for the Brothers

               F'   3:18–24: We Should Believe and *We Should Love One Another*

            E'   4:1–6: In This *You Know* the Spirit of God

         D'   4:7–12: God Has Sent *His Son* so that We Might Live through Him

      C'   4:13–5:2: Just as That One Is so We Are *in This World*

   B'   5:3–12: This Is *the Love of God* that *We Keep His Commandments*

A'   5:13–21: *All Unrighteousness* Is Sin

Preliminary Indications of Worship as the Main Theme of 1–3 John

As mentioned above, the subtitle chosen for this study, *Worship by Loving God and One Another to Live Eternally*, articulates what I am proposing as the main theme and overall concern of 1–3 John. In this section I will present an introductory overview of the indications that worship, understood in its most comprehensive and dynamic sense as including not only liturgical but ethical worship, serves as the main theme that organizes and unifies the whole of 1–3 John.

First of all, like the other epistolary literature in the New Testament, 1–3 John would have been performed in a setting of communal worship, heard by their audience in the order 3-2-1 John.[10] In 3 John the implied author, "the elder," the leader of the main Johannine community probably in Ephesus, addresses Gaius, evidently a leading member in one of the outlying churches within the Johannine network (1:1). Although addressed personally to Gaius, 3 John is nevertheless a communal letter meant to be heard by his entire local community assembled for worship. It concerns Gaius' relationship to his fellow believers within the Johannine community. After the elder affirms Gaius for the hospitality he has and will continue to extend to missionary "brothers," fellow believers (1:3–6), he draws his attention to "something I have written to the church" (1:9a), an apparent reference to the other two letters, 1–2 John.[11] The elder is implicitly authorizing Gaius to oversee and facilitate the public performance of 1 John in the sister church in which he is a leader and coworker of the elder (3 John 1:8).[12]

The elder, however, alerts Gaius of a possible hindrance to a favorable reception of 1 John by the church due to a certain Diotrephes, who does not properly receive and thus acknowledge the authority of the elder (3 John 1:9b). Not only does Diotrephes disparage the elder, but he does not properly receive or acknowledge the brothers (1:10) whom Gaius has assisted as a coworker of the elder (1:3–8). After the warning regarding Diotrephes, the elder recommends to Gaius a certain Demetrius, a universally attested individual either already in the sister church of Gaius or sent to it by the elder along with 1–3 John.[13] The implication is that Gaius ought to rely upon Demetrius to assist him in the implementation of the public performance of 1 John, the hortatory sermon written by the elder for the entire Johannine community, as part of a worship service in this

---

10. Heil, *Letters of Paul*; Heil, *Worship*; Heil, *James*; Heil, *1 Peter, 2 Peter, and Jude*; Heil, *Book of Revelation*.

11. Lorencin, "Hospitality," 165–74.

12. "The epistolary aorist ('written') seems not to refer to a previous communication but to the exhortation that the elder now wants read in the assembly—1 John" (Johnson, *Writings*, 498–99).

13. According to Marulli ("Letter," 203–23), Demetrius is not necessarily a letter bearer and 3 John is not a letter of recommendation but a rhetorical attempt to restore the elder's honor discredited by Diotrephes. But these are not necessarily mutually exclusive features of 3 John. See also Campbell, "Honor," 321–41.

local sister church. The communal nature of 3 John is confirmed at its conclusion when the elder directs Gaius to salute the friends by name in the sister church (1:15).

The elder addresses 2 John to "an elect lady and her children" (1:1). This is an apparent reference to the church, personified as a "lady," in which Gaius is a leader and whose "sister" is the church of the elder (1:13). This letter of 2 John is to function as an introductory cover letter for the performance of 1 John as an epistolary hortatory sermon to be heard in a context of worship. In 2 John the elder briefly introduces the topic of the commandment that we should love one another (1:4–6), which will be more fully developed in 1 John (2:3–4, 7–8; 3:22–24; 4:21; 5:2–3). In 2 John the elder directs his sister church not to receive or greet anyone who does not bring to them the teaching that implicitly includes the commandment that we should love one another (1:10). This underscores that 1 John, sent by the elder to the members of his sister church, does indeed bring them this teaching and thus prepares them to favorably receive it.

Second, acts of worship are performed within 1–3 John. Regarding Gaius, the addressee of 3 John, the elder performs a prayer of petition implicitly directed to God, "I pray [εὔχομαί] that you are prospering and in good health" (1:2),[14] and at the conclusion of the letter pronounces a prayerful greeting—"Peace to you" (1:15). At the beginning of 2 John the elder pronounces an epistolary greeting that functions as a petitionary prayer for the entire community—"Grace, mercy, and peace will be with us from God the Father and from Jesus Christ the Son of the Father in truth and love" (1:3).

An emphatic communal testimony regarding eternal life initiates 1 John: "What we have heard, what we have seen with our eyes, what we have looked upon and our hands have touched concerning the word of the life—and the life was manifested and we have seen and testified and declared to you the life eternal which was with the Father and manifested to us" (1:1–2). This authoritative testimony functions as a confession that amounts to an act of worship. It draws the audience into a fellowship of communal worship—"what we have seen and heard, we declare also to you, so that you also may have fellowship with us. And our fellowship

---

14. Although God is not explicitly mentioned, this can be considered a prayer rather than simply a wish, since "Gott gewährt Wohlergehen im umfassenden Sinn an Leib und Seele und in der Wahrheit" (Schnelle, *Johannesbriefe*, 36). "[I]n view of the content of 3 John as a whole, the verb [εὔχομαί] probably heralds the beginning of an actual prayer" (Smalley, *3 John*, 331).

is with the Father and with his Son Jesus Christ" (1:3). That 1 John is concerned with true worship is confirmed by the warning against false worship at its conclusion—"guard yourselves from the idols" (5:21).

And third, what the Gospel of John declares about true worship provides the background for additional preliminary indications of the prevalent concern for the dynamics of worship in 1–3 John. Regarding the controversy between Jews and Samaritans concerning the proper location for true worship in the Gospel of John, Jesus replied that "an hour is coming and now is, when true worshipers will worship the Father in Spirit and truth, for indeed the Father seeks such as those who worship him. God is Spirit, and those who worship him must worship in Spirit and truth" (John 4:23-24). To worship "in Spirit and truth" is to worship "in the Spirit of truth" that Jesus promised to send his disciples after his death and resurrection (14:17; 15:26; 16:13) as the advocate, the holy Spirit (14:16, 26; 15:26; 16:7), who will represent him and guide them in matters regarding the truth. Since there is a sense in which Jesus himself personifies the truth (14:6), to worship in Spirit and truth or in the Spirit of truth is ultimately to worship in very close union with Jesus.[15]

Central to the "truth" in John is the life eternal that came to be through Jesus Christ as the Word full of the divine gift of truth that came through him (1:4, 14, 17). In accord with this truth, "God so loved the world, that he gave his only begotten Son, so that everyone who believes in him might not perish but might have life eternal" (3:16). Included in this truth is the divine commandment that is life eternal (12:50), the commandment that gives life eternal to those who love one another as Jesus loved his disciples (13:34; 15:12) by laying down his life for them in his death on the cross (15:13). Eternal life is to know the only true God and the Jesus Christ (17:3) who loved by laying down his life so that believers might have eternal life. Believers may already live eternally, then, by practicing the commandment included in the truth, the commandment to love God, and thus worship God in an ethical way, by loving one another. Practicing this commandment of the truth is what it means

---

15. "Jesus reveals to the Samaritan woman the need to 'worship the Father in spirit and truth' (or 'Spirit of truth,' 4:23). . . . The friends of Jesus offer worship and adoration to the Father, through Jesus, as their part of the covenant, a worship that produces in disciples life, growth, and fruit" (Lee, "Friendship," 70-71). See also Thettayil, *In Spirit and Truth*, 106-65; Köstenberger, *Theology*, 429-30.

to worship the Father in Spirit and truth or in the Spirit of truth, and thereby experience life eternal through loving one another.[16]

What it means to be a true worshiper who worships God in Spirit and truth by loving one another and thereby living eternally is further developed in 1–3 John. The vocabulary of "truth/Spirit of truth," "life (eternal)," and the "commandment that we should love one another" occurs throughout 1–3 John. In 3 John "truth" (ἀλήθεια) occurs six times (1:1, 3 [2x], 4, 8, 12), in 2 John five times (1:1 [2x], 2, 3, 4), and in 1 John nine times (1:6, 8; 2:4, 21 [2x]; 3:18, 19; 4:6; 5:6). In 1 John 4:6 is a reference to "the Spirit of truth [τὸ πνεῦμα τῆς ἀληθείας]" (cf. John 14:17; 15:26; 16:13), and in 1 John 5:6 is a statement that "the Sprit is the truth" (τὸ πνεῦμά ἐστιν ἡ ἀλήθεια). Regarding the commandment that we should love one another, see 2 John 1:5; 1 John 2:10; 3:10–11, 14, 18, 23; 4:7, 11–12, 19–21; 5:1–2; cf. John 13:34; 15:12, 17.

The topic of eternal life is introduced at the very beginning of 1 John (1:1–2) and remains a primary theme throughout its discourse (2:25; 3:14–15; 5:11–13, 16), climaxing with a worshipful communal confession: "And we know that the Son of God has come and has given us understanding so that we might know the true one, and we are in the true one, in his Son Jesus Christ. This one is the true God and life eternal" (5:20). The topic of eternal life thus forms a literary inclusion framing the entire hortatory sermon that is 1 John. In addition and most noteworthy, however, are the statements in the central and pivotal unit of the macrochiastic structure of 1 John (3:13–17): "We know that we have moved from death to life, because we love the brothers" (3:14); and "in this we have known love, that that one for us laid down his life; so we ourselves ought for the brothers to lay down our lives" (3:16; cf. John 15:12–13).

These preliminary indications that "worship by loving God and one another to live eternally" expresses the main theme and concern of 1–3 John will be confirmed by the remainder of my exegetical, audience-oriented investigation into the chiastic structures of 1–3 John in the chapters to follow.

---

16. Moloney, *Love*, 192–203; Morgan-Wynne, *Cross*, 241–53.

Summary

1. There are thirteen distinct units in 1 John with each exhibiting its own microchiastic structure. Both 2 and 3 John also exhibit chiastic structures.

2. The thirteen units comprising 1 John operate as a macrochiastic structure with six pairs of parallel units and with the pivot of the entire macrochiastic structure occurring as the unparalleled central G unit in 3:13–17.

3. That 1–3 John was heard by their audience in a setting of worship, contain epistolary acts of worship, and develop the theme of worshiping God in Spirit and truth or in the Spirit of truth from the Gospel of John provide preliminary indications for worship, both liturgical and ethical, as their main organizing and unifying theme. More specifically, the subtitle, *Worship by Loving God and One Another to Live Eternally*, expresses the central and main concern of 1–3 John.

2

3 John
The Elder to Gaius

The Brothers Have Testified to
Your Love before the Church (1:1–8)

A   ¹The elder to Gaius the *beloved*, whom I *love* in truth. ²*Beloved*, concerning all things I pray that you are prospering and are in good health, just as your soul is prospering. ³ªFor I rejoiced greatly at *brothers* coming and *testifying* to your *truth*,

  B   ³ᵇjust as you in truth are *walking*.

    C   ⁴ªGreater joy than these things I do not have,

  B'   ⁴ᵇthat I hear that my children in the truth are *walking*.

A'   ⁵*Beloved*, a faithful thing you are doing in whatever you accomplish for the *brothers* and this even for strangers, ⁶who have *testified* to your *love* before the church, whom you will do well to send forth in a manner worthy of God. ⁷For on behalf of the name they have gone out, receiving nothing from the pagans. ⁸We then ought to support such as these, so that we may become coworkers to *the truth*.[17]

---

17. For the establishment of 3 John 1:1–8 as a chiasm, see ch. 1.

1:1–3a (A): The Brothers Are Testifying to Your Truth

The audience hear the A element (1:1–3a) of this chiastic unit as a chiastic pattern in itself:[18]

- a) The elder to Gaius the beloved, whom I love in *truth* (1:1).
  - b) Beloved, concerning all things I pray that you are *prospering* (1:2a)
    - c) and are in good health (1:2b),
  - b') just as your soul is *prospering* (1:2c).
- a') For I rejoiced greatly at brothers coming and testifying to your *truth* (1:3a).

The audience hear the words "and are in good health" (1:2b) as the unparalleled central and pivotal sub-element c) in this chiastic sub-unit. They then experience a pivot of parallels involving the only occurrences in 3 John of the verb "prosper." "You are prospering [εὐοδοῦσθαι]" in the b) sub-element (1:2a) progresses to "just as your soul is prospering [εὐοδοῦταί]" in the b') sub-element (1:2c). They then experience a progression of parallels involving the only occurrences in this sub-unit of the term "truth." "Whom I love in truth [ἀληθείᾳ]" in the a) sub-element (1:1) progresses to "testifying to your truth [ἀληθείᾳ]" in the a') sub-element (1:3a).

The designation of the sender of the letter of 3 John not just as "an" but as "*the* elder" (Ὁ πρεσβύτερος) already begins to engender in the audience a respectful hearing for whatever this venerable authoritative leader of the entire Johannine community has to communicate to them.[19] In accord with the communal nature of the letter, the addressee, before being directly addressed, is presented to the audience as "Gaius the be-

---

18. The term "audience" will be used throughout the work as a collective plural rather than singular noun to reflect the plurality of distinct individuals who compose the audience and who have responsibilities toward one another. Although 3 John is directly addressed to the individual Gaius, it is nevertheless a communal letter (see 1:15) concerned with the relationship between Gaius and other individuals within the Johannine community. It is meant to be performed in a context of communal worship and thus to be heard by the other individuals within the church of which Gaius is a leading member.

19. The designation, "the elder," "is meant to indicate a position of great dignity" (BDAG, 862).

loved." The elder affirms that Gaius is "beloved" (ἀγαπητῷ) implicitly not only by God and by the audience but, with the inclusion of the otherwise redundant personal pronoun, emphatically and explicitly by the elder himself—"whom *I* love [ἐγώ ἀγαπῶ] in truth" (1:1). That the elder loves the beloved Gaius in "truth" (ἀληθείᾳ) exemplifies for the audience the Johannine notion that the practice of the commandment to love one another (John 13:34; 15:12, 17) is a preeminent part of the "truth" (ἀληθείᾳ) by which one becomes a true worshiper of God (4:23-24) under the abiding guidance of the Spirit of truth (14:17; 15:26; 16:13).

The elder then underscores that he loves the beloved Gaius (3 John 1:1) by directly addressing him as "beloved" (Ἀγαπητέ). He then performs an act of worship, a prayer of petition for Gaius. Concerning all things "I pray" (εὔχομαί), says the elder, that Gaius is prospering and is in good health physically, just as spiritually his soul is prospering (1:2). The mention that the "soul" or "life" (ψυχή) of Gaius is prospering provides the audience with a hint that Gaius, like the elder, may also be engaged in practicing the truth of loving one another, as it recalls the Johannine notion that there is no greater love than to lay down, either literally or figuratively, one's "life" or "soul" (ψυχήν) for one's friends (John 15:13). The elder then reports that he rejoiced greatly at the "brothers" (ἀδελφῶν), that is, fellow believers who are members of the broader Johannine community, coming and testifying to "your truth [ἀληθείᾳ]" (3 John 1:3a). This further implies that Gaius, like the elder, who loves his fellow believer Gaius in "truth [ἀληθείᾳ]" (1:1), practices the truth of loving one another by loving the brothers.[20]

1:3b (B): Just as You in Truth Are Walking

The elder emphatically affirms the testifying by the brothers that Gaius practices the truth (1:3a) by adding, "just as you in truth are walking" (1:3b). This tells the audience that Gaius has not only loved the brothers who testified to the elder, but that "you are continually walking [περιπατεῖς]," that is, behaving or conducting his life by practicing the truth of loving one another.[21] In other words, loving one another has become part of his lifestyle, his

---

20. Trebilco, *Self-Designations*, 62–64. "The truth, moreover, is the essential sphere of reality in which mutual love (vv 1–2) exists" (Smalley, *3 John*, 331).

21. BDAG, 803.

"walking in the truth."²² And the progressive parallelism between "just as [καθώς] you in truth are walking" and "just as [καθώς] your soul is prospering" (1:2) further implies that the soul of Gaius is prospering because of his practice of the truth of loving one another.

1:4a (C): Greater Joy Than These Things I Do Not Have

The elder reinforces his statement that "I rejoiced" (ἐχάρην) greatly at the brothers testifying to the truth of Gaius loving the brothers and thus one another (1:3) by now declaring that greater "joy" (χαράν) than these things the elder does not have (1:4a).

1:4b (B'): That I Hear that My Children in the Truth Are Walking

The reason for the elder's great joy (1:4a) is "that I hear that my children in the truth are walking" (1:4b). At this point, after the unparalleled and central C element of this chiastic unit, "greater joy than these things I do not have" (1:4a), the audience experience a pivot of parallels from the B (1:3b) to the B' (1:4b) element. "Just as you," that is, Gaius, "in truth are walking [περιπατεῖς]" (1:3b) progresses to "that I," that is, the elder, "hear that my children in the truth are walking [περιπατοῦντα]" (1:4b). The elder's reference to "my children" further confirms the communal nature of the letter, as it includes not only Gaius but the other members of his community in the audience. Indeed, the elder affirms that not only Gaius but the communal audience of which he is a leading member are in the truth walking, that is, practicing the truth of loving one another. The designation "my children" reminds the audience that they are not only metaphorically "children" (τέκνα) of the elder, but "children" (τέκνα) of God (John 1:12; cf. 11:52) as believers who have been reborn into eternal life (1:4, 13).

1:5–8 (A'): The Brothers Have Testified to Your Love as a Worker to the Truth

At this point the audience experience progressions, via the chiastic parallels, from the A (1:1–3a) to the A' (1:5–8) element of this chiastic unit.

---

22. "That Gaius is walking in truth means that he is fulfilling the love command" (Painter, *3 John*, 370).

The elder's reference to Gaius as the "beloved [ἀγαπητῷ]" (1:1) and his address of him as "beloved [Ἀγαπητέ]" (1:2) are reinforced by his repeated address of him as "beloved [Ἀγαπητέ]" (1:5). "Whom I," the elder, "love [ἀγαπῶ]" (1:1) progresses to "your," Gaius's, "love [ἀγάπη]" (1:6). And the "brothers [ἀδελφῶν] coming and testifying [μαρτυρούντων] to your truth [τῇ ἀληθείᾳ]" (1:3a) progresses to the "brothers [ἀδελφούς]" (1:5) as those "who have testified [ἐμαρτύρησάν] to your love" (1:6) as a worker to "the truth [τῇ ἀληθείᾳ]" (1:8).

The audience heard Gaius addressed by the elder as "beloved" before he prayed for him (1:2). Now they again hear him addressed as "beloved," reinforcing the elder's and, by implication, the audience's esteem for Gaius, before the elder affirms Gaius is doing a faithful thing in whatever he accomplishes for the brothers, even if they are strangers (1:5). "Brothers" have come to the elder not only "testifying" to Gaius's truth (1:3a), but the "brothers" have "testified" publicly to Gaius's love before the church in an implied context of communal worship (1:6a). This fraternal testifying to both the truth and love of Gaius further indicates to the audience how loving one another is central to the practice of the truth. The elder is asking Gaius, who has already assisted brothers in the past, to continue this in the future by extending hospitality to brothers who come to him, even if they are strangers. Gaius is then to send them forth as travelling missionaries "in a manner worthy of God" (1:6b), that is, in accord with the love and true worship of God that consists in practicing the truth of loving one another.

These brothers went out as travelling evangelizers on behalf of "the name [ὀνόματος]" (1:7a), that is, the divine "name" (ὀνόματί) that God gave to Jesus Christ (John 17:11–12), the "name" (ὀνόματι) in which those who believe Jesus is the Christ, the Son of God, may have eternal life (20:31).[23] These brothers went out, receiving nothing from pagans (3 John 1:7b), so that they are dependent upon the hospitality and assistance—the love—of their fellow believing brothers. Consequently and emphatically, "we," the elder, Gaius, and by implication the audience, "ought" (ὀφείλομεν) to support such as these (1:8a).[24] This accords with

---

23. "'[T]he name' could have either God or Christ in mind, but in either case use of the one fully includes rather than excludes the identity and supporting activity of the other" (Yarbrough, *1–3 John*, 373). See also Olsson, *Letters*, 12.

24. "Since the brothers are accepting (receiving) [λαμβάνοντες, 1:7] nothing, we ought to support (receive) [ὑπολαμβάνειν, 1:8] them. A similar play on the two verbs is found in Acts 1:8–9" (Brown, *Epistles*, 713).

the teaching of Jesus that "you," his disciples, "ought" (ὀφείλετε) to "wash one another's feet" as a gesture of hospitable love (John 13:14) in accord with the new commandment of Jesus that you should love one another (13:34).[25] The elder, Gaius, and the audience may thereby become co-workers to "the truth" (3 John 1:8b), that is, those who cooperatively engage in the true worship, the worship in Spirit and truth (John 4:23–24), by loving God and one another to live eternally.

Diotrephes Does Not Acknowledge the Brothers but Demetrius Is Testified by All (1:9–15)

A [9]*I have written* something to the church, but that one who *likes to be first* among them, Diotrephes, does not acknowledge *us*. [10]Therefore, if I come, I will draw attention to his works which he is doing, with evil words disparaging *us*, and not being content with these things, he himself does not acknowledge the brothers and those wishing to do so he hinders and expels from the church.

B [11a]Beloved, do not imitate the *bad*

C [11b]but the *good*.

C' [11c]The one doing *good* is from God;

B' [11d]the one doing *bad* has not seen God.

A' [12]Demetrius is testified by all and by the truth itself, and *we* also testify, and you know that *our* testimony is true. [13]Many things I have to *write* to you, but I do not want through ink and pen to *write* to you. [14]I hope instead soon to see you, and we will speak face to face. [15]Peace to you. The *friends* (here) salute you. Salute the *friends* (there) by name.[26]

1:9–10 (A): I Have Written Something to the Church

The audience hear the A element (1:9–10) of this chiastic unit as a chiastic pattern in itself:

---

25. Brown, *Epistles*, 713; Schuchard, *1–3 John*, 679.
26. For the establishment of 3 John 1:9–15 as a chiasm, see ch. 1.

a) I have written something to the *church* (1:9a),

    b) but that one who likes to be first among them, Diotrephes, does not *acknowledge us* (1:9b).

        c) Therefore, if I come (1:10a),

    b') I will draw attention to his works which he is doing, with evil words disparaging *us*, and not being content with these things, he himself does not *acknowledge* the brothers (1:10b)

a') and those wishing to do so he hinders and expels from the *church* (1:10c).

The audience hear the words "therefore, if I come" (1:10a) as the unparalleled central and pivotal sub-element c) in this chiastic sub-unit. They then experience a pivot of parallels involving the only occurrences in 3 John of the verb "acknowledge" and in this sub-unit of the pronoun "us." "Diotrephes does not acknowledge [ἐπιδέχεται] us [ἡμᾶς]" in the b) sub-element (1:9b) progresses to "with evil words disparaging us [ἡμᾶς]" and "he himself does not acknowledge [ἐπιδέχεται] the brothers" in the b') sub-element (1:10b). They then experience a progression of parallels involving the only occurrences in this sub-unit of the term "church." "I have written something to the church [ἐκκλησίᾳ]" in the a) sub-element (1:9a) progresses to "expels from the church [ἐκκλησίας]" in the a') sub-element (1:10c).

The elder previously reported that brothers came to him and testified to Gaius's truth and love before the "church" (1:3, 6), the local worshiping assembly of the elder, probably in Ephesus. Now, however, he declares that "I have written something to the church" (1:9a), that is, to the entire Johannine community inclusive of the local churches outside of Ephesus.[27] As mentioned above, the "something" that the elder has written to the church most likely refers to 1–2 John, which 3 John is intended to introduce to the local church of which Gaius is a leading member.[28] This

---

27. "The 'church' in 3 Jn 6a appears to be the church of Ephesus, from which the elder writes, and the 'church' to which he refers here is the region-wide church of Asia Minor" (Schuchard, *1–3 John*, 681).

28. Johnson, *Writings*, 498-99. "The 'something' that John has written is likely to be 1 John, together with its introductory cover letter, 2 John" (Schuchard, *1–3 John*, 681). "If 2 John was a letter accompanying 1 John, as has been suggested, the Elder's indefinite reference here may take in both" (Painter, *3 John*, 376). See also Yarbrough, *1–3 John*, 377; Witherington, *Letters*, 586.

further confirms the communal concern of 3 John and begins to prepare its audience for a favorable reception of 1–2 John.

The elder, however, warns Gaius and the other members of his church, who constitute the audience of 3 John, about a certain Diotrephes. He likes to assert himself as first among "them" (1:9b), that is, among the members of the church for which the elder has written "something" (1:9a), 1–2 John. Diotrephes does not properly receive and thus acknowledge the authority of and the respect due to "us"[29]—the elder and his close associates, especially Gaius, as coworkers to the truth of loving one another (1:8).[30]

The audience are thus alerted that Diotrephes is a potential threat to a favorable reception of 1–2 John. The elder declares that if he comes, he will draw attention to the works Diotrephes is "doing [ποιεῖ]" (1:10b), in contrast to Gaius, "you who are doing [ποιεῖς] a faithful thing" (1:5), and "you who will do [ποιήσεις] well" to send forth the itinerant brothers in a manner worthy of God (1:6). With evil words Diotrephes disparages "us" (1:10b), as those whom he does not acknowledge (1:9b).[31] In actuality the elder already begins to accomplish through the letter of 3 John, as a substitute for his personal presence, what he intends to accomplish if he comes. As a speech act, the elder's words in the letter begin to have their effect on the audience now, as they hear them even before the elder arrives.[32]

Not only does Diotrephes not acknowledge "us" (1:9b)—the elder and his close associates, especially Gaius—but he does not properly receive or acknowledge the respect due to the itinerant brothers (1:10b). These are the brothers whom the elder and Gaius ought to support with hospitable assistance, so that they may become coworkers to the truth of loving one another (1:8). Furthermore, Diotrephes hinders those church members wishing to acknowledge the brothers with the loving support of their hospitality. Indeed, he even expels them from the "church" (1:10c), the "church" to which the elder has written the "something" that refers

---

29. The verb "receive" or "acknowledge" (ἐπιδέχεται) here refers to hospitable reception both in homes and in formal diplomatic relationships, and lexically does not include the notion of acknowledging someone's authority, according to Mitchell, "Diotrephes," 299–320. But the context seems to imply this. See also BDAG, 370.

30. "Diotrephes refuses to receive both the elder and those with whom the elder is most closely allied (cf. Jn 5:23). Instead of receiving these, he seeks to supplant them and every other authority" (Schuchard, 1–3 John, 682).

31. Marulli, "Letter," 220.

32. For a speech act analysis of 1 John, see Neufeld, Reconceiving.

to 1–2 John. The elder has thus singled out Diotrephes not only as a bad example for the audience as those who are to be coworkers with the elder to the truth of loving one another, but as a threat to a favorable hearing by all the members of the church who are to be the audience of 1–2 John.

1:11a (B): Do Not Imitate the Bad

The elder addresses Gaius for the third time as "beloved" (1:11a; cf. 1:2, 5), thus further recommending him rather than Diotrephes to the audience. He exhorts Gaius, and through him the broader communal audience, not to imitate "the bad" (1:11a). In the context this means that Gaius and his fellow church members are not to imitate Diotrephes in refusing to acknowledge the elder and the itinerant brothers, and in expelling those who wish to do so from the church (1:9–10).

1:11b (C): But the Good

Gaius and his fellow church members are not to imitate the bad (1:11a) but rather "the good" (1:11b). In the context this means that they are to imitate those who wish to acknowledge the itinerant brothers with hospitable support (1:10), and thus become coworkers to the truth of loving one another (1:8).

1:11c (C′): The One Doing Good Is from God

At this point the audience experience the pivot of parallels at the center of this chiastic unit. To imitate "the good [ἀγαθόν]" in the C element (1:11b) progresses to "the one doing good [ἀγαθοποιῶν] is from God" in the C′ element (1:11c).

That the one doing good is "from God [ἐκ τοῦ θεοῦ]" (1:11c) appeals to the audience as believers who have become children of God (John 1:12), living the divine eternal life (1:4) as those "born from God [ἐκ θεοῦ]" (1:13). The one who is "from God" (ἐκ τοῦ θεοῦ) hears the words of God (8:47) as spoken by Jesus, whose teaching is "from God [ἐκ τοῦ θεοῦ]" (7:17), especially his teaching of the commandment to love one another (13:34; 15:12, 17). As those who are "from God," then, the audience are to do good, especially the good of loving one another as part of their living eternally.

1:11d (B'): The One Doing Bad Has Not Seen God

At this point the audience experience a progression of parallels from the B (1:11a) to the B' (1:11d) element of this chiastic unit. "Do not imitate the bad [κακόν]" progresses to "the one doing bad [κακοποιῶν] has not seen God."

That the one doing bad, like Diotrephes who does not love the elder or the itinerant brothers (1:9-10), has not "seen" (ἑώρακεν) God (1:11d) reminds the audience that no one had ever "seen" (ἑώρακεν) God until Jesus made this possible (John 1:18). Not only has Jesus himself "seen" (ἑώρακεν) the Father (6:46), but whoever has seen Jesus has "seen" (ἑώρακεν) the Father (14:9). The audience has "seen" God as believers (20:29) in the sense of experiencing who God is as revealed by the Jesus who embodies God's love for the world by which believers may have eternal life (3:16). And the commandment central to doing the truth—to love one another as Jesus loved us (13:34; 15:12, 17)—is life eternal (12:50). The audience, then, are to be those who do the good of loving one another and living eternally as those who are not only "from God" (3 John 1:11c) but have "seen God" (1:11d).

1:12-15 (A'): Many Things I Have to Write to You

At this point the audience experience a progression of parallels from the A (1:9-10) to the A' (1:12-15) element of this chiastic unit. "I have written [ἔγραψά] something" (1:9) progresses to "many things I have to write [γράψαι] to you" and "to write [γράφειν] to you" (1:13); "who likes to be first [φιλοπρωτεύων]" (1:9) progresses by way of alliteration to "friends [φίλοι and φίλους]" (1:15); "does not acknowledge us [ἡμᾶς]" (1:9) and "disparaging us [ἡμᾶς]" (1:10) progress to "we [ἡμεῖς] also testify" (1:12) and "our [ἡμῶν] testimony is true" (1:12).

The audience hear the A' element (1:12-15) of this chiastic unit as a chiastic pattern in itself:

   a) Demetrius is *testified* by all and by the truth itself (1:12a),

     b) and *we* also *testify* (1:12b),

        c) and you *know* that our testimony is true (1:12c).

           d) Many things I have to *write to you* (1:13a),

e) but I do not want through ink and pen (1:13b)

d') to *write to you* (1:13c).

c') I hope instead soon to *see* you (1:14a),

b') and *we will speak* face to face (1:14b).

a') Peace to you. The friends (here) *salute* you. Salute the friends (there) by name (1:15).

The audience hear the words "but I do not want through ink and pen" (1:13b) as the unparalleled central and pivotal sub-element e) of this chiastic sub-unit. They then experience a pivot of parallels involving the only occurrences in 3 John of the expression "to write to you." "Many things I have to write to you [γράψαι σοι]" in the d) sub-element (1:13a) progresses to "to write to you" (σοι γράφειν) in the d') sub-element (1:13c). The audience then hear a progression of alliterative and lexically related parallels from "you know" (οἶδας) in the c) sub-element (1:12c) to "to see you" (σε ἰδεῖν) in the c') sub-element (1:14a).[33] Next the audience hear a progression of parallels involving the only occurrences in this sub-unit of first person plural verbs. "We also testify [μαρτυροῦμεν]" in the b) sub-element (1:12b) progresses to "we will speak" (λαλήσομεν) in the b') sub-element (1:14b). Finally, the audience hear a progression of parallels involving the only occurrences in this sub-unit of passive/middle verb forms. "Testified" (μεμαρτύρηται) in the a) sub-element (1:12a) progresses to "salute" (ἀσπάζονταί) in the a') sub-element (1:15).

In contrast to Diotrephes, who "likes to be first" and thus asserts himself over all the other members of the church (1:9), Demetrius "is testified by all and by the truth itself" (1:12a). That Demetrius is "testified" (μεμαρτύρηται) by all and by the "truth" (ἀληθείας) itself likens him to Gaius, to whose "truth" (ἀληθείᾳ) the brothers came "testifying" (μαρτυρούντων) to the elder (1:3), and to whose love the brothers "testified" (ἐμαρτύρησάν) before the church (1:6). And that Demetrius is testified by the truth itself suggests that he practices the truth of loving one another, so that the audience may consider him a model coworker to the "truth" (ἀληθείᾳ), along with the elder and Gaius (1:8). With an emphatic "we" (ἡμεῖς), referring to himself and those closely associated with him, the elder reinforces the testimony to Demetrius by all and by

---

33. BDAG, 279, 693.

the truth itself.³⁴ The elder declares that "we also testify" and that Gaius knows that "our" (ἡμῶν) testimony is true (1:12; cf. John 19:35; 21:24), despite Diotrephes not acknowledging "us [ἡμᾶς]" (1:9) and with evil words disparaging "us [ἡμᾶς]" (1:10).

Although the elder previously declared that "I have written" (ἔγραψά) something to the church (1:9), he now discloses that he has many other things "to write" (γράψαι) to Gaius, but he does not want through ink and pen "to write" (γράφειν) to him, as he is presently doing in this letter (1:13). The elder hopes instead soon "to see you [σε ἰδεῖν]" (1:14a) to further assure Gaius that "you know [οἶδας] that our testimony is true" regarding Demetrius (1:12c), and to draw his attention to the evil works of Diotrephes (1:10).³⁵ That "we will speak" (λαλήσομεν) face to face (literally "mouth to mouth," 1:14b) will allow the elder to personally assure Gaius that "we testify" (μαρτυροῦμεν) to the worth of Demetrius (1:12b).

Recalling the risen Jesus' greeting of "peace to you" (εἰρήνη ὑμῖν) to his disciples (John 20:19, 21, 26), suggesting the peace that the risen Jesus has made available to believers who may now live eternally, the elder begins to close the letter with his greeting of "peace to you" (εἰρήνη σοι) to Gaius, the main addressee of the letter (3 John 1:15a).³⁶ In contrast to Diotrephes, who "likes to be first" (φιλοπρωτεύων) among all church members (1:9), the "friends" (φίλοι) with the elder "salute" (ἀσπάζονταί) Gaius (1:15b), implicitly with the same greeting of peace, as those among all by whom Demetrius is "testified [μεμαρτύρηται]" (1:12). In turn, Gaius is to salute the "friends" (φίλους) with him, implicitly with the greeting of peace, very personally and individually "by name [κατ' ὄνομα]" (1:15c), recalling Jesus' commendation of the shepherd who "calls his own sheep by name [κατ' ὄνομα]" (John 10:3). This further confirms the communal nature of the letter as meant to be heard not only by Gaius but by the other members of his church as a plurality of distinct individuals worthy to be designated as "friends."

---

34. The elder "adds emphatic reference to the third testifier, ἡμεῖς, 'we,' which is exclusive of Gaius" (Schuchard, *1–3 John*, 663); it refers to "the author together with like-minded people at his location" (Clark, "Discourse," 113).

35. "The presbyter has already announced that he is to visit the congregation (v 10), so that he does not need to write more now. In any case, there were delicate matters—such as the case of Diotrephes—yet to be considered, and these were probably best dealt with in a personal interview" (Smalley, *3 John*, 349).

36. "'Peace to you' should probably be read more as a statement of fact than as a wish" (Olsson, *Letters*, 19).

The closing greeting of 3 John from "friends" (φίλοι) and to "friends" (φίλους) as members of the wider Johannine community (1:15) recalls the new status that Jesus conferred upon his followers. In his farewell discourse Jesus declared: "No one has greater love than this, that one lays down his life for his friends [φίλων]. You are my friends [φίλοι] if you do the things I command you. . . . I have said that you are friends [φίλους], because all the things I heard from my Father I have made known to you" (John 15:13-15).[37] This designation of "friends" for members of the Johannine community reminds the audience of 3 John that they are the "friends" of Jesus as those who do what he commanded, namely, to love one another as he loved them. This new commandment of love is central to the truth by which they may worship God in Spirit and truth (John 4:23-24), loving God and one another to live eternally.

Summary of 3 John

Although 3 John is sent by the venerable "elder," the leader of the broader Johannine community, to a certain Gaius (1:1), it is not just a personal letter but has a communal dimension. It was meant to be heard in a context of worship by a local church within the Johannine network, a church in which Gaius is a leading member. The chiastic unit (1:1-8) that comprises the first part of 3 John climaxes with an exhortation that the elder, Gaius, and the audience, his local church, may become coworkers to "the truth" by supporting itinerant believing brothers with hospitality as part of practicing the truth of loving one another (1:8). They may thus cooperatively engage in true worship, the worship in Spirit and truth (John 4:23-24), by loving God and one another to live eternally.

The chiastic unit (1:9-15) that comprises the second and final part of 3 John begins with the elder's announcement that "I have written something to the church" (1:9a), most likely a reference to 1-2 John, which 3 John, as a preliminary cover letter, is meant to introduce. Although a certain Diotrephes, who refuses to acknowledge the elder and the brothers, may prove to be a threat to a favorable hearing of 1-2 John by the church of Gaius (1:9b-10), the elder recommends to Gaius the well-attested Demetrius (1:12), suggesting that he can assist Gaius in implementing a favorable hearing of 1-2 John by the audience of 3 John. The closing greeting of "peace," a benefit of the risen, eternal life

---

37. Yarbrough, *1-3 John*, 386.

of Jesus, from "friends" and to "friends" as members of the wider Johannine community (1:15) reminds the audience of 3 John that they are the "friends" of Jesus as those who do what he commanded, namely, to love one another as he loved them. This new commandment of love is central to the truth by which they may worship God in Spirit and truth (John 4:23–24), loving God and one another for the peace of already beginning to live eternally.

3

2 John

The Elder to an Elect Lady

I Ask that We Love One Another (1:1–13)

A   ¹The elder to an *elect* lady and her *children*, whom I love in truth, and not I only but also all who know the truth, ²because of the truth that remains in us and with us will be forever. ³Grace, mercy, and peace will be with us from God the Father and from Jesus Christ the Son of the Father in truth and love. ⁴I *rejoiced* greatly because I have found some of your *children* walking in truth, just as we *received* a commandment from the Father. ⁵But now I ask you, lady, not as one *writing* a new commandment to you but that which we have had from the beginning, that we should love one another. ⁶And this is the love, that we walk according to his commandments. This is the commandment, just as you heard from the beginning, that in it you should walk. ⁷For *many* deceivers have gone out into the world, those not confessing Jesus Christ as *coming* in flesh. This is the deceiver and the antichrist. ⁸Watch yourselves, that you do not lose what we *worked* for but may obtain a *full* reward.

  B   ⁹ᵃEveryone going ahead and not *remaining in the teaching* of the Christ does not *have* God.

  B'   ⁹ᵇThe one *remaining in the teaching*, this one *has* both the Father and the Son.

A' ¹⁰If anyone comes to you and does not bring this teaching, do not *receive* him into a house and do not utter a *greeting* to him. ¹¹For the one uttering a *greeting* to him shares in his evil *works*. ¹²Having *many* things to *write* to you, I do not wish to do so through paper and ink, but I hope to be with you and to speak face to face, so that our *joy* may be *fulfilled*. ¹³The *children* of your *elect* sister salute you.³⁸

1:1–8 (A): I Rejoiced Greatly Because Your Children Are Walking in Truth

The audience hear the A element (1:1–8) of this chiastic unit as a chiastic pattern in itself:

a) The elder to an elect lady and her children, whom I love in truth, and not I only but also all who know the truth, because of the truth that remains in us and with us will be *forever*. Grace, mercy, and peace will be with us from God the Father and from *Jesus Christ* the Son of the Father in truth and love (1:1–3).

    b) I rejoiced greatly because I have found some of your children *walking* in truth, *just as* we received a commandment from the Father. But now I ask you, lady, not as one writing a new commandment to you but that which we have had *from the beginning* (1:4–5a),

        c) that we should love one another (1:5b).

    b') And this is the love, that we *walk* according to his commandments. This is the commandment, *just as* you heard *from the beginning*, that in it you should *walk* (1:6).

a') For many deceivers have gone out *into the world*, those not confessing *Jesus Christ* as coming in flesh. This is the deceiver and the antichrist. Watch yourselves, that you do not lose what we worked for but may obtain a full reward (1:7–8).

The audience hear the words "that we should love one another" (1:5b) as the unparalleled central and pivotal sub-element c) of this chiastic sub-unit. The audience, then, experience a pivot of parallels from the b) sub-element (1:4–5a) to the b') sub-element (1:6) involving the only occurrences

---

38. For the establishment of 2 John 1:1–13 as a chiasm, see ch. 1.

in 2 John of the verb "walk," the conjunction "just as," and the phrase "from the beginning." "Walking [περιπατοῦντας] in truth, just as [καθώς]" (1:4) and "that which we have had from the beginning [ἀπ' ἀρχῆς]" (1:5a) progress to "that we walk [περιπατῶμεν] according to his commandments" (1:6a), "just as [καθώς] you heard from the beginning [ἀπ' ἀρχῆς]" (1:6b), and "that in it you should walk [περιπατῆτε]" (1:6c). Finally, the audience hear a progression of parallels from the a) sub-element (1:1–3) to the a') sub-element (1:7–8) involving the only occurrences in this sub-unit of the preposition "into" and in 2 John of "Jesus Christ." "Forever [εἰς τὸν αἰῶνα]" (literally, "into the age," 1:2) and "from Jesus Christ" (1:3) progress to "into the world [εἰς τὸν κόσμον]" (1:7) and "confessing Jesus Christ" (1:7).

The audience hear the a) sub-element (1:1–3) of this chiastic sub-unit (1:1–8) as yet another chiastic pattern in itself:

(a) The elder to an elect lady and her children, whom I *love* in *truth*, and not I only but also all who know the *truth*, because of the *truth* that remains in us (1:1–2a)

  (b) and *with us will be* (1:2b)

    (c) forever (1:2c).

  (b') Grace, mercy, and peace *will be with us* (1:3a)

(a') from God the Father and from Jesus Christ the Son of the Father in *truth* and *love* (1:3b).

The audience hear the expression "forever" (1:2c) as the unparalleled central and pivotal sub-element (c) of this chiastic sub-unit. They then experience a pivot of parallels involving the only occurrences in 2 John of the expression "will be with us." "With us will be" (μεθ' ἡμῶν ἔσται) in the (b) sub-element (1:2b) progresses chiastically to "will be with us" (ἔσται μεθ' ἡμῶν) in the (b') sub-element (1:3a). Finally, the audience hear a progression of parallels involving the only occurrences in this sub-unit of expressions for "love" and "truth." "Whom I love [ἀγαπῶ] in truth [ἀληθείᾳ]" (1:1a), "all who know the truth [ἀλήθειαν]" (1:1b), and "because of the truth [ἀλήθειαν]" (1:2a) in the (a) sub-element (1:1–2a) progress to "in truth [ἀληθείᾳ] and love [ἀγάπη]" in the (a') sub-element (1:3b).

"*The* elder" (ὁ πρεσβύτερος), *the* venerable and authoritative leader of the Johannine network of local churches, who addressed 3 John to the individual Gaius (3 John 1:1a), addresses 2 John to "an elect lady and her children" (2 John 1:1a). Since 2 John is a circular cover letter for 1 John, "to an elect lady [ἐκλεκτῇ κυρίᾳ]" could refer to any of the local churches within the Johannine network.³⁹ But in this case it refers to the local church of which Gaius is a leading member and which is the audience of 1–3 John as a collective feminine personification (see the plural forms for the addressee in 1:6, 8, 10, 12), a noble "lady" with the status of being "elect" or "chosen" by God.⁴⁰ "And to her children [τέκνοις]" refers to the individual members of the local church, who are also among the "children" (τέκνα) of the elder (3 John 1:4), as well as "children" (τέκνα) of God as believers reborn into divine eternal life through the truth of Jesus Christ (John 1:4, 12–13, 17; 14:6).⁴¹

In 3 John the elder designated Gaius as the beloved "whom I love in truth [ἐγὼ ἀγαπῶ ἐν ἀληθείᾳ]" (3 John 1:1). In 2 John the elder explicitly extends his love for Gaius to all of the members of Gaius's local church. He designates the children of the elect lady as those "whom I love in truth [ἐγὼ ἀγαπῶ ἐν ἀληθείᾳ]" (2 John 1:1b). The elder then intensifies the emphatic "I" (ἐγώ) of this designation by adding that not only do "I" (ἐγώ) love them but also "all who know the truth" (1:1c). "All who know the truth [ἐγνωκότες τὴν ἀλήθειαν]" refers to all of the members of the Johannine community as believing disciples to whom Jesus promised that "you will know the truth [γνώσεσθε τὴν ἀλήθειαν]" (John 8:32). Indeed, Jesus promised that "you will know [γινώσκετε]" the "Spirit of truth [ἀληθείας]" (14:17), who will guide his followers in all the "truth [ἀληθείᾳ]" (16:13). And central to the truth is the commandment to love one another (13:34; 15:12, 17).⁴²

---

39. "So why was 2 John written? Answer: to provide a cover letter for 1 John that includes personal greetings from the elder to each of the Christian communities of the province of Asia Minor to which the companion pieces, 1 and 2 John, are being sent" (Schuchard, *1–3 John*, 612).

40. "In antiquity, a group of people, such as a city, could be referred to as 'lady,' *kyria*" (Olsson, *Letters*, 61). Disciples of Jesus are those whom "I have chosen [ἐξελεξάμην]" (John 6:70; 13:18; 15:16, 19).

41. "While 'lady' and 'sister' (2 Jn 13) designate local communities as a whole, 'children' refers to each community's—each mother's—believers" (Schuchard, *1–3 John*, 615–16).

42. "To '*know* the truth' is to accept the Christian message and to express that commitment in active love" (Smalley, *2 John*, 307; emphasis original). "Truth is the framework, the principle, that guides and gives genuine meaning to his expression of love" (Akin, *2 John*, 221).

The elder and all who know the truth love the members of this local church (2 John 1:1), "because of the truth that remains in us and with us will be [τὴν ἀλήθειαν τὴν μένουσαν ἐν ἡμῖν καὶ μεθ' ἡμῶν ἔσται] forever" (1:2). This further recalls Jesus' promise that his followers know the Spirit of "the truth" (τῆς ἀληθείας), "because beside you it remains and in you it will be [παρ' ὑμῖν μένει καὶ ἐν ὑμῖν ἔσται]" (John 14:17). And that the truth "with us will be forever [μεθ' ἡμῶν ἔσται εἰς τὸν αἰῶνα]" (2 John 1:2) recalls Jesus' promise that the Advocate, who is the Spirit of truth, is "to be with you forever [μεθ' ὑμῶν εἰς τὸν αἰῶνα ᾖ]" (John 14:16).[43] That the truth will be with us "forever [εἰς τὸν αἰῶνα]" (2 John 1:2) resonates with the eternal life made available through the truth of Jesus, by which one will live "forever [εἰς τὸν αἰῶνα]" (John 4:14; 6:51, 58; 8:51–52; 10:28; 11:26).

Not only the truth "will be with us" (μεθ' ἡμῶν ἔσται), the Johannine believers, forever in eternal life (2 John 1:2), but the divine benefits of that eternal life—"grace, mercy, and peace [εἰρήνη]"—"will be with us [ἔσται μεθ' ἡμῶν] from God the Father and from Jesus Christ the Son of the Father in truth and love" (1:3). The elder extended a prayerful greeting of "peace" (εἰρήνη) to Gaius at the close of 3 John (1:15), the "peace" (εἰρήνη) that is the benefit of the eternal life of the risen Jesus (John 20:19, 21, 26). And now the elder embellishes this peace with the closely related divine benefits of grace and mercy that accompany peace in his prayerful greeting at the beginning of 2 John.[44]

That the grace, mercy, and peace of eternal life will be with us "from God the Father [πατρός] and from Jesus Christ the Son [υἱοῦ] of the Father [πατρός] in truth and love [ἀγάπη]" (2 John 1:3) recalls Jesus' declaration that "the Father [πατήρ] loves [ἀγαπᾷ] the Son [υἱόν]" (John 3:35; cf. 17:26) and "whoever believes in the Son [υἱόν] has life eternal" (3:36). This grace, mercy, and peace from the divine Father and Son will be with us believers "in truth and love [ἐν ἀληθείᾳ καὶ ἀγάπῃ]" (2 John 1:3). Practicing the truth that includes the commandment to love one another, then, as exemplified by the elder who designated the audience as those whom "I

---

43. "What is said in John's Gospel about the Spirit of truth, that he will dwell in the disciples of Jesus (John 14:15–17), is referred here to the truth itself" (Smalley, 2 John, 308).

44. "Grace is God doing for us what we do not deserve, mercy is his not doing for us what we do deserve, and peace is God giving us what we need based upon his grace and mercy. The word order is significant. God's grace is always prior. Mercy and peace flow from it" (Akin, 2 John, 222).

love in truth [ἀγαπῶ ἐν ἀληθείᾳ]" (1:1), assures that divine grace, mercy and peace will be with us believers forever in eternal life.

In 3 John the elder declared to Gaius: "For I rejoiced greatly [ἐχάρην γὰρ λίαν] at brothers coming and testifying to your truth, just as you in truth are walking [ἐν ἀληθείᾳ περιπατεῖς]. Greater joy than these things I do not have, that I hear that my children [ἐμὰ τέκνα] in the truth are walking [ἐν τῇ ἀληθείᾳ περιπατοῦντα]" (1:3-4). In 2 John the elder associates his children and Gaius with the children of the elect lady, as he similarly declares to her, "I rejoiced greatly [ἐχάρην λίαν] because I have found some of your children [τέκνων σου] walking in truth [περιπατοῦντας ἐν ἀληθείᾳ]" (1:4a), "her children" (τέκνοις αὐτῆς) whom the elder loves "in truth [ἐν ἀληθείᾳ]" (1:1).

That they are walking in truth, "just as we received a commandment from the Father [ἐντολὴν ἐλάβομεν παρὰ τοῦ πατρός]" (1:4b), implies that walking in truth refers to their loving one another. It recalls Jesus' statement that "this commandment I received from my Father [ἐντολὴν ἔλαβον παρὰ τοῦ πατρός μου]" in reference to his laying down his life (John 10:18) as an act of the greatest love (15:13). Indeed, the "commandment" (ἐντολήν) the "Father" (πατήρ) gave Jesus to communicate (12:49) is a new "commandment" (ἐντολήν) he gave to love one another (13:34). This is in accord with his declaration that "this is my commandment [ἐντολή], that you love one another as I loved you" (15:12). The elder then makes explicit the implication that walking in truth refers to loving one another in accord with "a commandment [ἐντολήν] we received" (2 John 1:4), as he adds, "But now I ask you, lady, not as one writing a new commandment [ἐντολήν] to you but that which we have had from the beginning, that we love one another" (1:5).

The elder then declares that "this is love, that we walk [περιπατῶμεν] according to his commandments [ἐντολάς]" (1:6a), that "this is the commandment [ἐντολή]," and "that in it you should walk [περιπατῆτε]" (1:6b). These assertions emphatically confirm that "walking [περιπατοῦντας] in truth, just as we received a commandment [ἐντολήν] from the Father" (1:4) refers to loving one another. And the elder's reminder that "just as [καθώς] you heard from the beginning [ἀπ' ἀρχῆς]" (1:6b) reinforces his reminder that "just as [καθώς] we received a commandment from the

Father" (1:4) "which we have had from the beginning [ἀπ' ἀρχῆς], that we should love one another" (1:5).[45]

In contrast to the brothers, the members of the Johannine community, who "have gone out" (ἐξῆλθον) on behalf of the divine name, receive nothing from the pagans (3 John 1:7); "many deceivers have gone out [ἐξῆλθον] into the world [εἰς τὸν κόσμον]" (2 John 1:7a). This contradicts living eternally by practicing the truth of loving one another that with us will be "forever [εἰς τὸν αἰῶνα]" (1:2). That these many deceivers were not confessing "Jesus Christ" as coming in "flesh [σαρκί]" (1:7b) suggests that they denied that "Jesus Christ" is the incarnate Son of the Father (1:3). In other words, they denied the confession that "the Word became flesh [σάρξ] and dwelled among us, and we saw his glory, glory as of the only begotten one from the Father" (John 1:14).

These many deceivers are equivalent to one collective entity—"the deceiver and the antichrist" (2 John 1:7c).[46] Consequently, the elder warns the audience, the children of the elect lady (1:1), "watch yourselves, that you do not lose what we worked for [εἰργασάμεθα]" (1:8a), as those who are to become "coworkers" (συνεργοί) to the truth of loving one another to live eternally (3 John 1:8). This resonates with Jesus' exhortation, "Do not work [ἐργάζεσθε] for the food that perishes but for the food that remains for life eternal" (John 6:27). The elder exhorts his audience so that they rather "may obtain [ἀπολάβητε] a full reward" (2 John 1:8b), in accord with their practice of the commandment to love one another (1:5) that "we received" (ἐλάβομεν) from the Father (1:4). This "full [πλήρη] reward," from the one "full [πλήρης] of grace and truth" (John 1:14), includes the divine benefits of "grace, mercy, and peace" (2 John 1:3) that accompany living eternally by the practice of the truth, which amounts to true worship in Spirit and truth (John 4:23-24), the worship of loving God and one another.[47]

---

45. After employing singular forms to address the "lady" (1:5), the elder now employs plural forms (1:6). This indicates that the "lady" is a collective personification of the individual members of the local church, the "children" of the "elect lady" (1:1). "From the beginning" refers "to the original communication of the (Johannine) tradition in that church" (Painter, *2 John*, 348).

46. "The articles in front of 'deceiver' (ὁ πλάνος) and 'antichrist' (ὁ ἀντίχριστος) should be seen as marking out a certain category of persons" (Yarbrough, *1-3 John*, 344).

47. "To lose hold of the truth about Jesus is to lose hold of the Father and all his benefits, including eternal life and love in the community" (Witherington, *Letters*, 575).

1:9a (B): The One Not Remaining in the Teaching Does Not Have God

The elder then warns that "everyone going ahead and not remaining in the teaching [διδαχῇ] of the Christ does not have God [θεόν]" (1:9a).[48] This accords with Jesus' statement that "my teaching [διδαχή] is not my own but from the one who sent me" (John 7:16). In other words, concerning his "teaching" (διδαχῆς), it is "from God [ἐκ τοῦ θεοῦ]" (7:17), just as Jesus Christ himself is the one coming in flesh (2 John 1:7; John 1:14) "from God [ἐκ τοῦ θεοῦ]" (8:42). The "teaching of the Christ," then, refers both to what Christ taught, especially the commandment to love one another, and to the teaching about Christ as the one coming from God in flesh.[49] The implication is that in anyone not "remaining" (μένων) in the teaching of the Christ, the truth of loving one another is not "remaining [μένουσαν]" (2 John 1:2). That everyone not remaining in the teaching of the Christ "does not have God [θεόν]" resonates with "the one doing good is from God [θεοῦ]," whereas "the one doing bad has not seen God [θεόν]" (3 John 1:11), the God that can be seen in Jesus Christ as coming from God in flesh (John 1:18; 14:9).

1:9b (B'): The One Remaining in the Teaching Has Both the Father and the Son

At this point the audience experience the pivot of parallels at the center of this chiastic unit. "Not remaining in the teaching [μένων ἐν τῇ διδαχῇ] of the Christ" and "does not have [ἔχει] God" in the B element (1:9a) progress to "remaining in the teaching" (μένων ἐν τῇ διδαχῇ) and "this one has [ἔχει] both the Father and the Son" in the B' element (1:9b). The one remaining in the teaching, the teaching of the truth of loving one another, has not just "God [θεόν]" (1:9a) but both the divine "Father" (πατέρα) and the divine "Son [υἱόν]" (1:9b). This means that such a person has the divine benefits of the "grace, mercy, and peace" of eternal life

---

48. "'Goes ahead' likely means 'goes too far' or 'goes beyond' and thus 'leaves behind' the sound teaching" (Schuchard, *1–3 John*, 630).

49. With reference to Wendland ("What Is Truth," 310), Kruse (*Letters*, 212n15) notes that both the subjective (what Christ taught) and objective (teaching about Christ) meanings are intended here: "That is, it was important not only to confess that Jesus Christ had come in the flesh (teaching about Christ), but also to acknowledge and obey Christ's teaching/command to love one another."

that "will be with us from God [θεοῦ] the Father [πατρός] and from Jesus Christ the Son [υἱοῦ] of the Father [πατρός] in truth and love" (1:3).

1:10-13 (A'): That Our Joy May Be Fulfilled

At this point the audience experience the following progression of parallels from the A (1:1-8) to the A' (1:10-13) element of this chiastic unit: From "an elect [ἐκλεκτῇ] lady and her children [τέκνοις]" (1:1) and "your children [τέκνων]" (1:4) to "the children [τέκνα] of your elect [ἐκλεκτῆς] sister" (1:13); from "I rejoiced [ἐχάρην] greatly" (1:4) to "greeting [χαίρειν]" (1:10, 11) and "our joy [χαρά]" (1:12); from "we received [ἐλάβομεν] a commandment" (1:4) to "do not receive [λαμβάνετε] him" (1:10); from "writing [γράφων] a new commandment" (1:5) to "to write [γράφειν] to you" (1:12); from "many [πολλοί] deceivers" (1:7) to "many [πολλά] things" (1:12); from "coming [ἐρχόμενον] in flesh" (1:7) to "if anyone comes [ἔρχεται] to you" (1:10); from "what we worked for [εἰργασάμεθα]" (1:8) to "evil works [ἔργοις]" (1:11); and from "full [πλήρη] reward" (1:8) to "may be fulfilled [πεπληρωμένη]" (1:12).

The audience hear the A' element (1:10-13) of this chiastic unit as a chiastic pattern in itself:

a) If anyone comes *to you* and does not bring this teaching (1:10a),

  b) do not receive him into a house and do not *utter* a *greeting* to him (1:10b).

  b') For the one *uttering* a *greeting* to him shares in his evil works (1:11).

a') Having many things to write to you, I do not wish to do so through paper and ink, but I hope to be *with you* and to speak face to face, so that our joy may be fulfilled. The children of your elect sister salute you (1:12-13).

At the center of this chiastic sub-unit the audience experience a pivot of parallels involving the only occurrences in this sub-unit of the terms "utter" and "greeting." "Do not utter [λέγετε] a greeting [χαίρειν]" in the b) sub-element (1:10b) progresses to "the one uttering [λέγων] a greeting [χαίρειν]" in the b') sub-element (1:11). The audience then hear a progression of parallels involving the only occurrences in 2 John of the prepositional phrase "to/with you." "If anyone comes to you [πρὸς ὑμᾶς]" in the a) sub-element (1:10a) progresses to "I hope to be with you [πρὸς ὑμᾶς]" (1:12) in the a') sub-element (1:12-13).

"If anyone comes [ἔρχεται] to you and does not bring this teaching [διδαχήν]" (1:10a) refers to the "teaching [διδαχῇ] of the Christ" (1:9), as the one from God "coming [ἐρχόμενον] in flesh" (1:7) and teaching the commandment that we should love one another (1:5). In accord with this commandment that "we received" (ἐλάβομεν) from the Father (1:4), the audience are not to "receive" (λαμβάνετε) such a person who rejects the teaching that Christ came from God in flesh and taught that we should love one another into a house or even utter a greeting to him (1:10b).[50] This is in contrast to the elder's exhortation that we ought to "support" (ὑπολαμβάνειν) with hospitable love those brothers (3 John 1:8) who have gone out on behalf of the divine name, "receiving" (λαμβάνοντες) nothing from the pagans (1:7). Indeed, the one uttering a greeting of hospitality to such a person would share in his evil "works [ἔργοις]" (2 John 1:11), which contradicts what "we worked for [εἰργασάμεθα]" (1:8) as "coworkers" (συνεργοί) to the truth (3 John 1:8) of loving one another as taught by the Christ who came from God in flesh.

In view of the fact that "many" (πολλοί) deceivers have gone out into the world (2 John 1:7), and although he is not "writing" (γράφων) a new commandment (1:5), the elder has "many" (πολλά) additional things to "write" (γράφειν) to the audience (1:12a). In 3 John the elder told Gaius, "Many things I have to write to you [σοι], but I do not want through ink and pen to write to you [σοι]. I hope instead soon to see you [σε], and we will speak face to face" (1:13-14). And now in 2 John he extends what he told Gaius and thus reinforces it for the wider audience: "Having many things to write to you [ὑμῖν], I do not wish to do so through paper and ink, but I hope to be with you [ὑμᾶς] and to speak face to face" (1:12).[51] The elder hopes to be "with you" (πρὸς ὑμᾶς), the audience, to speak

---

50. "This could well be a reference to refusing to provide hospitality to such itinerant false teachers, but it is also plausible that 'house' here refers to the house-church meeting, in which case the reference is not to general hospitality, but rather to allowing these people opportunities in Christian worship to spread their false views" (Witherington, *Letters*, 577). Olsson (*Letters*, 55) also argues that this refers to not "receiving someone into the house where one gathers for worship." The elder "prohibits not any and all forms of greeting. Rather, he prohibits one that would have been customary in welcoming a person into the fellowship of a house, especially that of a house church (see 2 Jn 13; 3 Jn 15)" (Schuchard, *1-3 John*, 633).

51. "References to having much to write but preferring a personal visit is standard in Hellenistic letters" (Painter, *2 John*, 356).

further with them regarding anyone who comes "to you" (πρὸς ὑμᾶς) not bringing the teaching of the Christ (1:10).

The elder wishes to come and speak with the audience in person, "so that our joy may be fulfilled" (1:12). This "joy" (χαρά) includes what the elder previously declared, namely, that "I rejoiced" (ἐχάρην) greatly over those in the audience who are walking in the truth (1:4) of loving one another (1:5). In 3 John he declared that he has no greater "joy" (χαράν) than to hear that his children in the truth are walking (1:4). This joy stands in contrast to the joy connoted in the "greeting" (χαίρειν) to be denied one who does not bring the teaching of the Christ (1:10-11). That the joy of the elder and the audience may be "fulfilled" (πεπληρωμένη) reinforces his exhortation for them to obtain a "full" (πλήρη) reward (1:8), including the divine grace, mercy, and peace (1:3) that accompany living eternally by the worship that consists of loving God and one another. It recalls Jesus' farewell address to his disciples that "my joy [χαρά] may be in you and your joy [χαρά] may be fulfilled [πληρωθῇ]" (John 15:11; cf. 16:24; 17:13), as those who practice his commandment "to love one another as I have loved you" (15:12; cf. 15:10).

The elder closes the letter of 2 John with the greeting that "the children [τέκνα] of your elect [ἐκλεκτῆς] sister salute you" (1:13), that is, the "children" (τέκνοις) of the "elect" (ἐκλεκτῇ) lady to whom the letter is addressed (1:1), some of whose "children" (τέκνων) are walking in the truth (1:4) of loving one another (1:5). "Your elect sister" thus refers to the main church led by the elder as a sister church to the local church addressed in 2 John and designated "an elect lady." "Your elect sister" are the "friends" (φίλοι) who "salute you" (ἀσπάζονταί σε), Gaius, at the close of 3 John (1:15a). As the children of your elect sister, they now "salute you" (ἀσπάζεταί σε), the elect lady, the associate children and "friends" (φίλους) of the elect sister whom Gaius is to salute (3 John 1:15b).[52]

The closely related final greetings of 2 and 3 John together reinforce that the members, the "children" (τέκνα), of the sister churches (2 John 1:1, 4, 13) in the Johannine community are not only "children" (τέκνα) of the elder (3 John 1:4) but "children" (τέκνα) of God as believers who

---

52. "Despite his senior and supervisory status, he [the elder] writes as a fellow member of the body of Christ that he oversees. Moreover, the ecclesial bodies connected by his epistle are 'family'—members are 'children,' and a fellow church can be viewed corporately as a 'sister'" (Yarbrough, *1–3 John*, 359). "The greeting conveyed by the presbyter adds the authority of the Johannine community itself to this own as well as including his personal expression of Christian fellowship and love" (Smalley, *2 John*, 323).

are reborn into the divine eternal life of God (John 1:4, 12; 3:16, 36; 5:24; 6:40, 47; 11:25; 20:31). They are also the "friends" (φίλοι) of Jesus (15:14), who are to practice his commandment "to love one another as I have loved you" (15:12). Indeed, as children of God they are to live eternally as friends of Jesus who practice the true worship and love of God, the worship in Spirit and truth (4:23–24), by loving one another (2 John 1:5).

Summary of 2 John

In 3 John the elder indirectly addressed the communal audience assembled for worship by directly addressing Gaius (1:1), one of their leading members, regarding "something I have written to the church" (1:9), an apparent reference to 1–2 John. In 2 John the elder addresses this same audience as "an elect lady and her children" (1:1). He prays that the divine benefits of the "grace, mercy, and peace" that accompany eternal life will be with us as those who practice the truth of loving one another (1:3–5). As those who remain in the teaching of the Christ, the teaching that Christ came from God in flesh (1:7) and taught us God's commandment to love one another (1:4–5), the audience may have these divine benefits of eternal life from the Father and the Son (1:9).

As coworkers to the truth of loving one another to live eternally, the elder, Gaius, and the audience, as members of the Johannine community, ought to support with hospitable love those believing brothers who have gone out on behalf of the divine name (3 John 1:7–8). But the many deceivers who have gone out into the world the audience is not to receive with hospitable love, because they do not confess Jesus Christ as coming from God in flesh and they reject the teaching of the Christ to love one another (2 John 1:7–11). Before the elder comes to the audience to speak with them further in person (3 John 1:13–14; 2 John 1:12), they are to listen to 1 John, included in "something I have written to the church" (3 John 1:9), as a substitute for his personal presence. As fellow "children" not only of elect sister churches (2 John 1:1, 13) but of God (John 1:12), the audience, as members of the Johannine community, are to live eternally as fellow "friends" (3 John 1:15) of Jesus who practice the true worship and love of God, the worship in Spirit and truth (John 4:23–24), by loving one another (2 John 1:3–5).

4

1 John 1:1–10

He Will Cleanse Us from All Unrighteousness

If in the light we are walking, we have fellowship with one another

A   ^{1:1}What was from the beginning, what we have heard, what we have seen with our eyes, what we observed and our hands touched concerning the *word* of the life—²indeed the life was manifested and we have seen and testify and declare to you the life eternal which was with the Father and manifested to us—³what we have seen and heard, we declare also to you, so that you also may have fellowship with us. And the fellowship that is ours is with the Father and with *his Son Jesus* Christ. ⁴And these things indeed we are writing, so that our joy may be fulfilled.

⁵ᵃAnd this is the message which we have heard from him and announce to you,

  B   ⁵ᵇthat God is *light* and there is no darkness in him at all. ⁶ᵃIf we say that *fellowship we have* with him yet in the darkness are *walking*,

    C   ⁶ᵇwe are lying and not doing the truth.

B' ⁷ᵃBut if in the *light* we are *walking* as he is in the *light, fellowship we have* with one another

A' ⁷ᵇand the blood of *Jesus his Son* cleanses us from all sin. ⁸If we say that sin we do not have, we are deceiving ourselves and the truth is not in us. ⁹If we confess our sins, he is faithful and righteous, so that he will forgive us the sins and cleanse us from all unrighteousness. ¹⁰If we say that we have not sinned, we make him a liar and his *word* is not in us.[53]

1:1–5a (A): The Word of Life Eternal and Fellowship with the Father and His Son Jesus Christ

The audience hear the A element (1:1–5a) of this chiastic unit as a chiastic pattern in itself:

a) What was from the beginning, what we have *heard*, what we have seen with our eyes, what we observed and our hands touched concerning the word of the life—indeed the life was manifested and we have seen and testify and *declare to you* the life eternal which was with the Father and manifested to us—what we have seen and *heard*, we *declare* also *to you* (1:1–3a),

b) so that you also may have *fellowship* with us (1:3b).

b') And the *fellowship* that is ours is with the Father and with his Son Jesus Christ (1:3c).

a') And these things indeed we are writing, so that our joy may be fulfilled. And this is the message which we have *heard* from him and *announce to you* (1:4–5a).

At the center of this chiastic sub-unit the audience experience a pivot of parallels involving the only occurrences in this sub-unit of the term "fellowship." "You also may have fellowship [κοινωνίαν] with us" in the b) sub-element (1:3b) progresses to "our fellowship [κοινωνία]" in the b') sub-element (1:3c). The audience then hear a progression of parallels involving the only occurrences in this sub-unit of the verb "hear" and the expression "we declare/announce to you." "What we have heard [ἀκηκόαμεν]" (1:1, 3a), "we declared to you [ἀπαγγέλλομεν ὑμῖν]" (1:2), and "we declare also to you [ἀπαγγέλλομεν καὶ ὑμῖν]" (1:3a) in the a) sub-element

---

53. For the establishment of 1 John 1:1–10 as a chiasm, see ch. 1.

(1:1–3a) progress to "the message which we have heard [ἀκηκόαμεν]" (1:5a) and "we announce to you [ἀναγγέλλομεν ὑμῖν]" (1:5a) in the a') sub-element (1:4–5a).

The audience hear the a) sub-element (1:1–3a) of this chiastic sub-unit as yet another chiastic pattern in itself:

(a) What was from the beginning, what we have *heard*, what we have seen with our eyes, what we observed and our hands touched (1:1a)

  (b) concerning the word of the *life*—indeed the *life* was *manifested* (1:1b–2a),

    (c) and we have seen and testify (1:2b)

  (b') and declare to you the *life* eternal which was with the Father and *manifested* to us (1:2c)—

(a') what we have seen and *heard*, we declare also to you (1:3a).

The audience hear the expression "and we have seen and testify" (1:2b) as the unparalleled central and pivotal (c) sub-element of this chiastic sub-unit. They then experience a pivot of parallels involving the only occurrences in this chiastic sub-unit of the noun "life" and the verb "manifest." "The word of the life [ζωῆς] and the life [ζωή] was manifested [ἐφανερώθη]" in the (b) sub-element (1:1b–2a) progresses to "the life [ζωήν] eternal" and "manifested [ἐφανερώθη] to us" in the (b') sub-element (1:2c). The audience then hear a progression of parallels involving the only occurrences in this sub-unit of the verb "hear." "What we have heard [ἀκηκόαμεν]" in the (a) sub-element (1:1a) progresses to "what we have seen and heard [ἀκηκόαμεν]" in the (a') sub-element (1:3a).

Having heard the introductory cover letters of 3 and 2 John, the audience, assembled as a local church, an "elect lady and her children" (2 John 1:1), a "sister" to the main Johannine church led by the elder (1:13), are well disposed for listening to 1 John in a context of communal worship. In 3 John the elder recommended to them both the beloved Gaius (1:1), a leading member of the local church, and Demetrius, a well-attested member of the Johannine community (1:12). In view of the threat that Diotrephes poses to the proper reception of the "something"—1 and 2 John—that the elder has written to the church (1:9), he has entrusted Gaius, assisted by Demetrius, with the public performance of these documents before this particular local church. In 2 John the elder exhorted the audience to love one another in accord with the commandment of the truth, so that the divine benefits of "grace, mercy, and peace" that accompany living eternally may be with them "from God the Father and from Jesus Christ the Son of the Father in truth and love" (1:3). This prepares the audience for a fuller development of this theme in 1 John.

The opening of 1 John presents the audience with a profession of faith regarding "the" divine and eternal life proclaimed by an authoritative communal "we," which includes the elder and his associates as the foundational witnesses for this faith.[54] The profession begins with a rhythmic progression of emphatic assertions introduced by the neuter relative pronoun "what" (ὅ) to refer in a general and comprehensive way to all of the items of evidence for this faith: "What [ὅ] was from the beginning, what [ὅ] we have heard, what [ὅ] we have seen with our eyes, what [ὅ] we observed and our hands touched concerning the word of the life" (1:1). All of the various elements of this progression recall and resonate with, but also in some ways develop, what the audience remember from the Gospel of John.[55]

First of all, "what was from the beginning [ὅ ἦν ἀπ' ἀρχῆς] ... concerning the word [λόγου] of the life [ζωῆς]" (1:1) recalls "in the beginning was the Word [ἐν ἀρχῇ ἦν ὁ λόγος], and the Word [λόγος] was with God, and the Word [λόγος] was God. He was in the beginning [ἐν ἀρχῇ] with God ... what [ὅ] came to be in him was life [ζωή], and the life [ζωή] was the light for human beings" (John 1:1-4).[56] "What" (ὅ) was from the beginning concerning the word of the "life" (ζωῆς) in 1 John resonates with "what" (ὅ) came to be in him was "life" (ζωή) in John. But whereas at this point in John λόγος refers to the personified Word, Jesus Christ (1:17), in whom came to be eternal life (cf. 14:6), in 1 John λόγος can

---

54. The elder uses "we" rather than the singular "I" in order "to deflect attention away from the author as if he were speaking only on his own authority or of something that ultimately depends only on his experience and on his interpretation of it" (Lieu, *Commentary*, 39).

55. "In the Gospel of John, the neuter can be used to refer to persons of a certain type or quality. See, e.g., John 6:37. Thus, here in 1 John it is Jesus who is in view, with all that Jesus is and stands for, his being, his person, his words and deeds, i.e., Jesus as the revealed God and the divine life (1 John 5:20)" (Olsson, *Letters*, 74).

56. In John 8:44 Jesus declares that the devil "was from the beginning" (ἦν ἀπ' ἀρχῆς) a murderer, which involves the verb "was" in a predicate construction with "murderer," whereas "what was from the beginning" (ὅ ἦν ἀπ' ἀρχῆς) in 1 John 1:1 involves the verb "was" to express existence itself.

refer to both the personified Word and to the word spoken by this Word concerning eternal life.[57]

Indeed, Jesus, the Word, declared that whoever hears my "word" (λόγον) and believes the one who sent me has "life" (ζωήν) eternal (John 5:24). He went on to warn that on the last day the "word" (λόγος) that he spoke will condemn the one who rejects him, because Jesus did not speak on his own, but the Father who sent him gave him a commandment to reveal and communicate, and his commandment is "life" (ζωή) eternal (12:48–50). In other words, believers who practice Jesus' commandment to love one another as he loved them (13:34; 15:12) have divine eternal life. By loving one another, then, they are already living eternally. Thus, "concerning the word [λόγου] of the life [ζωῆς]" (1 John 1:1) refers to both the personified Word who brings about the eternal life, indeed who is "the life [ζωή]" (John 14:6), as well as the word spoken by Jesus, the Word, especially the commandment to love one another, which leads to the eternal life.[58]

In the proclamation, "what was from the beginning" (1 John 1:1a), "what" (ὅ) functions as the subject referring to the eternal life as "what" (ὅ) came to be in the personified Word that was in the beginning (John 1:1, 3–4). This progresses to "what we have heard" (1 John 1:1b), with "what" (ὅ) now functioning as the object and referring to the word spoken by Jesus as a basis for coming to believe. "What we have heard [ἀκηκόαμεν]" recalls and resonates with what the Samaritans in John proclaimed when they came to believe in Jesus: "For we ourselves have heard [ἀκηκόαμεν] and we know that this is truly the savior of the world" (John 4:42). This illustrates how "many more believed on account of his word [λόγον]" (4:41) and points to "what we heard" concerning the "word" (λόγου) of the eternal life (1 John 1:1) for those who believe (John 3:15–16, 36; 5:24; 6:40, 47; 11:25; 20:31). And "what we have heard from the beginning [ἀπ' ἀρχῆς]" recalls what the audience heard in 2 John about the commandment to love one another, which "you heard from the beginning [ἠκούσατε ἀπ' ἀρχῆς]" (1:6).

"What we have heard" (1 John 1:1b) then progresses to "what we have seen," intensified with a redundant "with our eyes" (1:1c). "What we have seen [ἑωράκαμεν]" concerning the word of the eternal life resonates with

---

57. "Jesus gave the word and embodied it" (Houlden, *Commentary*, 52).

58. "Against those who have favored an either/or, the phrase 'word of life' evokes instead a both/and: *both* (1) he who is ὁ λόγος, 'the Word,' and ἡ ζωή, 'the Life,' *and* (2) the things for which he who is the Word and the Life is himself responsible, which are word and life" (Schuchard, *1–3 John*, 87; emphases original).

what Jesus, speaking on behalf of believers, tells Nicodemus as the representative of unbelieving Jews, regarding seeing as a basis for faith: "We testify about what we have seen [ἑωράκαμεν], but you do not accept our testimony" (John 3:11). He adds that "if I have told you about earthly things and you do not believe, how if I tell you about heavenly things will you believe?" (3:12). Similarly, the disciples' proclamation that "we have seen [ἑωράκαμεν] the Lord" (20:25) implies their faith in the risen Jesus, who brings eternal life (10:28; 11:25–26; 17:2; 20:31), in contrast to Thomas who declares, "I will not believe," until he likewise sees (20:25). The redundant but emphatic "with our eyes [ὀφθαλμοῖς]" presents a contrast with John's quotation of Isa 6:10, "they would not see with their eyes [ὀφθαλμοῖς]" (12:40), as the explanation for the reason "they could not believe" (12:39).

The next in the series of assertions in this communal profession of faith, "what we observed [ἐθεασάμεθα]" (1 John 1:1d), resonates with the communal profession of faith in the prologue of John: "And the Word became flesh and dwelled among us, and we observed [ἐθεασάμεθα] his glory, glory as of the only begotten one from the Father" (1:14). This assertion in 1 John is followed by "and our hands [χεῖρες] touched" (1:1e), recalling how Thomas came to share in the communal faith of the other disciples after he put his "hand" (χεῖρά) into the side of the risen Jesus, the source of eternal life (John 20:27; cf. 10:28; 11:25–26; 17:2; 20:31). Similarly, "what we observed and our hands touched" implicitly invites the audience to share the faith of this authoritative and communal "we," the faith concerning the word of the eternal life (1 John 1:1).

The focus of this communal profession of faith concerning the word of "the life [τῆς ζωῆς]" (1:1) continues with "indeed the life [ἡ ζωή] was manifested [ἐφανερώθη]" (1:2a), recalling that the risen Jesus, the source of eternal life, was "manifested" (ἐφανερώθη) three times to his disciples (John 21:14; cf. 21:1). The profession goes on to emphasize that "the life," now explicitly identified as the eternal life, was indeed manifested "to us": "and we have seen and testify and declare to you the life eternal [τὴν ζωὴν τὴν αἰώνιον] which was with the Father and manifested [ἐφανερώθη] to us" (1 John 1:2).[59] "We have seen and testify" (ἑωράκαμεν καὶ μαρτυροῦμεν) reinforces the recall of "about what we have seen we

---

59. "The Greek word for 'eternal' (αἰώνιον) suggests more a quality than a measure of time: almost 'of divine character,' 'belonging to another world.' Being eternal is a characteristic belonging to God" (Olsson, *Letters*, 76). "'Eternal life' is a spiritual *quality* of life, which God gives to every believer through Jesus his Son (cf. John 3:16; 17:2–3)" (Smalley, *1 John*, 9; emphasis original).

testify" (ὃ ἑωράκαμεν μαρτυροῦμεν) as a basis for believing (John 3:11). That "we declare to you" (ἀπαγγέλλομεν ὑμῖν) the life eternal that was "with the Father" (πρὸς τὸν πατέρα), recalling the life that was in the Word who was "with God [πρὸς τὸν θεόν]" (John 1:1-2, 4) resonates with Jesus' promise to his disciples that "concerning the Father [πατρός] I will declare to you [ἀπαγγελῶ ὑμῖν]" (16:25).

This communal profession of faith continues with "what we have seen and heard [ὃ ἑωράκαμεν καὶ ἀκηκόαμεν]" (1 John 1:3a), reinforcing the initial assertion, "what we have heard [ὃ ἀκηκόαμεν], what we have seen [ὃ ἑωράκαμεν] with our eyes" (1:1). The pronouncement that "we have seen and testify and declare [ἀπαγγέλλομεν] to you [ὑμῖν] the life eternal which was with the Father and manifested to us [ἡμῖν]" (1:2) then progresses to the emphatic assertion that this life eternal "we declare [ἀπαγγέλλομεν] also to you [καὶ ὑμῖν]" (1:3a). This life eternal was manifested *to us* and now "we" declare it *also to you.* In other words, the communal and foundational "we," representative of the main Johannine church led by the elder, are inviting the communal "you," the audience who are an associated "sister" church (2 John 1:1, 13), to accept and to assent to their authoritative witness and thus share their faith in the life eternal that has been manifested to them.

This is confirmed as the pronouncement regarding the life eternal that was manifested "to us [ἡμῖν]" (1 John 1:2) and that "we declare also to you [καὶ ὑμῖν]" (1:3a) is followed by "so that you also [καὶ ὑμεῖς]," as a worshiping community, "may have fellowship with us [ἡμῶν]" (1:3b), as the goal of this profession of faith, an act of worship in itself. Instead of being one who "shares" (κοινωνεῖ) in the evil works of someone (2 John 1:11) who does not remain in the teaching of the Christ that we should love one another (1:5, 9), the audience may have "fellowship" (κοινωνίαν) with the foundational and authoritative "us." And this "fellowship" (κοινωνία) that is "ours" (ἡμετέρα), the fellowship that the authoritative "we" share with "you," the audience as fellow worshipers, involves living the life eternal, the divine life, which was "with the Father [πρὸς τὸν πατέρα]" (1 John 1:2).

Not only do "you" share this life "with us [μεθ᾽ ἡμῶν]" (1:3b), but together "we" and "you" share this divine eternal life "with the Father [μετὰ τοῦ πατρός] and with his Son [μετὰ τοῦ υἱοῦ αὐτοῦ] Jesus Christ" (1:3c). This fellowship that is "ours" (ἡμετέρα) includes the "grace, mercy and peace" that "will be with us [μεθ᾽ ἡμῶν] from God the Father [πατρός] and from Jesus Christ the Son of the Father [υἱοῦ τοῦ πατρός] in truth and love" (2 John 1:3). That this fellowship includes the sharing of the divine eternal life of the Father and of the Son accords with Jesus' pronouncement that "just as the Father [πατήρ] has life in himself, so also he granted the Son [υἱῷ] to have life in himself" (John 5:26).[60]

In 3 John the elder disclosed that "I have written [ἔγραψά] something to the church" (1:9), an apparent reference to 1–2 John. But now in 1 John the individual writer is pluralized to "these things indeed we are writing [ταῦτα γράφομεν], so that [ἵνα] our joy may be fulfilled" (1:4), with an emphatic "we" (ἡμεῖς) including not just the elder but the foundational and authoritative witnesses associated with him in the main Johannine church.[61] This statement of the purpose for writing recalls and resonates with the stated purpose toward the conclusion of the Gospel of John that "these things [ταῦτα] are written [γέγραπται] so that [ἵνα] you may believe that Jesus is the Christ, the Son of God and so that [ἵνα], believing, you may have life in his name" (20:31). But the "our" (ἡμῶν) of "our joy" (1 John 1:4) is not limited to the "we" who are writing. It includes the "you" of the audience, their fellow worshipers, as those who are to share in this fellowship, the living of eternal life by loving one another, the fellowship that is "ours [ἡμετέρα]" (1:3).[62]

"So that our joy may be fulfilled [ἵνα ἡ χαρὰ ἡμῶν ᾖ πεπληρωμένη]" (1:4) repeats for the audience exactly what the elder told them in 2 John, "so that our joy may be fulfilled [ἵνα ἡ χαρὰ ἡμῶν ᾖ πεπληρωμένη]" (1:12), as the reason for his communicating with them. Their joy may be fulfilled when they experience the full joy of living eternally by practicing the truth of the commandment to love one another. This accords with the great "joy" (χαράν) the elder has when he hears that his "children," fellow believers, are "walking in the truth" (3 John 1:4). Indeed the elder said that "I rejoiced" (ἐχάρην) greatly at learning that Gaius is "walking in the truth" (1:3), and that "I rejoiced" (ἐχάρην) greatly because "children" are walking in truth (2 John 1:4) in accord with the commandment that we love one another (1:5).[63]

---

60. On "fellowship" (κοινωνία) in 1 John as a joint sharing in a common divine and eternal life with God and fellow believers, see Combs, "Meaning of Fellowship," 3–16.

61. "ταῦτα, 'these things,' does not refer either to what directly precedes or to what follows, but to the content of 1 John as a whole" (Smalley, *1 John*, 14).

62. "The expression of 'our,' a post-positive ἡμετέρα, normally carries special emphasis" (Olsson, *Letters*, 77). See also Yarbrough, *1–3 John*, 41n29.

63. On the oral performance of 1 John 1:1–4, see Brickle, *Aural Design*; see also Schuchard, *1–3 John*, 61–97; Morgen, "Le prologue," 55–75; Watson, "Keep Yourselves from Idols," 281–302.

In John, Jesus said that "the reaper" (the Father) is gathering fruit for eternal life, so that "the sower" (the Son) and "the reaper" can "rejoice" (χαίρῃ) together (4:36), indicating that joy is derived when people come to believe to live eternally. Jesus told his disciples to keep his commandments (15:10), especially his commandment to love one another as he loved them (15:12), so that his "joy" (χαρά) may be in them and their "joy" (χαρά) may be "fulfilled [πληρωθῇ]" (15:11). And to his disciples Jesus went on to say, "so that your joy may be fulfilled [ἵνα ἡ χαρὰ ὑμῶν ᾖ πεπληρωμένη]" (16:24), as the reason they should ask the Father in his name for whatever they need (16:23). This implies that they should ask for what they need to practice the truth of the commandment to love one another in order to experience the fulfilled joy of living eternally. Indeed Jesus himself prayed that his disciples may have "the joy that is mine" (τὴν χαρὰν τὴν ἐμήν), the joy of the divine eternal life he shares with the Father, "fulfilled" (πεπληρωμένην) in themselves (17:13).[64]

The pronouncements of "what we have heard [ἀκηκόαμεν]" (1 John 1:1) and "what we have seen and heard [ἀκηκόαμεν]" (1:3) progress to "this is the message which we have heard [ἀκηκόαμεν] from him," that is, from Jesus Christ, the Son of the Father (1:3), "and announce to you [ἀναγγέλλομεν ὑμῖν]" (1:5a). This recalls and resonates with Jesus' farewell promise to his followers that when the Spirit of truth comes, "he will guide you in all the truth" and "he will speak whatever he hears [ἀκούσει], and announce to you [ἀναγγελεῖ ὑμῖν] the things that are coming" (John 16:13; cf. 16:14-15). Thus, the authoritative "we"—the elder and his associates—are playing a role similar to the Spirit of truth, implying that the message they are now going to announce to "you," the audience, has to do with being guided in all the truth involved in worshiping in Spirit and truth (4:23-24). The audience have thus been prepared for an elaboration of this message.

1:5b-6a (B): Fellowship We Have with God Who Is Light

The message that "we" have heard from "him," namely, the Son Jesus Christ (1:3), and now announce to "you" (1:5a) is "that God is light [φῶς] and there is no darkness [σκοτία] in him at all" (1:5b). This reminds the

---

64. "As is the case in John's Gospel, 'joy' designates an eschatological benefit reserved for those who have entered into the community of John made possible by Jesus" (Schuchard, *1-3 John*, 95-96). On the relation of 1 John 1:1-4 to the Gospel of John, see Heckel, "Historisierung," 425-43.

audience that Jesus, the Word who was God (John 1:1, 18; 20:28), declared, "I am the light [φῶς] of the world. The one who follows me will never walk in the darkness [σκοτίᾳ], but will have the light [φῶς] of the life" (8:12). He similarly declared, "While I am in the world, I am the light [φῶς] of the world" (9:5), and "I came as light [φῶς] into the world, so that everyone who believes in me might not remain in the darkness [σκοτίᾳ]" (12:46). But if "we," the author and his associates as well as the audience, who have the fellowship that is ours (1 John 1:3), say we have fellowship with "him," that is, with God who is light (1:5b), "yet in the darkness [σκότει] are walking" (1:6a), then this involves us in a contradiction.

1:6b (C): We Are Lying and Not Doing the Truth

Indeed, if we say that fellowship we have with the God who is light yet in darkness are walking (1:6a), then "we are lying and not doing the truth" (1:6b). That in the darkness "we are walking" (περιπατῶμεν) means that "we are walking" (περιπατῶμεν) not according to his commandments (2 John 1:6), the preeminent of which is that we love one another (1:5). It also means we are not "children walking [περιπατοῦντα] in the truth [ἀληθείᾳ]" (3 John 1:4; cf. 2 John 1:4). That is why, if we are in darkness walking, we are lying and not "doing the truth [ποιοῦμεν τὴν ἀλήθειαν]" (1 John 1:6b), not practicing the truth of the commandment to love one another in order to live eternally and thus have fellowship with the God who is "light [φῶς]" (1:5b). Indeed, the one who "does the truth [ποιῶν τὴν ἀλήθειαν] comes to the light [φῶς], so that his works may be manifested that in God they have been worked" (John 3:21).

1:7a (B'): Walking in Light We Have Fellowship with One Another

At this point, after the central and unparalleled C element, "we are lying and not doing the truth" (1:6b), the audience experience a pivot of parallels from the B (1:5b–6a) to the B' (1:7a) element of this chiastic unit. "God is light [φῶς]" (1:5b) progresses to "if in the light [φωτί] we are walking as he is in the light [φωτί]" (1:7a). And "if we say that fellowship we have [κοινωνίαν ἔχομεν] with him yet in the darkness are walking [περιπατῶμεν]" (1:6a) progresses to "if in the light we are walking [περιπατῶμεν] as he is in the light, fellowship we have [κοινωνίαν ἔχομεν] with one another" (1:7a).

But if in the light we are walking as he is in the light (1:7a), since God is light (1:5b), then we are not walking in the darkness and may have fellowship with him, with the God who is light (1:6a). If in the light we are walking, then we may have fellowship not only with the God who is light, but with "one another [ἀλλήλων]" (1:7a). This is because walking in the light means practicing the truth (1:6b) of the commandment that we love "one another [ἀλλήλους]" (2 John 1:5). This fellowship we have with one another as fellow worshipers, the fellowship that is ours as we love one another, is the sharing of the divine life eternal with the Father and with his Son Jesus Christ (1 John 1:3).[65]

1:7b–10 (A'): The Blood of Jesus His Son and His Word

At this point, the audience hear a progression of parallels from the A (1:1–5a) to the A' (1:7b–10) element of this chiastic unit. The "word [λόγου] of the life" (1:1) progresses to "his word [λόγος] is not in us" (1:10). And the fellowship that is ours "with his Son Jesus [τοῦ υἱοῦ αὐτοῦ Ἰησοῦ] Christ" (1:3) progresses to "the blood of Jesus his Son [Ἰησοῦ τοῦ υἱοῦ αὐτοῦ]" (1:7b).

The audience hear the A' element (1:7b–10) of this chiastic unit as a chiastic pattern in itself:

a) and the blood of Jesus his Son *cleanses us from all sin. If we say that sin we do not have*, we are deceiving ourselves and the truth *is not in us. If we confess our sins* (1:7b–9a),

b) he is *faithful* (1:9b)

b') and *righteous* (1:9c),

a') so that he will forgive us the *sins* and *cleanse us from all unrighteousness. If we say that we have not sinned*, we make him a liar and his word *is not in us* (1:9d–10).

At the center of this chiastic sub-unit the audience experience a pivot of parallels involving a pair of alliterative and conceptually similar adjectives. "Faithful [πιστός]" in the b) sub-element (1:9b) progresses to "righteous [δίκαιος]" in the b') sub-element (1:9c). The audience then

---

65. "Consequently 1 John argues that those who mutually share the life from God are brought into relationship with each other, and this is the basis of the Johannine understanding of the possibility and obligation of mutual love" (Painter, *1 John*, 137).

hear a progression of several parallels from the a) sub-element (1:7b–9a) to the a') sub-element (1:9d–10): "cleanses us from all sin [καθαρίζει ἡμᾶς ἀπὸ πάσης ἁμαρτίας]" (1:7b) to "will cleanse us from all unrighteousness [καθαρίσῃ ἡμᾶς ἀπὸ πάσης ἀδικίας]" (1:9d); "if we say that sin we do not have [ἐὰν εἴπωμεν ὅτι ἁμαρτίαν οὐκ ἔχομεν]" (1:8) to "if we say that we have not sinned [ἐὰν εἴπωμεν ὅτι οὐχ ἡμαρτήκαμεν]" (1:10); "the truth is not in us [οὐκ ἔστιν ἐν ἡμῖν]" (1:8) to "his word is not in us [οὐκ ἔστιν ἐν ἡμῖν]" (1:10); and "confess our sins [ἁμαρτίας]" (1:9a) to "forgive us the sins [ἁμαρτίας]" (1:9d).

With its allusion to sacrificial atonement, "the blood of Jesus his Son cleanses us from all sin [ἁμαρτίας]" (1:7b) recalls and resonates with the proclamation that Jesus is "the lamb of God who takes away the sin [ἁμαρτίαν] of the world" (John 1:29).[66] We need to be cleansed from all sin so that we do not die in our "sin [ἁμαρτίᾳ]" (8:21), deprived of eternal life, not believing that Jesus is "the way, and the truth, and the life" (14:6; cf. 8:24). If we say that "sin" (ἁμαρτίαν) we do not have (1 John 1:8), in other words, that we do not need to be cleansed by the blood of Jesus, then we are "deceiving" (πλανῶμεν) ourselves, becoming like the many "deceivers" (πλάνοι) who do not confess the significance of Jesus Christ as coming in flesh (2 John 1:7). Consequently, "the truth [ἀλήθεια] is not in us [ἐν ἡμῖν]" (1 John 1:8), contradicting "the truth [ἀλήθειαν] that remains in us [ἐν ἡμῖν]" (2 John 1:2), in accord with Jesus' promise that the Spirit of "truth" (ἀληθείας) "will be in you [ἐν ὑμῖν]" (John 14:17). This is the truth of living eternally as "true worshipers" (4:23–24) by loving one another (2 John 1:1–5).

If we "confess" (ὁμολογῶμεν) our "sins" (ἁμαρτίας) as an act of communal worship, and thus acknowledge our need to be cleansed from all "sin" (ἁμαρτίας) by the blood of Jesus (1 John 1:7b), in contrast to the many deceivers not "confessing" (ὁμολογοῦντες) Jesus Christ as coming in flesh (2 John 1:7), "he is faithful and righteous" (1 John 1:9a).[67] That

---

66. "The term αἷμα, 'blood,' is a symbol for the crucifixion of Christ, and its background is to be located in Jewish sacrifice. In the OT blood was regarded as the seat of life (Lev 17:11). In terms of sacrifice, as a means of atonement ('at-one-ment' between humanity and God), the 'blood' of a victim was thus its life yielded up in death, and the 'sprinkling' of that blood guaranteed for the worshiper the effectiveness of any sacrifice (cf. Exod 30:10; Lev 16:15–19). . . . Thus to say here that the blood of Jesus 'purifies us from every sin' means that in the cross of Christ our sin is effectively and repeatedly removed" (Smalley, *1 John*, 23).

67. "The intention is not only an inner admission, but also an open confession of sins before God" (Hofius, "ὁμολογέω," 2.515). It is "possible that there was already

he is "faithful" (πιστός) recalls that the risen Jesus enabled an "unbelieving" (ἄπιστος) disciple to become one who is "believing [πιστός]" (John 20:27). That he is "righteous" (δίκαιος) recalls that Jesus is truthful as the one who seeks the glory of the God who sent him, so that there is no "unrighteousness" (ἀδικία) in him (7:18). Consequently, in accord with his authority to command that those whose "sins" (ἁμαρτίας) you "forgive" (ἀφῆτε) they are "forgiven" (ἀφέωνται) them (20:23), "he will forgive [ἀφῇ] us the sins [ἁμαρτίας] and cleanse [καθαρίσῃ] us from all unrighteousness [ἀδικίας]" (1 John 1:9b), since his blood "cleanses" (καθαρίζει) us from all "sin [ἁμαρτίας]" (1:7b).[68]

Being cleansed of all unrighteousness (1:9) enables the truth of living eternally as true worshipers by practicing the commandment to love one another to be in us (1:8c). If we say not only that we do not have sin (1:8a), but that we have not sinned, we not only are deceiving ourselves (1:8b), but we make him a "liar [ψεύστην]" (1:10), thus likening him to the devil, who is a "liar" (ψεύστης), "because there is no truth in him [ἀλήθεια ἐν αὐτῷ]" (John 8:44).[69] Indeed, if Jesus were to say that he does not know the Father, he would be a "liar" (ψεύστης), but he knows him and keeps his "word [λόγον]" (8:55). Consequently, if we make him a liar, then not only the "truth" (ἀλήθεια) is not "in us [ἐν ἡμῖν]" (1 John 1:8), but his "word" (λόγος), the "word" (λόγου) of the life eternal (1:1), is not "in us [ἐν ἡμῖν]" (1:10).

Summary of 1 John 1:1–10

The authoritative "we" representative of the elder and his associates in the main Johannine church testify and declare to "you," an elect sister church as the audience of 1 John gathered as a worshiping assembly, the life eternal that was with the Father (1:1–2). "We" declare this to "you," so that "you" may have fellowship as true fellow worshipers with "us." And the worshiping fellowship that is "ours"—of both "we" and "you"—is living

---

a liturgical custom of confessing one's sins before the assembled congregation" (Schnackenburg, *Johannine Epistles*, 82). "All the parallels and background given thus far suggest that the Johannine expression refers to a public confession rather than a private confession by the individual to God" (Brown, *Epistles*, 208).

68. Roitto, "Practices of Confession," 235–53; Glasscock, "Forgiveness and Cleansing," 217–31.

69. "From the Johannine standpoint, lies and lying (like murder) are the special province of the devil (John 8:44)" (Yarbrough, *1–3 John*, 66).

divine eternal life with the Father and with his Son Jesus Christ (1:3). The purpose and goal for the writing of 1 John is so that the joy of the elder and his associates as well as of the audience may be fulfilled when they experience the full joy of living eternally as true worshipers by practicing the truth of the commandment to love one another (1:4).

If we say we have fellowship with God, who is light, yet we walk in the darkness as those not practicing the commandment to love one another, we are lying and not doing the truth (1:5–6). But if in the light we are walking, then the fellowship of living eternally we have not only with one another, as those who love one another, but with God, who is light (1:7a). Since the blood of Jesus cleanses us from all sin, if we confess our sins as an act of communal worship, he will cleanse us from all unrighteousness, so that not only the truth but his word of life eternal may be in us. We may thereby worship God in the truth (John 4:23–24) of practicing the commandment to love one another (2 John 1:1–5), and thus live eternally by the true worship of loving God and one another (1 John 1:7b–10).

5

1 John 2:1–14

If We Keep His Commandments the Love of God Has Been Perfected

You have known the one who is from the beginning

A   ²:¹My *little children*, these things I am writing to you so that you may not sin. But if anyone sins, we have an advocate with the Father, Jesus Christ the righteous one. ²And he himself is the expiation for our *sins*, not for ours only but also for the whole world. ³And in this we *know* that we have *known* him, if we keep his commandments. ⁴The one saying, "I have *known* him," but not keeping his commandments, is a liar and the truth is not in this one. ⁵But whoever keeps his word, truly in this one the love of God has been perfected. In this we *know* that we are in him.

    B   ⁶The one saying that he remains in him ought, just as that one *walked*, he himself thus to *walk*.

        C   ⁷ᵃBeloved, not a *new commandment am I writing to you* but an old commandment which you have had from the beginning. The old commandment

            D ⁷ᵇis the word which you heard.

        C' ⁸ᵃOn the other hand, a *new commandment I am writing to you*, which is true in him and in you,

B' ⁸ᵇbecause the darkness is passing away and the true light already is shining. ⁹The one saying that he is in the light but hating his brother is still in the darkness. ¹⁰The one loving his brother remains in the light and there is no fault in him. ¹¹But the one hating his brother is in the darkness and in the darkness is *walking* and does not know where he is going, because the darkness has blinded his eyes.

A' ¹²I am writing to you, *little children*, because the *sins* have been forgiven for you on account of his name. ¹³I am writing to you, fathers, because you have *known* the one who is from the beginning. I am writing to you, young men, because you have conquered the evil one. ¹⁴I have written to you, young children, because you have *known* the Father. I have written to you, fathers, because you have *known* the one who is from the beginning. I have written to you, young men, because you are strong and the word of God in you remains and you have conquered the evil one.⁷⁰

2:1–5 (A): Jesus Christ Is Himself the Expiation for Our Sins

The audience hear the A element (2:1–5) of this chiastic unit as a chiastic pattern in itself:

a) My little children, these things I am writing to you so that you may not sin. But if anyone sins, we have an advocate with the Father, Jesus Christ the righteous one. And he himself is the expiation for our sins, not for ours only but also for the whole world. And *in this we know* (2:1–3a)

   b) that we have *known him*, if we keep *his commandments* (2:3b).

   b') The one saying, "I have *known him*," but not keeping *his commandments* (2:4a),

a') is a liar and the truth is not *in this one*. But whoever keeps his word, truly *in this one* the love of God has been perfected. *In this we know* that we are in him (2:4b–5).

At the center of this chiastic sub-unit the audience experience a pivot of parallels involving the only occurrences in this sub-unit of "known

---

70. For the establishment of 2:1–14 as a chiasm, see ch.1.

him" and "his commandments." "That we have known him [ἐγνώκαμεν αὐτόν], if we keep his commandments [ἐντολὰς αὐτοῦ]" in the b) sub-element (2:3b) progresses to "I have known him [ἔγνωκα αὐτόν], but not keeping his commandments [ἐντολὰς αὐτοῦ]" in the b') sub-element (2:4a). The audience then hear a progression of parallels from the a) sub-element (2:1–3a) to the a') sub-element (2:4b–5) involving the only occurrences in this sub-unit of "in this [one]" and "we know." "In this we know [ἐν τούτῳ γινώσκομεν]" (2:3a) progresses to "not in this one [ἐν τούτῳ]" (2:4b), "in this one [ἐν τούτῳ]" (2:5), and "in this we know [ἐν τούτῳ γινώσκομεν]" (2:5).

The audience hear the a) sub-element (2:1–3a) of this chiastic sub-unit as yet another chiastic pattern in itself:

(a) My little children, these things I am writing to you so that you may not *sin*. But if anyone *sins* (2:1a),

(b) we have an advocate with the Father, Jesus Christ the righteous one (2:1b).

(a') And he himself is the expiation for our *sins*, not for ours only but also for the whole world. And in this we know (2:2–3a).

The audience hear the expression "we have an advocate with the Father, Jesus Christ the righteous one" (2:1b) as the unparalleled central and pivotal (b) sub-element of this chiastic sub-unit. The audience then experience a pivot of parallels from the (a) sub-element (2:1a) to the (a') sub-element (2:2–3a) involving the only occurrences in this sub-unit of expressions for "sin." "You may not sin [ἁμάρτητε]" and "if anyone sins [ἁμάρτῃ]" (2:1a) progress to "he himself is the expiation for our sins [ἁμαρτιῶν]" (2:2).

And the audience hear the a') sub-element (2:4b–5) of this chiastic sub-unit as yet another chiastic pattern in itself:

(a) is a liar and the *truth is* not *in this one* (2:4b).

(b) But whoever keeps his word (2:5a),

(a') *truly in this one* the love of God has been perfected. *In this* we know that we *are* in him (2:5b).

The audience hear the expression "but whoever keeps his word" (2:5a) as the unparalleled central and pivotal (b) sub-element of this chiastic sub-unit. They then experience a pivot of parallels involving the only occurrences in this sub-unit of expressions for "truth," the verb "to be," and "in this [one]." "The truth [ἀλήθεια] is [ἔστιν] not in this one [ἐν τούτῳ]" in the (a) sub-element (2:4b) progresses to "truly [ἀληθῶς] in this one [ἐν τούτῳ]" and "in this [ἐν τούτῳ] we know that we are [ἐσμεν] in him" in the (a') sub-element (2:5b).

Reminiscent of the affectionate yet authoritative way that Jesus in his farewell discourse addressed his disciples as "little children [τεκνία]" (John 13:33), the elder similarly addresses his audience as "my little children [τεκνία]" (1 John 2:1a).[71] The progression from "these things [ταῦτα] indeed we are writing [γράφομεν]" (1:4a) to "these things [ταῦτα] I am writing [γράφω] to you" (2:1) emphasizes the personal authority yet individual concern the elder himself has for his audience of "little children." That he is writing these things "so that [ἵνα] you may not sin" (2:1a) suggests that not sinning will contribute to the purpose and goal of writing 1 John, namely, "so that [ἵνα] our joy may be fulfilled" (1:4b). And with the words, "so that you may not sin [ἁμάρτητε]," the audience hear the transitional term that links this chiastic unit (2:1–14) to the preceding one (1:1–10), whose conclusion began with the statement, "if we say that we have not sinned [ἡμαρτήκαμεν]" (1:10). Merely saying that we have not sinned thus progresses to the concern of not actually sinning.[72]

But if anyone in the audience does sin (2:1a), then we believers "have an advocate [παράκλητον] with the Father, Jesus Christ the righteous one" (2:1b). This recalls Jesus' reference to himself as "another advocate [παράκλητον]" when he promised his disciples to ask the Father to send them the other advocate to be with them forever (John 14:16), the holy Spirit of truth (14:26; 15:26; 16:7).[73] That our advocate Jesus is now "with the Father" (πρὸς τὸν πατέρα) recalls that the life eternal that was "with the Father [πρὸς τὸν πατέρα]" (1 John 1:2) came to be in Jesus (John 1:3–4), who was with God in the beginning (1:1–2), but who through his death and resurrection returned to be "with the Father [πρὸς τὸν πατέρα]" (13:1; 14:12, 28; 16:10, 17, 28; 20:17). And that in our

---

71. The elder is thus "imitating Jesus' affectionate address for his disciples at the Last Supper as he gave them the commandment to love (John 13:33). In this father-to-children pattern the implicit authority is that of a tradition-bearer; the implicit age is that of an elder in Christianity" (Brown, *Epistles*, 214).

72. On "you may not sin" (ἁμάρτητε) as the preferred reading here, see Do, "That You May Not Sin," 77–95.

73. On the significance of "advocate" (παράκλητος) here, see Shelfer, "Legal Precision," 131–50. "'Advocate' in the legal sense or 'intercessor' or 'mediator' are therefore apt translations of the word" (Yarbrough, *1–3 John*, 76).

advocate Jesus Christ we have the "righteous one" (δίκαιον) recalls that he is faithful and "righteous" (δίκαιος), so that he will forgive the sins of anyone who sins and cleanse that one of all "unrighteousness [ἀδικίας]" (1 John 1:9), thus enabling the truth of living eternally by practicing the commandment to love one another to be in him (1:8).

Indeed, if anyone "sins [ἁμάρτῃ]" (2:1a), our advocate Jesus Christ himself is the expiation or the atoning sacrifice "for our sins [ἁμαρτιῶν], not for ours only but also for the whole world [κόσμου]" (2:2). This recalls and resonates with the sacrificial blood of Jesus that cleanses us from all "sin [ἁμαρτίας]" (1:7b). And this is the Jesus, who, as the sacrificial Lamb of God, "takes away the sin [ἁμαρτίαν] of the world [κόσμου]" (John 1:29).[74]

In this we know (1 John 2:3a) that we have known "him [αὐτόν]" (2:3b), Jesus Christ the righteous one (2:1), who "himself" (αὐτός) is the expiation for our sins (2:2), "if we keep his [αὐτοῦ] commandments" (2:3b). In other words, the way that we know that we have known him as the one who forgives our sins and cleanses us of all unrighteousness is by keeping his commandments, the preeminent of which is that we should love one another (2 John 1:5–7) to live eternally (John 12:50; 13:34).[75] Then, in contrast to the Jews who declared that "now we have known [ἐγνώκαμεν]" that Jesus has a demon (8:55), but together with Peter, the spokesman for the disciples, who confessed that "we have believed and have known [ἐγνώκαμεν]" that Jesus is the Holy One of God (6:69) who has the words of life eternal (6:68), we know that "we have known" (ἐγνώκαμεν) him.

"If we keep his commandments [ἐὰν τὰς ἐντολὰς αὐτοῦ τηρῶμεν]" (1 John 2:3b), preeminent of which is that we should love one another (2 John 1:5), then we are also loving Jesus, who declared, "If you love me, you will keep my commandments [τὰς ἐντολὰς τὰς ἐμὰς τηρήσετε]" (John 14:15). He went on to say that "whoever has my commandments [ἐντολάς] and keeps [τηρῶν] them is the one who loves me, and whoever loves me will be loved by my Father, and I will love him and reveal myself to him" (14:21). And again he stated that "if you keep my commandments [ἐὰν τὰς ἐντολάς μου τηρήσητε], you will remain in my love, just

---

74. "While Jesus's death certainly has the effect of expiating sin (wiping away its penalty), it is difficult to avoid the impression that it also propitiates (turns away the wrath of) God's promised punishment of sins and sinners whose transgressions are not atoned for on the last day—a day of condemnation spoken of by Jesus in John 12:48)" (Yarbrough, *1–3 John*, 78). See also Do, "1 John 2,2," 415–35.

75. "The commandments in 1 John 2:3 are equivalent to Jesus's 'word' in 2:5. Jesus's 'commandment' and 'word' to love are identical in 2:7" (Yarbrough, *1–3 John*, 83).

as I have kept [τετήρηκα] the commandments [ἐντολάς] of my Father and remain in his love" (15:10). The goal of being loved by God the Father is living eternally, in accord with Jesus' pronouncement that "God so loved the world that he gave his only Son, so that everyone who believes in him might not perish but might have life eternal" (3:16).

The one saying "I have known him [αὐτόν]," but not keeping "his" [αὐτοῦ] commandments (1 John 2:4a), the commandments of Jesus, who "himself" (αὐτός) is the expiation for our sins (2:2), "is a liar and the truth is not in this one" (2:4b). Whereas if we say we have not sinned, we make him a "liar" (ψεύστην) and "his word is not in us [οὐκ ἔστιν ἐν ἡμῖν]" (1:10); the one saying that "I have known him," but not keeping his commandments, is a "liar" (ψεύστης) and "the truth is not in this one [ἐν τούτῳ ἡ ἀλήθεια οὐκ ἔστιν]" (2:4). This recalls that "if we say that sin we do not have, we are deceiving ourselves and the truth is not in us [ἡ ἀλήθεια οὐκ ἔστιν ἐν ἡμῖν]" (1:8). Indeed, "if we say that fellowship we have with him yet in the darkness are walking, we are lying [ψευδόμεθα] and not doing the truth [ἀλήθειαν]" (1:6). This means that the truth of practicing the commandment that we should love one another in order to live eternally, the truth by which one worships in Spirit and truth (John 4:23–24), is not in one who says he has known Jesus but does not keep his commandments.

Although the one saying he has known Jesus but does not keep his commandments is a liar and "the truth is not in this one [ἐν τούτῳ ἡ ἀλήθεια οὐκ ἔστιν]" (1 John 2:4), whoever keeps his word (2:5a), "truly in this one [ἀληθῶς ἐν τούτῳ] the love of God has been perfected" (2:5b). "Whoever keeps his word [τηρῇ αὐτοῦ τὸν λόγον]," synonymous with keeping his commandment that we should love one another (John 15:10, 12), recalls Jesus' pronouncement that "if anyone loves me, he will keep my word [τὸν λόγον μου τηρήσει], and my Father will love him" (14:23). In such a person the love of God has been perfected, since the goal of God's love for the world is to live eternally by believing in Jesus (3:16) and loving one another (2 John 1:1–5). That in the one who does this the "love" (ἀγάπη) of God "has been perfected" (τετελείωται) by God (divine passive) thus recalls and resonates with Jesus' prayer to the Father that his disciples "may be perfected [τετελειωμένοι] as one, so that the world may know that you sent me and loved [ἠγάπησας] them as you loved [ἠγάπησας] me" (John 17:23).[76]

If we keep the commandments of Jesus, particularly his main commandment or word that we should love one another in order to live eternally, then not only "in this do we know [ἐν τούτῳ γινώσκομεν] that we have known him" (1 John 2:3), but "in this we know [ἐν τούτῳ γινώσκομεν] that we are in him" (2:5). That in this "we know" (γινώσκομεν) that "we have known" (ἐγνώκαμεν) him and are in him resonates with the pronouncement of Jesus in his prayer to the Father that "this is eternal life, that they know [γινώσκωσιν] you, the only true God, and the one whom you sent, Jesus Christ" (John 17:3). That we are "in him" (ἐν αὐτῷ) thus means that we are living eternally by believing in him and by keeping his commandment that we should love one another as he loved us (15:12). This recalls and resonates with the pronouncement that eternal life came to be "in him [ἐν αὐτῷ]" (1:4), and that everyone who believes "in him" (ἐν αὐτῷ) may have eternal life (3:15).

2:6 (B): The One Remaining in Jesus Ought to Walk as He Walked

The one saying he remains in him, in Jesus, and thus lives eternally, ought, just as that one "walked" (περιεπάτησεν), he himself thus to "walk [περιπατεῖν]" (1 John 2:6). This means walking in the light, as it recalls that if in the light "we are walking" (περιπατῶμεν) as he, Jesus, is in the light (1:7a), then the fellowship of divine eternal life we have with him (1:6a) and with one another (1:7a). This resonates with Jesus' exhortation to "walk" (περιπατεῖτε) while you have the light, since the one "walking" (περιπατῶν) in darkness does not know where he is going (John 12:35). Jesus himself is the light, so that the one who follows him will never "walk" (περιπατήσῃ) in the darkness, but will have the light of eternal life (8:12; cf. 9:5).

To remain in Jesus and thus live eternally one "ought" (ὀφείλει) thus to "walk," that is, to conduct himself, as Jesus did by loving one another (1 John 2:6). This resonates with Jesus' declaration to his disciples that you "ought" (ὀφείλετε) to wash the feet of one another, as he washed their

---

76. "Although the context is concerned with what believers do, it seems best to understand the reference here as to the love that comes from God" (Lieu, *Commentary*, 71). "Τελειόω (perfect, complete) occurs only in the passive in 1 John, and only in connection with the noun 'love.' In every case divine activity can be understood as lying behind the passive voice. In John's Gospel the perfect tense divine passive of τελειόω is likely at 17:23 and 19:28" (Yarbrough, *1–3 John*, 86n30).

feet, as a humble gesture of loving one another (John 13:14). To "remain" (μένειν) in Jesus, as he directed his disciples to "remain" (μείνατε) in him (15:4; cf. 15:4-7), means to "remain" (μείνατε) in his love (15:9). And "you will remain" (μενεῖτε) in his love by keeping his commandments (15:10), particularly his main commandment that we love one another as he has loved us (13:34; 15:12, 17) to live eternally (12:50).

2:7a (C): Not a New Commandment Am I Writing to You

Having affectionately addressed his audience as "my little children" (2:1), the elder now affectionately addresses them as "beloved [ἀγαπητοί]" (2:7a), reminiscent of his address of Gaius in 3 John as "beloved [ἀγαπητῷ]" (1:1; cf. 1:2, 5, 11), with a connotation of being loved by God, the elder, and fellow believers.[77] To his beloved audience the elder declares that "not a new commandment am I writing to you [οὐκ ἐντολὴν καινὴν γράφω ὑμῖν] but an old commandment which you have had from the beginning [ἣν εἴχετε ἀπ' ἀρχῆς]" (2:7a).[78] And this is the commandment that we should love one another, as it recalls his similar declaration to the audience in the introductory cover letter of 2 John: "But now I ask you, lady, not as one writing a new commandment to you [οὐχ ὡς ἐντολὴν καινὴν γράφων σοι] but that which we have had from the beginning [ἣν εἴχομεν ἀπ' ἀρχῆς], that we should love one another" (1:5).

2:7b (D): The Word Which You Heard

That the old commandment the audience had "from the beginning [ἀπ' ἀρχῆς]" (2:7a) is the "word" (λόγος) which "you heard [ἠκούσατε]" (2:7b) recalls that whoever keeps his "word" (λόγον), "truly in this one the love of God has been perfected" (2:5). And it recalls and reinforces the elder's previous declaration that "this is the love, that we walk according to his commandments. This is the commandment, just as you heard [ἠκούσατε] from the beginning [ἀπ' ἀρχῆς], that in it you should walk"

---

77. The elder's "first use of the adjective 'beloved' is filled with meaning for a community of love (2:5b, 10) whose model figure is the disciple whom Jesus loved (Jn 13:23; 19:26; 20:2; 21:7, 20), whose own are both beloved and love one another (1 Jn 2:5b, 10), because God was first to love them (4:7-10). The vocative has a hortatory force" (Schuchard, *1-3 John*, 187-88).

78. "The imperfect indicative εἴχετε is emphatic" (Schuchard, *1-3 John*, 168). See also Voelz, *Grammar*, 56-60.

(2 John 1:6). The word the audience heard from the beginning is thus the same as the commandment that we should love one another.

2:8a (C'): A New Commandment I Am Writing to You

At this point, after the central and unparalleled D element, "is the word which you heard" (2:7b), the audience experience a pivot of parallels from the C to the C' element of this chiastic unit. "Not a new commandment am I writing to you [οὐκ ἐντολὴν καινὴν γράφω ὑμῖν]" (2:7a) progresses to "on the other hand, a new commandment I am writing to you [ἐντολὴν καινὴν γράφω ὑμῖν]" (2:8a).

The old commandment the audience had from the beginning (2:7) is at the same time a new commandment (2:8a) they always and continually need to hear anew.[79] That the new commandment the elder is writing to the audience is true "in him [ἐν αὐτῷ]" (2:8a) reinforces that one remains "in him" (ἐν αὐτῷ), in Jesus, by "walking" in and thus practicing the truth of the commandment to love one another in order to live eternally (2:6). In contrast to the "truth" (ἀλήθεια) not being "in this one" (ἐν τούτῳ), one not keeping his commandments (2:4), the new commandment of loving one another is "true" (ἀληθές) "in you [ἐν ὑμῖν]" (2:8a), in those who practice it. Indeed, whoever keeps his word, his commandment to love one another, and thus live eternally, "truly" (ἀληθῶς) "in this one" (ἐν τούτῳ) "the love of God has been perfected" (2:5).

2:8b-11 (B'): The One Hating His Brother in the Darkness Is Walking

At this point, the audience hear a progression of parallels from the B (2:6) to the B' (2:8b-11) element of this chiastic unit. "The one saying that he remains in him ought, just as that one walked [περιεπάτησεν], he himself thus to walk [περιπατεῖν]" (2:6) progresses to "the one hating his brother is in the darkness and in the darkness is walking [περιπατεῖ]" (2:11).

---

79. Although the commandment to love one another was new when Jesus gave it (John 13:34), "it had often been heard before by the readers. In that sense it was no longer 'new' but 'old.'... Yet there was a sense in which the writer could refer to the commandment as 'new.' It remains new in that it remains true and is continually being realized and actualized in the life of Jesus and his followers in the new age" (Marshall, *Epistles*, 129).

The audience hear the B' element (2:8b–11) of this chiastic unit as a chiastic pattern in itself:

a) because the *darkness* is passing away and the true *light* already is shining. The one saying that he is in the *light* but *hating* his brother is still in the *darkness* (2:8b–9).

b) The one loving his brother (2:10a)

a') remains in the *light* and there is no fault in him. But the one *hating* his brother is in the *darkness* and in the *darkness* is walking and does not know where he is going, because the *darkness* has blinded his eyes (2:10b–11).

After the central and unparalleled b) sub-element of this chiastic sub-unit, "the one loving his brother" (2:10a), the audience experience a pivot of parallels from the a) to the a') sub-element involving the only occurrences in this sub-unit of the terms "darkness," "light," and "hating." "Because the darkness [σκοτία] is passing away and the true light [φῶς] already is shining. The one saying that he is in the light [φωτί] but hating [μισῶν] his brother is still in the darkness [σκοτίᾳ]" (2:8b–9). This progresses to "remains in the light [φωτί] and there is no fault in him. But the one hating [μισῶν] his brother is in the darkness [σκοτίᾳ] and in the darkness [σκοτίᾳ] is walking and does not know where he is going, because the darkness [σκοτία] has blinded his eyes" (2:10b–11).

And the audience hear the a) sub-element (2:8b–9) of this chiastic sub-unit as yet another chiastic pattern in itself:

(a) because the *darkness* is passing away (2:8b)

(b) and the true *light* already is shining (2:8c).

(b') The one saying that he is in the *light* (2:9a)

(a') but hating his brother is still in the *darkness* (2:9b).

At the center of this chiastic sub-element the audience experience a pivot of parallels from the (b) to the (b') sub-element involving the only occurrences in this sub-unit of the term "light." "The true light [φῶς] already is shining" (2:8c) progresses to "the one saying that he is in the light [φωτί]" (2:9a). The audience then hear a progression of parallels from the (a) to the (a') sub-element involving the only occurrences in this sub-unit of the term "darkness." "The darkness [σκοτία] is passing away" (2:8b) progresses to "still in the darkness [σκοτία]" (2:9b).

The elder is writing a new commandment, which is true both "in him," in Jesus, and "in you" (2:8a), that is, it involves the truth of living eternally by loving one another, "because the darkness [σκοτία] is passing away and the true light [τὸ φῶς τὸ ἀληθινόν] already is shining [φαίνει]" (2:8b). This recalls and resonates with the pronouncement that "the light [φῶς]," which is eternal life (John 1:4), "shines [φαίνει] in the darkness [σκοτίᾳ], but the darkness [σκοτία] did not overcome it" (1:5). Indeed, "the true light [τὸ φῶς τὸ ἀληθινόν], which enlightens every person, was coming into the world" (1:9) in the person of Jesus, who is light (8:12; 9:5; 12:46) and life (14:6).[80]

"The one saying" (ὁ λέγων) that he is in the light, and thus living eternally, but hating his brother, his fellow believer (cf. 3 John 1:3, 5, 10), is actually still in the "darkness [σκοτίᾳ]" (1 John 2:9), the "darkness" (σκοτία) that is passing away with the arrival of the true light of eternal life (2:8b). This reinforces the exhortation that "the one saying" (ὁ λέγων) he remains in Jesus ought to "walk" and thus conduct himself as he did (2:6), by loving one another. And it confirms the warning that "the one saying" (ὁ λέγων) that he knows Jesus but does not keep his commandment of loving one another in order to live eternally "is a liar and the truth is not in this one" (2:4).[81]

The one "loving" (ἀγαπῶν) his brother (2:10a), in accord with the commandment that "we should love" (ἀγαπῶμεν) one another (2 John 1:5), "remains" (μένει) in the light (1 John 2:10b), and thus "remains" (μένειν) in Jesus (2:6), "and there is no fault in him" (2:10c).[82] He actually remains in the "light" (φωτί), in contrast to the one merely saying that he is in the "light [φωτί]" (2:9a). But the one "hating his brother is in the darkness [μισῶν τὸν ἀδελφὸν αὐτοῦ ἐν τῇ σκοτίᾳ ἐστίν]" (2:11a). This reiterates and thus reinforces that "the one saying that he is in the light but hating his brother is still in the darkness [τὸν ἀδελφὸν αὐτοῦ μισῶν ἐν τῇ σκοτίᾳ ἐστὶν ἕως ἄρτι]" (2:9), indeed the "darkness" (σκοτία) that is passing away with the arrival of the true light of eternal life (2:8b).

---

80. Here the elder "testifies to a time in which the light Jesus promised is an increasing reality in the community he founded" (Yarbrough, *1–3 John*, 102).

81. "To hate would then mostly mean to lack love, and not so much to have feelings of hatred or enmity" (Olsson, *Letters*, 111).

82. On the translation "fault" for σκάνδαλον in 1 John 2:10, see BDAG, 926.

The one hating his brother is "walking" (περιπατεῖ) in the darkness (2:11b), whereas he ought to "walk" (περιπατεῖν) as Jesus "walked [περιεπάτησεν]" (2:6) by loving one another. That the one hating his brother is walking in darkness and "does not know where he is going [οὐκ οἶδεν ποῦ ὑπάγει]" (2:11c) resonates with an exhortation of Jesus. He urged unbelievers to "walk" (περιπατεῖτε) while they have the light, so that the darkness does not overcome them. Indeed the one who "walks" (περιπατῶν) in the darkness "does not know where he is going [οὐκ οἶδεν ποῦ ὑπάγει]" (John 12:35), suggesting that he has lost the way to eternal life. That the one hating his brother does not know where he is going, "because the darkness has blinded his eyes [ἐτύφλωσεν τοὺς ὀφθαλμοὺς αὐτοῦ]" (1 John 2:11d), recalls that God "blinded their eyes [τετύφλωκεν αὐτῶν τοὺς ὀφθαλμούς]" (John 12:40) as the reason people could not believe (12:39).[83] But the darkness of unbelief is passing away with the arrival of the true light that already is shining (1 John 2:8b), the light of the truth of living eternally by loving one another.

2:12–14 (A'): Sins Have Been Forgiven for You on Account of His Name

At this point the audience hear a progression of parallels from the A (2:1–5) to the A' (2:12–14) element of this chiastic unit: from "my little children [τεκνία]" (2:5) to "little children [τεκνία]" (2:12); from "expiation for our sins [ἁμαρτιῶν]" (2:2) to "the sins [ἁμαρτίαι] have been forgiven" (2:12); from "we know [γινώσκομεν] that we have known [ἐγνώκαμεν] him" (2:3), "I have known [ἔγνωκα] him" (2:4), and "in this we know [γινώσκομεν]" (2:5) to "you have known [ἐγνώκατε] the one who is from the beginning" (2:13, 14) and "you have known [ἐγνώκατε] the Father" (2:14).

The audience hear the A' element (2:12–14) of this chiastic unit as a chiastic pattern in itself:

a) I am writing to you, little children, because the sins have been forgiven for you on account of his name. I am writing to you, *fathers, because you have known the one who is from the beginning.* I am writing to you, *young men, because you have conquered the evil one* (2:12–13).

---

83. "Particularly striking is that whereas John 12:40 leaves it open as to who 'blinded'—most naturally it is God, as in Isaiah—1 John specifies that it is 'the darkness'" (Lieu, *Commentary*, 83).

b) I have written to you, young children, because you have known the Father (2:14a).

a') I have written to you, *fathers, because you have known the one who is from the beginning.* I have written to you, *young men,* because you are strong and the word of God in you remains and *you have conquered the evil one* (2:14b).

After the central and unparalleled b) sub-element of this chiastic sub-unit, "I have written to you, young children, because you have known the Father" (2:14a), the audience experience a pivot of parallels from the a) sub-element (2:12–13) to the a') sub-element (2:14b). "I am writing to you, fathers, because you have known the one who is from the beginning [πατέρες, ὅτι ἐγνώκατε τὸν ἀπ' ἀρχῆς]" (2:13) progresses to "I have written to you, fathers, because you have known the one who is from the beginning [πατέρες, ὅτι ἐγνώκατε τὸν ἀπ' ἀρχῆς]" (2:14b). And "I am writing to you, young men [νεανίσκοι], because you have conquered the evil one [νενικήκατε τὸν πονηρόν]" (2:13) progresses to "I have written to you, young men [νεανίσκοι], because . . . you have conquered the evil one [νενικήκατε τὸν πονηρόν]" (2:14b).

And the audience hear the a) sub-element (2:12–13) of this chiastic sub-unit as yet another chiastic pattern in itself:

(a) *I am writing to you,* little children, because the sins have been forgiven for you on account of his name. *I am writing to you,* fathers (2:12–13a),

(b) because you have known the one who is from the beginning (2:13b).

(a') *I am writing to you,* young men, because you have conquered the evil one (2:13c).

After the central and unparalleled (b) sub-element of this chiastic sub-unit, "because you have known the one who is from the beginning" (2:13b), the audience experience a pivot of parallels from the (a) sub-element (2:12–13a) to the (a') sub-element (2:13c). "I am writing to you [γράφω ὑμῖν], little children" (2:12) and "I am writing to you [γράφω ὑμῖν], fathers" (2:13a) progress to "I am writing to you [γράφω ὑμῖν], young men" (2:13c).

After addressing his audience as "my little children [τεκνία]," the elder states that "these things I am writing to you [γράφω ὑμῖν] so that you may not sin [ἁμάρτητε]. But if anyone sins [ἁμάρτῃ], we have an advocate with the Father, Jesus Christ the righteous one. And he himself is the expiation for our sins [ἁμαρτιῶν]" (2:1–2). And now he emphatically reinforces that indeed their sins have been forgiven: "I am writing to you [γράφω ὑμῖν], little children [τεκνία], because the sins [ἁμαρτίαι] have been forgiven for you on account of his name" (2:12). Their sins "have been forgiven" (ἀφέωνται) for them on account of his "name" (ὄνομα), that is, the divine character of Jesus Christ, our advocate with the Father, who gave him his divine "name [ὄνομα]" (John 17:11–12).[84] He is the one with the authority to declare that "whose sins [ἁμαρτίας] you forgive [ἀφῆτε] are forgiven [ἀφέωνται] them" (20:23). And he is the faithful and righteous one who "will forgive [ἀφῇ] us the sins [ἁμαρτίας] and cleanse us from all unrighteousness" (1 John 1:9), so that the truth of living eternally by loving one another may be in us (1:8).

The elder is writing not only to the "little children," a designation for the audience as a whole (2:12; cf. 2:1), but "I am writing to you, fathers" (2:13a), the married men who lead the households. He affirms them "because you have known [ἐγνώκατε] the one who is from the beginning" (2:13b).[85] This recalls that the one saying, "I have known [ἔγνωκα] him," but does not keep his commandments, is a liar and the truth is not in him (2:4). The implication, then, is that the fathers do keep his commandments, so that the truth of living eternally by keeping the commandment to love one another is in them. They thus have known the one who is "from the beginning" (ἀπ' ἀρχῆς), the Jesus in whom life eternal came to be "from the beginning [ἀπ' ἀρχῆς]" (1:1; cf. John 1:2–4). This is in contrast to unbelievers, "you who have not known [ἐγνώκατε] him" (John 8:55), that is, the Father made known by Jesus (1:18). Indeed, Jesus stated

---

84. "On account of his name [διὰ τὸ ὄνομα αὐτοῦ]" (1 John 2:12) refers to the divine character or status of Jesus in accord with his warning to his disciples that "they will do these things to you on account of my name [διὰ τὸ ὄνομά μου], because they do not know the one who sent me" (John 15:21). In other words, they do not know the divine Father who sent his divine Son (3:16–17) and gave him his divine name (17:11–12). "In an Old Testament perspective a person's name stands for his or her identity and power" (Olsson, *Letters*, 126).

85. The elder praises "each father of every household belonging to one of the house churches" in the audience for which the elder "holds the greater responsibility as the region's elder father. . . . for even such fathers are themselves his 'children.'" The elder then addresses "those who like him are fathers in relationship to the rest of the children" (Schuchard, *1–3 John*, 218–19). "To appeal to Christians as fathers was to evoke their sense of responsibility and their humble yet lofty privilege under the Father par excellence" (Yarbrough, *1–3 John*, 117).

that "if you have known [ἐγνώκατε] me, you will also know my Father" (14:7), the God with whom Jesus, the Word, was "in the beginning [ἐν ἀρχῇ]" (1:1–2).

The elder proclaims that he is writing not only to the "fathers," the married leaders of households (1 John 2:13a), but also to the "young men" (νεανίσκοι), the not yet married future leaders, "because you have conquered the evil one [νενικήκατε τὸν πονηρόν]" (2:13c).[86] They have conquered the evil one in and through Jesus, who proclaimed that "I myself have conquered [νενίκηκα] the world" (John 16:33). He went on to pray that the Father not take his disciples out of the world but keep them from "the evil one [τοῦ πονηροῦ]" (17:15), from the devil, who, because he was a murderer from the beginning and does not stand in the truth (8:44), poses a threat to the truth of living eternally by loving one another. But thanks to Jesus the young men have conquered the threat of the evil one, so that they may live eternally by the truth of loving one another.

The elder reinforces his previous assertions of the purpose for his writing, that "I am writing to you [γράφω ὑμῖν]" (1 John 2:1, 7, 8, 12, 13a, 13c), by now emphasizing the completed goal of his writing, that "I have written to you [ἔγραψα ὑμῖν]" (2:14a).[87] Having addressed his entire audience as "little children [τεκνία]" (2:1, 12), characterizing the affectionate relationship they have with him, the elder now addresses them as "young children [παιδία]" (2:14a), implying that they are in a relationship of learning from the elder as well as from their "fathers" and "young men" (2:13), their older and younger local leaders.[88] The elder has

---

86. A νεανίσκος was "a young man beyond the age of puberty, but normally before marriage" (Culy, *Handbook*, 40). "Here, however, his addressees are those who have emerged from adolescence and now stand at the onset of adulthood" (Schuchard, *1–3 John*, 219).

87. "It is standard in Greek letters to use both the present, 'I am writing,' reflecting the author's standpoint, and the past 'I have written,' reflecting the readers' standpoint (cf. 2:1 and 5:13)" (Lieu, *Commentary*, 86). "Whereas γράφω comported with John's *act* of writing, ἔγραψα views the *fact* of having written, regarded in its entirety" (Yarbrough, *1–3 John*, 121; emphases original). At this point the elder thus "prepares his hearers for the remainder of his letter in which the aorist tense forms of γράφω will predominate [see 2:14, 21, 26; 5:13]" (Schuchard, *1–3 John*, 206).

88. In the Gospel of John, Jesus addresses his disciples both as "little children [τεκνία]" (13:33) and as "young children [παιδία]" (21:5). The term παιδίον can refer to "one who is open to instruction" (BDAG, 749). The elder "addresses the whole of his audience under two general terms of endearment (τεκνία and παιδία) and then, more specifically, subdivided into the older and the younger" (Yarbrough, *1–3 John*, 114).

written to his audience, characterized as young children, "because you have known the Father" (2:14a).

The elder's affirmation that "you" young children "have known" (ἐγνώκατε) the Father (2:14a) thus complements his affirmation that "you" fathers "have known" (ἐγνώκατε) the one who is from the beginning (2:13), Jesus Christ. Indeed, Jesus asserted that "if you have known [ἐγνώκατε] me, you will also know [γνώσεσθε] my Father" (John 14:7; cf. 16:3). And that believers "know" (γινώσκωσιν) the only true God and the one whom he sent, Jesus Christ, is what constitutes living eternally (17:3). That the audience know both the Father and Jesus his Son thus implies that they are keeping the commandments of Jesus, especially that we should love one another, since "in this we know [γινώσκομεν] that we have known [ἐγνώκαμεν] him, if we keep his commandments" (1 John 2:3). The elder, then, has implicitly affirmed that the truth of living eternally by loving one another is in the audience (2:4–5).

The elder reinforces his assertion that "I am writing [γράφω] to you, fathers, because you have known the one who is from the beginning" (2:13) by now reiteratively emphasizing that "I have written [ἔγραψα] to you, fathers, because you have known the one who is from the beginning" (2:14b). He then reinforces and develops his assertion that "I am writing [γράφω] to you, young men, because you have conquered the evil one" (2:13) by now emphasizing that "I have written [ἔγραψα] to you, young men, because you are strong and the word of God in you remains and you have conquered the evil one" (2:14b). That the young men are "strong" (ἰσχυροί) implies that they are loving their brothers, so that there is no "fault" (σκάνδαλον) in them (2:10).[89]

In contrast to unbelievers, who do not have "his word" (τὸν λόγον αὐτοῦ), that of God, "in you remaining [ἐν ὑμῖν μένοντα]" (John 5:38), in the young men, as the elder affirms, "the word of God in you remains [ὁ λόγος τοῦ θεοῦ ἐν ὑμῖν μένει]" (1 John 2:14b). This implies that they are keeping "his word [αὐτοῦ τὸν λόγον]" (2:5), the "word" (λόγος) which is synonymous with the commandment (2:7) that we should love one another, so that in them "the love of God" (ἡ ἀγάπη τοῦ θεοῦ) has been perfected (2:5). The elder is thus implicitly affirming that "his word" (ὁ λόγος αὐτοῦ) is in the young men (1:10), a sub-group within but also representative of

---

89. "As young men, they are now explicitly said to be strong, and the reason for their strength is given: the word of God lives in them" (Marshall, *Epistles*, 141).

the entire audience, as "the word" (τοῦ λόγου) of the life (1:1) that they are keeping and thus living eternally by loving one another.[90]

Summary of 1 John 2:1–14

In this we know (2:3a) that we have known "him" (2:3b), Jesus Christ the righteous one (2:1), who "himself" is the expiation for our sins (2:2), "if we keep his commandments" (2:3b). In other words, the way we know we have known him as the one who forgives our sins and cleanses us of all unrighteousness is by keeping his commandments, the preeminent of which is that we should love one another (2 John 1:5–7) to live eternally (John 12:50; 13:34). Although the one saying he has known Jesus but does not keep his commandments is a liar and "the truth," the truth by which one worships in Spirit and truth (4:23–24), "is not in this one" (1 John 2:4), whoever keeps his word (2:5a), "truly in this one the love of God has been perfected" (2:5b). In such a person the love of God has been perfected, since the goal of God's love for the world is to live eternally by believing in Jesus (John 3:16) and loving one another (2 John 1:1–5).

"The one saying" that he is in the light, and thus living eternally, but hating his brother, his fellow believer (cf. 3 John 1:3, 5, 10), is actually still in the "darkness" (1 John 2:9), the "darkness" that is passing away with the arrival of the true light of eternal life (2:8b). This reinforces the exhortation that "the one saying" he remains in Jesus ought to "walk" and thus conduct himself as he did (2:6), by loving one another. And it confirms the warning that "the one saying" he knows Jesus but does not keep his commandment of loving one another in order to live eternally "is a liar and the truth is not in this one" (2:4).

The one "loving" his brother (2:10a), in accord with the commandment that "we should love" one another (2 John 1:5), "remains" in the light (1 John 2:10b), and thus "remains" in Jesus (2:6), "and there is no fault in him" (2:10c). He actually remains in the "light," in contrast to the one merely saying that he is in the "light" (2:9a). But the one "hating his brother is in the darkness" (2:11a). This reiterates and thus reinforces that "the one saying that he is in the light but hating his brother is still in

---

90. "In the prologue 'the word' belonged to the experience that 'we' proclaimed to 'you'; here it belongs firmly and without mediation or dependence to 'you,' the young men but also the whole community addressed" (Lieu, *Commentary*, 91).

the darkness" (2:9), indeed the "darkness" that is passing away with the arrival of the true light of eternal life (2:8b).

The one hating his brother is "walking" in the darkness (2:11b), whereas he ought to "walk" as Jesus "walked" (2:6) by loving one another. That the one hating his brother is walking in darkness and "does not know where he is going" (2:11c) resonates with an exhortation of Jesus. He urged unbelievers to "walk" while they have the light, so that the darkness does not overcome them. Indeed the one who "walks" in the darkness "does not know where he is going" (John 12:35), suggesting that he has lost the way to eternal life. That the one hating his brother does not know where he is going, "because the darkness has blinded his eyes" (1 John 2:11d), recalls that God "blinded their eyes" (John 12:40) as the reason people could not believe (12:39). But the darkness of unbelief is passing away with the arrival of the true light that already is shining (1 John 2:8b), the light of the truth of living eternally by loving one another.

The elder's affirmation of the audience as "you" young children who "have known" the Father (2:14a) complements his affirmation that "you" fathers, the older leaders within the audience, "have known" the one who is from the beginning (2:13), Jesus Christ. Indeed, Jesus asserted that "if you have known me, you will also know my Father" (John 14:7; cf. 16:3). And that believers "know" the only true God and the one whom he sent, Jesus Christ, is what constitutes living eternally (17:3). That the audience know both the Father and Jesus his Son thus implies that they are keeping the commandments of Jesus, especially that we should love one another, since "in this we know that we have known him, if we keep his commandments" (1 John 2:3). The elder, then, has implicitly affirmed that the truth of living eternally by loving one another is in the audience (2:4–5).

In contrast to unbelievers, who do not have "his word," that of God, "in you remaining" (John 5:38), in the young men within the audience, as the elder affirms, "the word of God in you remains" (1 John 2:14b). This implies that they are keeping "his word" (2:5), the "word" which is synonymous with the commandment (2:7) that we should love one another, so that in them "the love of God" has been perfected (2:5). The elder is thus implicitly affirming that "his word" is in the young men (1:10), a separate sub-group within but also representative of the entire audience, as "the word" of *the* life (1:1) that they are keeping and thus living eternally by loving one another.

6

1 John 2:15–17

Do Not Love the Things in the World

The one doing the will of God remains forever

A   ¹⁵Do not love *the world* or the things in *the world*. If anyone loves *the world*, the love of *the Father is not* in him, ¹⁶ᵃbecause all that is in *the world*—*the desire* of the flesh and *the desire* of the eyes

      B   ¹⁶ᵇand the arrogance concerning the livelihood,

A'   ¹⁶ᶜ*is not* from *the Father* but is from *the world*. ¹⁷Yet *the world* is passing away and *the desire* concerning it, but the one doing the will of God remains forever.⁹¹

2:15–16a (A): Do Not Love the World or the Things in the World

The audience hear the A element (2:15–16a) of this chiastic unit as a chiastic pattern in itself:

a) Do not love *the world* or the things in *the world*. If anyone loves *the world* (2:15a),

---

91. For the establishment of 2:15–17 as a chiasm, see ch. 1.

b) the love of the Father is not in him (2:15b),

a') because all that is in *the world*—the desire of the flesh and the desire of the eyes (2:16a).

After the central and unparalleled b) sub-element, "the love of the Father is not in him" (2:15b), the audience experience a pivot of parallels from the a) to the a') sub-element involving the only occurrences in this sub-unit of the term "the world." "Do not love the world [τὸν κόσμον] or the things in the world [τῷ κόσμῳ]. If anyone loves the world [τὸν κόσμον]" (2:15a) progresses to "all that is in the world [τῷ κόσμῳ]" (2:16a). And with the phrase, "love of the Father [πατρός]" (2:15b), the audience hear the transitional term that links this unit (2:15–17) to the previous unit (2:1–14), which concludes with a reference to knowing "the Father [πατέρα]" (2:14).

The elder's command for his audience not to "love" (ἀγαπᾶτε) the world or the things in the world (2:15a) reinforces his exhortation for every member of his audience rather to be one who "loves" (ἀγαπῶν) his brother, his fellow believer, and thus remains in the light (2:10) of eternal life (John 1:4).[92] Indeed, if anyone "loves" (ἀγαπᾷ) the world (1 John 2:15a), the "love" (ἀγάπη) of God the Father is not in him (2:15b), because it is in the one who keeps the word, the commandment, to love one another that the "love" (ἀγάπη) of God has been perfected (2:5).[93] And for the love of God "the Father [πατρός]" not to be in anyone who loves the world would contradict the elder's affirmation of the audience as the "young children" who have known "the Father [πατέρα]" (2:14).[94]

---

92. The elder "seems to be suggesting that the love of any Christian may be directed, rightly and creatively, toward the faithful (cf. v 10), as a mark of 'living in the light.' But it may also be bestowed, wrongly and selfishly, on the world and on worldly values" (Smalley, *1 John*, 78).

93. The "love of the Father/God" is purposefully ambiguous. It can connote our love for God and/or God's love for us. "Given 1 John's many ambiguities of expression, however, it may be mistaken to ask of his thought a precision that it did not have" (Lieu, *Commentary*, 93).

94. "From a dualistic perspective, 'the world' takes on a powerfully negative connotation, especially in John 13–17 and 1 John. . . . The world in the Johannine writings is at enmity with God and his people; it is evil and doomed to destruction. . . . However, in some places the word 'world' stands for the entire human race, which God wants to save (John 3:16; 4:42; 6:33, 51; 8:12; 1 John 2:2; 4:14). . . . Here in v. 15, 'the world' can have yet a third meaning, the material world and everything that belongs to it, the values, related to the concept 'mammon' in Matt 6:24, that can lure humanity away from God" (Olsson, *Letters*, 128).

The audience are not to love the world or the things in the world (2:15a) because of all that is in the world. This includes the desire of the flesh and the desire of the "eyes [ὀφθαλμῶν]" (2:16a). It recalls that the one hating his brother is in the darkness, rather than in the light of eternal life, because the darkness has blinded his "eyes [ὀφθαλμούς]" (2:11). And this is in contrast to what concerns the word of eternal life, "what we have seen with our eyes [ὀφθαλμοῖς]" (1:1).

2:16b (B): The Arrogance Concerning the Livelihood

All of the things in the world, which the audience are not to love (2:15), include not only the desire of the flesh and the desire of the eyes (2:16a) but also "the arrogance concerning livelihood" (2:16b), that is, the arrogance involved in the pursuit and pride of possessing a material livelihood, in contrast to living eternally by loving one another.[95]

2:16c-17 (A'): The World Is Passing Away

After the central and unparalleled B element, "and the arrogance concerning the livelihood" (2:16b), the audience experience a pivot of parallels from the A (2:15-16a) to the A' element (2:16c-17): from "the world [κόσμον]," "in the world [κόσμῳ]," and "the world [κόσμον]" (2:15a) to "from the world [κόσμου]" (2:16c) and "the world [κόσμος]" (2:17); from "the love of the Father [πατρός] is not [οὐκ ἔστιν] in him" (2:15a) to "is not [οὐκ ἔστιν] from the Father [πατρός]" (2:16c); and from "the desire [ἐπιθυμία] of the flesh and the desire [ἐπιθυμία] of the eyes" (2:16a) to "the desire [ἐπιθυμία] concerning it" (2:17).

"The love of the Father" (2:15b) is not in the one who loves the world (2:15a), because all that is in the world (2:16a) is not "from the Father but is from the world [ἐκ τοῦ κόσμου]" (2:16c). This is in marked contrast to Jesus and his disciples as those who are not "from the world [ἐκ τοῦ κόσμου]" (John 17:14, 16). Yet, just as the darkness "is passing away [παράγεται]" (1 John 2:8), the world "is passing away [παράγεται] and the desire concerning it" (2:17a). This includes the "desire" of the

---

95. "Arrogance concerning the livelihood" refers to "the boastful possessions of life" (Painter, *1 John*, 192) or to "boasting over what one is, has, and owns. The word ἀλαζονεία means pride, arrogance, boasting/boastfulness. The word βίος means livelihood, what one has to live on, sustenance, or life" (Olsson, *Letters*, 130).

flesh and the "desire" of the eyes (2:16a), as well as "the arrogance concerning the livelihood" (2:16b). Although the world is passing away, "the one doing the will of God remains [μένει] forever" (2:17). This resonates with "the one loving his brother remains [μένει] in the light" (2:10) of eternal life. It includes the young men, as representative of the audience, in whom "remains" (μένει) the word of God, the commandment that we love one another to live eternally.

That "the one doing [ποιῶν] the will [θέλημα] of God remains forever [μένει εἰς τὸν αἰῶνα]" (2:17) recalls that Jesus came down from heaven not "so that I may do [ποιῶ] my own will [θέλημα] but the will [θέλημα]" of the God who sent him (John 6:38; cf. 4:34; 5:30). As the Son of God and the Christ, Jesus not only "remains forever [μένει εἰς τὸν αἰῶνα]" (8:35; 12:34), but provides the way to living eternally by the truth (14:6) of practicing the commandment, and thus doing the will of God, that we should love one another (12:50; 13:34; 15:12).[96]

Summary of 1 John 2:15-17

Since the world, with its desires for pursuing material livelihood (2:16), is passing away, one should do the will of God—love one another—rather than the will of the world, so that the love of the Father is in him (2:15). The one doing this will of God the Father, like Jesus, remains forever (2:17) and thus lives eternally.

---

96. "The loving Christian 'remains' (μένει) for ever, and by living 'as Jesus lived' (1 John 2:6) the believer remains as Christ himself remains (John 12:34)" (Smalley, *1 John*, 84).

7

1 John 2:18–27

The One Confessing the Son Also Has the Father

Remain in him who promised us life eternal

A   ¹⁸Young children, it is the last hour, and just as you *heard* that the antichrist is coming, so now many antichrists have appeared. Thus we know that it is the last hour. ¹⁹From us they have gone out but they were not from us. For if they were from us, they would have *remained* with us, but rather so that they may be manifested that they all are not from us. ²⁰But you have an *anointing* from the holy one and all of you know. ²¹*I have written to you* not because you do not know the *truth*, but because you know it, and because every *lie* is not from the *truth*.

    B   ^{22a}Who is the liar but the one who *denies*, saying, "Jesus *is not the Christ*?"

    B'   ^{22b}This *is the antichrist*, the one who *denies* the Father and the Son. ²³Everyone who *denies* the Son does not have the Father. The one confessing the Son also has the Father.

A'   ²⁴As for you, what you *heard* from the beginning, in you let it *remain.* If in you *remains* what from the beginning you *heard*, you also will *remain* in the Son and in the Father. ²⁵And this is the promise that he himself promised to us—the life eternal. ²⁶These things *I have written to you* concerning those deceiving you. ²⁷And as for you, the *anointing* that you received from him *remains* in you and you do not have need that anyone teach you. But as his *anointing* teaches you concerning all things, indeed it is *true* and is not a *lie*, and just as it has taught you, *remain* in him.⁹⁷

2:18–21 (A): You Have an Anointing and You Know the Truth

The audience hear the A element (2:18–21) of this chiastic unit as a chiastic pattern in itself:

- a) Young children, it *is* the last hour, and just as you heard that the antichrist is coming, so now many antichrists have appeared. Thus we know that it *is* the last hour (2:18).

  - b) From us they have gone out but *they were not from us* (2:19a).

  - b') For if *they were from us*, they would have remained with us (2:19b),

- a') but rather so that they may be manifested that they all *are* not from us. But you have an anointing from the holy one and all of you know. I have written to you not because you do not know the truth, but because you know it, and because every lie *is* not from the truth (2:19c–21).

At the center of this chiastic sub-unit the audience experience a pivot of parallels from the b) to the b') sub-element involving the only occurrences in this sub-unit of the expression "they were/were not from us." "But they were not from us [οὐκ ἦσαν ἐξ ἡμῶν]" (2:19a) progresses to "if they were from us [ἐξ ἡμῶν ἦσαν]" (2:19b). And with the notice that "they would have remained [μεμενήκεισαν] with us" (2:19b), the audience hear the transitional term that links this chiastic unit (2:18–27) to the preceding one (2:15–17), which concluded with the notice that "the one doing the will of God remains [μένει] forever" (2:17). The audience then hear a progression of parallels from the a) sub-element (2:18) to the a') sub-element (2:19c–21) involving the only occurrences in this sub-unit of the present tense of the verb "to be." "It is [ἐστίν] the last hour" and "we know that it is [ἐστίν] the last hour" (2:18) progress to "they

---

97. For the establishment of 2:18–27 as a chiasm, see ch. 1.

all are [εἰσίν] not from us" (2:19c) and "every lie is [ἔστιν] not from the truth" (2:21).

The audience hear the a) sub-element (2:18) of this chiastic sub-unit as yet another chiastic pattern in itself:

(a) Young children, it *is the last hour* (2:18a),

   (b) and just as you heard that the *antichrist* is coming (2:18b),

   (b') so now many *antichrists* have appeared (2:18c).

(a') Thus we know that it *is the last hour* (2:18d).

At the center of this chiastic sub-unit the audience experience a pivot of parallels from the (b) to the (b') sub-element involving the only occurrences in this sub-unit of the term "antichrist." "The antichrist [ἀντίχριστος] is coming" (2:18b) progresses to "many antichrists [ἀντίχριστοι] have appeared" (2:18c). The audience then hear a progression of parallels from the (a) to the (a') sub-element involving the only occurrences in 1 John of the expression "last hour." "It is the last hour [ἐσχάτη ὥρα ἐστίν]" (2:18a) progresses to "we know that it is the last hour [ἐσχάτη ὥρα ἐστίν]" (2:18d).

And the audience hear the a') sub-element (2:19c–21) of this chiastic sub-unit as yet another chiastic pattern in itself:

(a) but rather so that they may be manifested that they all *are not from us* (2:19c).

   (b) But you have an anointing from the holy one and all of *you know* (2:20).

      (c) I have written to you (2:21a)

   (b') not because *you* do not *know* the truth, but because *you know* it (2:21b),

(a') and because every lie *is not* from the truth (2:21c).

After the central and unparalleled (c) sub-element, "I have written to you" (2:21a), the audience experience a pivot of parallels from the (b) to the (b') sub-element involving the only occurrences in this sub-unit of the expression "you know." "All of you know [οἴδατε]" (2:20) progresses to "not because you do not know [οἴδατε] the truth, but because you know [οἴδατε] it" (2:21b). The audience then hear a progression of parallels from the (a) to the (a') sub-element involving the only occurrences in this sub-unit of the expression "is/are not." "They all are not [οὐκ εἰσίν] from us" (2:19c) progresses to "every lie is not [οὐκ ἔστιν] from the truth" (2:21c).

The elder previously addressed his entire audience as "young children" (παιδία) to whom he has written this letter because they have known the Father (2:14). And now after he again addresses them as "young children" (παιδία), characterizing them as open to and in need of instruction, he instructs them that "it is the last hour, and just as you heard that the antichrist is coming, so now many antichrists have appeared. Thus we know that it is the last hour" (2:18). Having heard that the darkness and the world are passing away (2:8, 17), the audience are now informed that "it is the last hour [ἐσχάτη ὥρα]" (2:18a), indicating that the final period of tribulation preceding final salvation has arrived.[98]

"Just as you heard" (καθὼς ἠκούσατε) that the antichrist is coming (2:18b) reminds the audience of a threat to their keeping the commandment, the word "you heard [ἠκούσατε]" (2:7), that we should love one another (2 John 1:5), "just as you heard" (καθὼς ἠκούσατε) from the beginning (1:6). The "antichrist" (ἀντίχριστος) whom they heard is "coming" (ἔρχεται) and the "many antichrists" (ἀντίχριστοι πολλοί) who have now appeared (1 John 2:18bc) refer to those not confessing Jesus "Christ" (Χριστόν) as "coming" (ἐρχόμενον) in flesh. This is the deceiver and the "antichrist" (ἀντίχριστος), the "many" (πολλοί) deceivers who have gone out into the world (2 John 1:7). If any one of these antichrists who do not bring the teachings of Christ, which includes that we should love one another, "comes" (ἔρχεται) to the audience, they are not to receive or greet him (1:10). Now that they have appeared "we know" (γινώσκομεν) indeed that it is the last hour (1 John 2:18cd), "we" who "know" (γινώσκομεν) that we have known the Christ and are in him, if we keep his commandments (2:3, 5) that we should love one another.[99]

From us the many antichrists (2:18) "have gone out [ἐξῆλθαν]" (2:19a), that is, the many deceivers "have gone out [ἐξῆλθον] into the

98. For a possible allusion to "that hour" (ὥραν ἐκείνην) as the eschatological hour in Dan 12:1, see Beale, "Last Hour," 231–54. "First John uses, but only here, the distinctive phrase 'the last hour'; 'hour' can indicate not a specific measure of time but a significant moment" (Lieu, *Commentary*, 99).

99. The elder "speaks of the personified expectation of an ever-present evil, whose disposition is 'against' Christ. If Christ has come, comes, and is to come, then antichrist also comes, whose embodied presence and demonic influence takes a multitude of forms" (Schuchard, *1–3 John*, 264).

world" (2 John 1:7). But they were not from us (1 John 2:19a). "For if they were from us, they would have remained [μεμενήκεισαν] with us" (2:19b). Each of them could then "remain" (μένει) forever by doing the will of God (2:17), "remain" (μένει) in the light by loving his brother (2:10), and thus "remain" (μένειν) in Jesus Christ (2:6).[100] That they would have remained "with us" (μεθ᾽ ἡμῶν) means that they, like the audience, would have fellowship "with us" (μεθ᾽ ἡμῶν), the elder and his associates, the fellowship that is ours with the Father and with his Son Jesus Christ (2:3). They would experience the truth that remains in us and "with us" (μεθ᾽ ἡμῶν) will be forever (2 John 1:2), the grace, mercy, and peace that will be "with us" (μεθ᾽ ἡμῶν) from God the Father and from Jesus Christ the Son of the Father in truth and love (1:3), the truth of doing the commandment that we should love one another to live eternally.

That from us the antichrists have gone out and not remained with us (1 John 2:19ab) happened so that, in contrast to the eternal life that was "manifested [ἐφανερώθη]" (1:2), "they may be manifested [φανερωθῶσιν] that they all are not from us" (2:19c). Although from us they have gone out, they all presently "are" (εἰσίν) not from us. This confirms that we know that indeed it presently "is" (ἐστίν) the last hour (2:18).

In emphatic contrast to "all" (πάντες) who are not from us (2:19), "you" (ὑμεῖς), the audience, "have an anointing from the holy one and all [πάντες] of you know" (2:20). That they have an "anointing" (χρῖσμα) confirms their association with Jesus Christ as the "anointed one [Χριστός]" (1:3; 2:1) rather than with the "antichrists [ἀντίχριστοι]" (2:18).[101] That they have an anointing from the "holy" (ἁγίου) one recalls that the risen Jesus Christ bestowed the "holy" (ἅγιον) Spirit upon his disciples (John 20:22). And in his farewell address Jesus promised that the "holy" (ἅγιον) Spirit that the Father will send in his name will teach his disciples all things and remind them of all the things he told them (14:26).[102] In contrast to the one who hates his brother so that he walks

---

100. "The occurrence here of the verb μεμενήκεισαν, whose root is μένω, should not be overlooked in a context where the steadfastness implied by the verbal actions of remaining or abiding is the paraenetic center of the discourse" (Yarbrough, *1–3 John*, 147).

101. "A play on words is apparent in this passage" (Smalley, *1 John*, 100). For a discussion regarding a possible significance of this anointing for the situation of the audience, see Connell, "Chrism," 212–34.

102. "Most rightly see the referent of the 'anointing' as the Holy Spirit" (Schuchard, *1–3 John*, 269). "The author presumably has in mind the Spirit, i.e., the spirit of truth who mediates the truth to Jesus' disciples" (Olsson, *Letters*, 144). "Here and in verse

in the darkness and does not "know [οἶδεν] where he is going" (1 John 2:11), all of "you," the audience, "know [οἴδατε]" (2:20), resonating with the elder's affirmation of Gaius that "you know [οἶδας] that our testimony is true" (3 John 1:12).

The elder previously stated that "I have written to you, young children [ἔγραψα ὑμῖν, παιδία], because you have known the Father" (1 John 2:14). And now he tells his "young children [παιδία]" (2:18) that "I have written to you [ἔγραψα ὑμῖν] not because you do not know [οἴδατε] the truth, but because you know [οἴδατε] it, and because every lie is not from the truth" (2:21). This further specifies what it is that "all of you know [οἴδατε]" (2:20). That he has written to them because they know the "truth" (ἀλήθειαν) and because every "lie" (ψεῦδος) is not from the "truth" (ἀληθείας) means that the "truth" (ἀλήθεια) of keeping the commandments to love one another to live eternally is in them so that they are not "liars [ψεύστης]" (2:4). Of those who have gone out, including those who know the "truth," "all are not from us [οὐκ εἰσὶν πάντες ἐξ ἡμῶν]," which associates them with "every lie" (πᾶν ψεῦδος) that "is not from the truth [ἐκ τῆς ἀληθείας οὐκ ἔστιν]" (2:21).

2:22a (B): Who Is the Liar but the One Who Denies that Jesus Is the Christ?

Not only is the one saying he has known Jesus Christ, but not keeping his commandments, a "liar [ψεύστης]" (2:4), but the "liar" (ψεύστης) is the one who denies that Jesus is the Christ (2:22a). This means denying that Jesus is the Christ who is the righteous one, the advocate we have with the Father (2:1), and that Jesus is the Christ who is the Son of the Father (1:3; 2 John 1:3). The one who denies that Jesus is the Christ is an associate of "the many deceivers who have gone out into the world, those not confessing Jesus Christ as coming in flesh" (2 John 1:7).

---

27 the anointing is linked to knowledge and to teaching; it is most likely that the term does itself refer to the readers' possession of true understanding, an internalization of the teaching that had transformed and shaped them" (Lieu, *Commentary*, 103).

2:22b-23 (B'): The Antichrist Is the One
Who Denies the Father and the Son

At this point the audience experience a pivot of parallels from the B (2:22a) to the B' (2:22b-23) element of this chiastic unit. The "one who denies [ἀρνούμενος], saying, 'Jesus is not the Christ [οὐκ ἔστιν ὁ Χριστός]'" (2:22a) progresses to "this is the antichrist [ἐστιν ὁ ἀντίχριστος], the one who denies [ἀρνούμενος] the Father and the Son" (2:22b) and "everyone who denies [ἀρνούμενος] the Son does not have the Father" (2:23).

That "this is the antichrist [οὗτός ἐστιν ὁ ἀντίχριστος]" (2:22b), the "antichrist" (ἀντίχριστος) the audience have heard is coming (2:18), recalls that "this is the deceiver and the antichrist [οὗτός ἐστιν ὁ πλάνος καὶ ὁ ἀντίχριστος]," namely, the many deceivers who "have gone out into the world, those not confessing Jesus Christ as coming in flesh" (2 John 1:7). In "denying" (ἀρνούμενος) that Jesus is the Christ (2:22a), the antichrist "denies" (ἀρνούμενος) the Father and the Son (2:22b). And everyone who "denies" (ἀρνούμενος) the Son does not have the Father. Whereas, in contrast to those not "confessing" (ὁμολογοῦντες) Jesus Christ as coming in flesh (2 John 1:7), "the one confessing [ὁμολογῶν] the Son also has the Father [τὸν υἱὸν καὶ τὸν πατέρα ἔχει]" (1 John 2:23). This recalls that the one remaining in the teaching of the Christ "has both the Father and the Son [τὸν πατέρα καὶ τὸν υἱὸν ἔχει]" (2 John 1:9). And this means having the fellowship of living eternally by loving one another that is ours "with the Father and with his Son [μετὰ τοῦ πατρὸς καὶ μετὰ τοῦ υἱοῦ αὐτοῦ] Jesus Christ" (1 John 1:3).

2:24-27 (A'): The Anointing that
You Have Received Is True

At this point the audience experience a progression of parallels from the A (2:18-21) to the A' (2:24-27) element of this chiastic unit: from "just as you heard [ἠκούσατε]" (2:18) to "what you heard [ἠκούσατε] from the beginning" and "what from the beginning you heard [ἠκούσατε]" (2:24); from "they would have remained [μεμενήκεισαν] with us" (2:19) to "in you let it remain [μενέτω]," "if in you remains [μείνῃ]," "you also will remain [μενεῖτε]" (2:24), "remains [μένει] in you," and "remain [μένετε] in him" (2:27); from "you have an anointing [χρῖσμα]" (2:20) to "the anointing [χρῖσμα] that you received" (2:27); from "I have written to you [ἔγραψα ὑμῖν]" (2:21) to "these things I have written to you [ἔγραψα ὑμῖν]" (2:26); from "not because you do not know the truth [ἀλήθειαν]" and "because every lie [ψεῦδος] is not from the truth [ἀληθείας]" (2:21) to "it is true [ἀληθές] and is not a lie [ψεῦδος]" (2:27).

The audience hear the A' element (2:24–27) of this chiastic unit as a chiastic pattern in itself:

a) As for *you*, what you heard from the beginning, in *you* let it *remain*. If in *you remains* what from the beginning you heard, *you* also will *remain* in the Son and in the Father (2:24).

b) And this is the *promise* (2:25a)

b') that he himself *promised* to us—the life eternal (2:25b).

a') These things I have written to *you* concerning those deceiving *you*. And as for *you*, the anointing that you received from him *remains* in *you* and you do not have need that anyone teach *you*. But as his anointing teaches *you* concerning all things, indeed it is true and is not a lie, and just as it has taught you, *remain* in him (2:26–27).

At the center of this chiastic sub-unit the audience experience a pivot of parallels from the b) to the b') sub-element involving the only occurrences in 1 John of expressions for "promise." "And this is the promise [ἐπαγγελία]" (2:25a) progresses to "that he himself promised [ἐπηγγείλατο]" (2:25b). The audience then hear a progression of parallels from the a) to the a') sub-element involving the only occurrences in this sub-unit of the pronoun "you" and the verb "remain." "As for you [ὑμεῖς], what you heard from the beginning, in you [ὑμῖν] let it remain [μενέτω]. If in you [ὑμῖν] remains [μείνῃ] what from the beginning you heard, you [ὑμεῖς] also will remain [μενεῖτε] in the Son and in the Father" (2:24). This progresses to: "These things I have written to you [ὑμῖν] concerning those deceiving you [ὑμᾶς]. And as for you [ὑμεῖς], the anointing that you received from him remains [μένει] in you [ὑμῖν] and you do not have need that anyone teach you [ὑμᾶς]. But as his anointing teaches you [ὑμᾶς] concerning all things, it is true and is not a lie, and just as it has taught you, remain [μένετε] in him" (2:26–27).

The audience hear the a) sub-element (2:24) of this chiastic sub-unit as yet another chiastic pattern in itself:

(a) As for *you* (2:24a),

(b) what you *heard* (2:24b)

    (c) *from the beginning* (2:24c)

        (d) in *you* let it remain (2:24d).

        (d') If in *you* remains (2:24e).

    (c') what *from the beginning* (2:24f)

(b') you *heard* (2:24g)

(a') *you* also will remain in the Son and in the Father (2:24h).

At the center of this chiastic sub-unit the audience experience a pivot of parallels from the (d) to the (d') sub-element involving the only occurrences in this sub-unit of the dative plural second person pronoun. "In you [ὑμῖν] let it remain" (2:24d) progresses to "if in you [ὑμῖν] remains" (2:24e). The audience hear a progression of parallels from the (c) to the (c') sub-element involving the only occurrences in this sub-unit of "from the beginning." "From the beginning [ἀπ' ἀρχῆς]" (2:24c) progresses to "what from the beginning [ἀπ' ἀρχῆς]" (2:24f). The audience then hear a progression from the (b) to the (b') sub-element involving the only occurrences in this sub-unit of "you heard." "What you heard [ἠκούσατε]" (2:24b) progresses to "you heard [ἠκούσατε]" (2:24g). And finally, the audience hear a progression from the (a) to the (a') sub-element involving the only occurrences in this sub-unit of the nominative plural second person pronoun. "As for you [ὑμεῖς]" (2:24a) progresses to "you [ὑμεῖς] also" (2:24h).

And within the a') sub-element (2:26–27) of this chiastic sub-unit the audience hear yet another chiastic pattern in itself:

(a) And as for you, the anointing that you received from him *remains in* you (2:27a)

    (b) and you do not have need that anyone *teach you*. But as his anointing *teaches you* concerning all things (2:27b),

        (c) indeed it *is* true (2:27c)

        (c') and *is* not a lie (2:27d),

    (b') and just as it *has taught you* (2:27e),

(a') *remain in* him (2:27f).

At the center of this chiastic sub-unit the audience experience a pivot of parallels from the (c) to the (c') sub-element involving the only occurrences in this sub-unit of the verb "to be." "Indeed it is [ἐστιν] true" (2:27c) progresses to "and is [ἐστιν] not a lie" (2:27d). The audience then hear a progression of parallels from the (b) to the (b') sub-element involving the only occurrences in 1 John of expressions for "teaching you." "That anyone teach you [διδάσκῃ ὑμᾶς]" and "his anointing teaches you [διδάσκει ὑμᾶς]" (2:27b) progress to "just as it has taught you [ἐδίδαξεν ὑμᾶς]" (2:27e). Finally, the audience hear a progression from the (a) to the (a') sub-element involving the only occurrences in this sub-unit of the verb "remain." "Remains in [μένει ἐν] you" (2:27a) progresses to "remain in [μένετε ἐν] him" (2:27f).

As for the audience, "what you heard from the beginning [ἠκούσατε ἀπ' ἀρχῆς], in you let it remain [μενέτω]" (2:24). This refers to the commandment "you heard from the beginning [ἠκούσατε ἀπ' ἀρχῆς]" (2 John 1:6), namely, "that we should love one another" (1:5). If in them "remains [μείνῃ] what from the beginning you heard [ἀπ' ἀρχῆς ἠκούσατε]" (1 John 2:24), then, although some have gone out and not "remained [μεμενήκεισαν] with us" (2:19), "you will remain [μενεῖτε] in the Son and in the Father" (2:24). This recalls that the one "remaining" (μένων) in the teaching of the Christ, including especially that we should love one another, "has both the Father and the Son" (2 John 1:9). This means that even though some have abandoned them, if the audience continue to practice the commandment to love one another, they will maintain their fellowship that "is with the Father and with his Son Jesus Christ" (1 John 1:3).

That "this is the promise that he himself promised us—the life eternal [τὴν ζωὴν τὴν αἰώνιον]" (2:25) recalls and reinforces the assertion of the elder and his associates that "we have seen and testify and declare to you the life eternal [τὴν ζωὴν τὴν αἰώνιον] which was with the Father and manifested to us" (1:2). In other words, the promise that the audience will remain in the Son and in the Father, if they continue to practice the commandment they heard from the beginning to love one another (2:24), is the divine promise of the life eternal. By continuing to love one another they thus live eternally in the fellowship they share "with the Father and with his Son Jesus Christ" (1:3).

That the elder has written these things to the audience concerning those "deceiving" (πλανώντων) them (2:26) refers to the many "deceivers" (πλάνοι) who "have gone out into the world, those not confessing Jesus Christ as coming in flesh" (2 John 1:7a). Indeed, "this is the deceiver [πλάνος] and the antichrist" (1:7b). But as for the audience, the "anointing" (χρῖσμα) that they received from him remains in them (1 John 2:27a), recalling that they have an "anointing" (χρῖσμα) from the holy one (2:20). That the anointing they received from the holy one, the holy Spirit (John 14:26), "remains" (μένει) in them resonates with Jesus' farewell assertion to his disciples that the Spirit of truth "remains" (μένει) with them and will be in them (14:17). Thus the audience do not have a need that anyone "teach" (διδάσκῃ) them, since his anointing "teaches" (διδάσκει) them concerning "all things [πάντων]" (1 John 2:27b). This accords with Jesus' promise that the holy Spirit "will teach" (διδάξει) his followers "all things" (πάντα) and will remind them of "all things" (πάντα) that he told them (John 14:26).[103]

The anointing teaches that which is "true [ἀληθές]" (1 John 2:27c), recalling and reinforcing that the new commandment to love one another is "true [ἀληθές]" (2:8). The emphatic assertion that it is therefore not a "lie [ψεῦδος]" (2:27d) recalls and reinforces that every "lie" (ψεῦδος) is not from the truth, but the audience know the truth (2:21). Consequently, the audience are able to worship God in the Spirit of truth (John 4:23-24) by continuing to love one another.

"It has taught [ἐδίδαξεν]" (2:27e), that is, the true anointing "teaches" (διδάσκει) the audience concerning all things, so that they do not need anyone to "teach" (διδάσκῃ) them (2:27b). Therefore, just as the anointing they received "from him remains in" (ἀπ᾽ αὐτοῦ μένει ἐν) them (2:27a), so they are to "remain in him [μένετε ἐν αὐτῷ]" (2:27f). This reinforces that anyone in the audience "remaining" (μένων) in the "teaching" (διδαχῇ) of the Christ has both the Father and the Son (2 John 1:9). If the audience remain in the teaching to love one another, and thus become true worshipers of God in the Spirit of truth (John 4:23-24), they are living the divine life eternal (1 John 2:25) in the fellowship that is theirs with the Father and with his Son Jesus Christ (1:3).

---

103. The elder "obviously uses slight irony here. If they had no need for instruction beyond some inner light imparted by their anointing, his epistle would be unnecessary" (Yarbrough, *1-3 John*, 166). "The teaching they are given by the anointing is comprehensive, 'about everything,' but the present tense 'teaches' here shows that this is an ongoing experience and so requires that they continue to be dependent on the anointing" (Lieu, *Commentary*, 113).

Summary of 1 John 2:18-27

The elder previously stated that "I have written to you, young children, because you have known the Father" (1 John 2:14). And now he tells his "young children" (2:18) that "I have written to you not because you do not know the truth, but because you know it, and because every lie is not from the truth" (2:21). This further specifies what it is that "all of you know" (2:20). That he has written to them because they know the "truth" and because every "lie" is not from the "truth" means that the "truth" of keeping the commandments to love one another to live eternally is in them, so that they are not a "liar" (2:4). Of those who have gone out, including those who know the "truth," "all are not from us," which associates them with "every lie" that "is not from the truth" (2:21).

That "this is the antichrist" (2:22b), the "antichrist" the audience have heard is coming (2:18), recalls that "this is the deceiver and the antichrist," namely, the many deceivers who "have gone out into the world, those not confessing Jesus Christ as coming in flesh" (2 John 1:7). In "denying" that Jesus is the Christ (2:22a), the antichrist "denies" the Father and the Son (2:22b). And everyone who "denies" the Son does not have the Father. Whereas, in contrast to those not "confessing" Jesus Christ as coming in flesh (2 John 1:7), "the one confessing the Son also has the Father" (1 John 2:23). This recalls that the one remaining in the teaching of the Christ "has both the Father and the Son" (2 John 1:9). And this means having the fellowship of living eternally by loving one another that is ours "with the Father and with his Son Jesus Christ" (1 John 1:3).

"It has taught" them (2:27e), that is, the true anointing "teaches" the audience concerning all things, so that they do not need anyone to "teach" them (2:27b). Therefore, just as the anointing they received "from him remains in" them (2:27a), so they are to "remain in him" (2:27f). This reinforces that anyone in the audience "remaining" in the "teaching" of the Christ has both the Father and the Son (2 John 1:9). If the audience remain in the teaching to love one another, and thus become true worshipers of God in the Spirit of truth (John 4:23-24), they are living the divine life eternal (1 John 2:25) in the fellowship that is theirs with the Father and with his Son Jesus Christ (1:3).

8

1 John 2:28—3:6
You Know Whoever Does Righteousness Has Been Begotten from Him

> Everyone who sins has neither
> seen him nor known him

A   ²⁸And now, little children, *remain in him*, so that when he is *manifested* we may have confidence and not be shamed away from him at his coming. ²⁹If you *know* that he is righteous, you *know* that also *everyone who does* righteousness from him has been begotten. ³:¹*See* what sort of love the Father has given us, that we may be called children of God, and indeed we are. For this reason the world does not *know* us, because it did not *know* him. ²Beloved, now we are children of God, but it has not yet been *manifested* what we will be. We *know* that when it is *manifested*, we will be like him, because we will *see* him just as he is.

B   ³ªAnd everyone who has this hope in him *purifies* himself,

B'   ³ᵇjust as that one is *pure*.

A'   ⁴*Everyone who does* sin also does lawlessness, indeed sin is lawlessness. ⁵And you *know* that that one was *manifested*, so that he might take away sins, but sin is not in him. ⁶Everyone who *in* *him remains* does not sin. Everyone who sins has neither *seen* him nor *known* him.[104]

2:28–3:2 (A): Remain in Him as Children of God

The audience hear the (A) element (2:28–3:2) of this chiastic unit as a chiastic pattern in itself:

a) And now, little children, remain in him, so that *when he is manifested* we may have confidence and not be shamed away from him at his coming. If you *know* that he *is* righteous, you know that also everyone who does righteousness from him has been begotten (2:28–29).

  b) See what sort of *love* the Father has given us, that we may be called *children of God*, and indeed *we are* (3:1a).

   c) For this reason the world *does not know* us (3:1b),

   c') because it *did not know* him (3:1c).

  b') *Beloved*, now *we are children of God* (3:2a),

a') but it has not yet been *manifested* what we will be. We *know* that *when it is manifested*, we will be like him, because we will see him just as he *is* (3:2b).

At the center of this chiastic sub-unit the audience experience a pivot of parallels from the c) to the c') sub-element involving the only occurrences in this sub-unit of the expression "do not know." "The world does not know [οὐ γινώσκει] us" (3:1b) progresses to "because it did not know [οὐκ ἔγνω] him" (3:1c). The audience then hear a progression of parallels from the b) to the b') sub-element involving the only occurrences in this sub-unit of expressions for "love," "children of God, " and "we are." "What sort of love [ἀγάπην] the Father has given us, that we may be called children of God [τέκνα θεοῦ], and indeed we are [ἐσμέν]" (3:1a) progresses to "beloved [ἀγαπητοί], now we are children of God [τέκνα θεοῦ ἐσμεν]" (3:2a).

And finally, the audience hear a progression of parallels from the a) sub-element (2:28–29) to the a') sub-element (3:2b) involving the only

---

104. For the establishment of 2:28–3:6 as a chiasm, see ch. 1.

occurrences in this sub-unit of the expressions "manifest," "know," and "is." "When he is manifested [ἐὰν φανερωθῇ]" (2:28) progresses to "it has not yet been manifested [ἐφανερώθη]" and "when it is manifested [ἐὰν φανερωθῇ]" (3:2b); and "if you know [εἰδῆτε] that he is [ἐστιν] righteous" (2:29) progresses to "we know [οἴδαμεν] . . . and will see him just as he is [ἐστιν]" (3:2b). Additionally, when the audience hear "remain in him [μένετε ἐν αὐτῷ]" (2:28) at the beginning of this chiastic unit (2:28–3:6), they hear the transitional terms that link this unit to the preceding one (2:18–27), which concluded with the exhortation to "remain in him [μένετε ἐν αὐτῷ]" (2:27).

Having previously addressed his audience as his "little children [τεκνία]" (2:1, 12), the elder again addresses them as "little children" (τεκνία) with the exhortation for them to "remain in him [μένετε ἐν αὐτῷ]" (2:28). This repeats and thus emphatically reinforces his preceding exhortation for them to "remain in him [μένετε ἐν αὐτῷ]" (2:27), that is, in the Son Jesus Christ (2:6, 24). By remaining in him, we may have confidence and not be shamed away from him at his final coming, when he is "manifested [φανερωθῇ]" (2:28), as the one in whom life eternal was "manifested [ἐφανερώθη]" (1:2), in contrast to those "manifested [φανερωθῶσιν] that they all are not from us" (2:19).

If the audience, "you" who "know [οἴδατε] the truth" (2:21), "know [εἰδῆτε] that he is righteous [δίκαιός]" (2:29a), then they know Jesus Christ as the "righteous one [δίκαιον]" (2:1), the one who is "faithful and righteous [δίκαιος], so that he will forgive us the sins and cleanse us from all unrighteousness [ἀδικίας]" (1:9).[105] And they know "that also everyone who does righteousness [ποιῶν τὴν δικαιοσύνην] from him has been begotten [ἐξ αὐτοῦ γεγέννηται]" (2:29b). This recalls and resonates with the assertion that "the one doing [ποιῶν] the will of God remains forever" (2:17). Indeed, it recalls that Jesus Christ gave believers the authority to become children of God (John 1:12) as those "from God begotten [ἐκ θεοῦ ἐγεννήθησαν]" (1:13) into the divine life eternal (1:4).[106]

---

105. Thus Jesus Christ is the antecedent of δίκαιός in 2:29, and not God the Father, contra von Wahlde, "Stereotyped Structure," 319–38.

106. "As does his Father, Jesus, who is himself born of God, gives birth by means of the anointing seed of God (see 3:9; see also Jn 3:3–8). This seed, the Spirit of Truth (Jn 14:17; 16:13), the baptized receive so that all might 'be like him' (Jesus) as they share now and forever in Jesus' identity as *child* of God (1 Jn 3:2; see also Jn 1:12–13)" (Schuchard, *1–3 John*, 285–86; emphasis original).

That those begotten from him (1 John 2:29) have been given the authority to become "children of God [τέκνα θεοῦ]" (John 1:12) is confirmed as the elder declares, "See what sort of love [ἀγάπην] the Father [πατήρ] has given us, that we may be called children of God [τέκνα θεοῦ], and indeed we are" (1 John 3:1a). This reinforces the exhortation for the audience not to love the world, since the "love of the Father" (ἀγάπη τοῦ πατρός) is not in anyone who loves the world (2:15). But whoever keeps his word, the commandment that we should love one another to live eternally, "truly in this one the love of God [ἀγάπη τοῦ θεοῦ] has been perfected" (2:5).

The reason the "world" (κόσμος) does not "know" (γινώσκει) us (3:1b) is that it "did not know him [οὐκ ἔγνω αὐτόν]" (3:1c). This recalls that although Jesus Christ, the Word, was in the "world" (κόσμῳ), and the "world" (κόσμος) came to be through him, "the world did not know him [κόσμος αὐτὸν οὐκ ἔγνω]" (John 1:10). The world thus does not know the audience, including those who "have known [ἐγνώκατε] the one from the beginning" (1 John 2:13). In contrast to the world, then, the audience are "we" who "know [γινώσκομεν] that we have known him [ἐγνώκαμεν αὐτόν]," since "we keep his commandments" (2:3), preeminent of which is that we should love one another to live eternally as children of God.

The elder emphatically underlines "the sort of love [ἀγάπην] the Father has given us, that we may be called children of God [τέκνα θεοῦ], and indeed we are [ἐσμέν]" (3:1a), with his address to the audience as "beloved [ἀγαπητοί], now we are children of God [τέκνα θεοῦ ἐσμεν]" (3:2a). They are children of God as the "beloved" (ἀγαπητοί) who practice the commandment that we should love one another (2:7). "But it has not yet been manifested [ἐφανερώθη] what we will be" (3:2b), when he is "manifested [φανερωθῇ]" (2:28). "We know [οἴδαμεν] that when it is manifested [φανερωθῇ], we will be like him," as those who do righteousness, "because we will see him just as he is [ἐστιν]" (3:2b), that is, as the one whom "you know" (εἰδῆτε) "is" (ἐστιν) righteous (2:29).

3:3a (B): Everyone Who Has This Hope in Him Purifies Himself

"Everyone [πᾶς] who has this hope in him" (3:3a), that is, the hope that "we will be like him, because we will see him just as he is" (3:2), "purifies himself" (3:3a). This implies that "everyone [πᾶς] who does righteousness," as he is righteous (2:29), is one who "purifies" (ἁγνίζει) himself, a cultic act to describe a qualification for proper worship, here used figuratively for the behavior needed for proper ethical worship.[107] In contrast to saying that "sin we do not have," so that "we are deceiving ourselves [ἑαυτούς] and the truth is not in us" (1:8), the one who "purifies himself [ἑαυτόν]" does righteousness, which includes doing the truth of loving one another to live eternally as children of God.

3:3b (B'): Just as That One Is Pure

At this point the audience experience a pivot of parallels from the B to the B' element of this chiastic unit. "Purifies [ἁγνίζει] himself" (3:3a) progresses to "just as that one is pure [ἁγνός]" (3:3b). Everyone who hopes to see Jesus Christ "just as he is [καθὼς ἐστιν]" (3:2), as the one who "is" (ἐστιν) righteous (2:29), purifies himself, "just as that one [καθὼς ἐκεῖνος] is [ἐστιν] pure."[108] This recalls and reinforces the assertion that "the one saying that he remains in him ought, just as that one [καθὼς ἐκεῖνος] walked, he himself thus to walk" (2:6). This means practicing the truth of the commandment (2:7-8) to love one another to live eternally as children of God, as true worshipers of God the Father in the Spirit of truth (John 4:23-24).

3:4-6 (A'): Everyone Who in Him Remains Does Not Sin

Next the audience hear a progression of parallels from the A (2:28-3:2) to the A' (3:4-6) element of this chiastic unit: from "remain in him [μένετε ἐν αὐτῷ]" (2:28) to "everyone who in him remains [ἐν αὐτῷ μένων]" (3:6); from "when he is manifested [φανερωθῇ]" (2:28), "it has not yet been manifested [ἐφανερώθη]" (3:2), and "when it is manifested [φανερωθῇ]" (3:2) to "that one was manifested [ἐφανερώθη]" (3:5); from "if you know [εἰδῆτε] that he is righteous, you know [γινώσκετε]" (2:29), "the world does not know [γινώσκει] us, because it did not know [ἔγνω] him" (3:1),

---

107. Balz, "ἁγνίζω," 23. This notion of purification "recalls OT prescriptions regarding the need of the worshiper for ritual cleansing (see Ex 19:10-11; Num 8:21)" (Schuchard, *1-3 John*, 299). "The verb ἁγνίζω (to cleanse, purify) can have either a ceremonial (John 11:55; Acts 21:24, 26: 24:18) or ethical (James 4:8; 1 Pet. 1:22) connotation. Here the latter is in view" (Yarbrough, *1-3 John*, 180n15).

108. "The words 'just as he is pure' now lead the Elder back to the statement 'he is righteous' in v. 29 and thus to the theme of righteousness and sin" (Olsson, *Letters*, 163).

and "we know [οἴδαμεν]" (3:2) to "you know [οἴδατε]" (3:5) and "known [ἔγνωκεν] him" (3:6); from "everyone who does [πᾶς ὁ ποιῶν] righteousness" (2:29) to "everyone who does [πᾶς ὁ ποιῶν] sin" (3:4); from "see [ἴδετε] what sort of love" (3:1) and "we will see [ὀψόμεθα] him" (3:2) to "seen [ἑώρακεν] him" (3:6).

The audience hear the A' element (3:4–6) of this chiastic unit as a chiastic pattern in itself:

a) *Everyone* who does *sin* also does lawlessness, indeed *sin is* lawlessness (3:4).

b) And you know that that one was manifested (3:5a),

a') so that he might take away *sins*, but *sin is* not in him. *Everyone* who in him remains does not *sin*. *Everyone* who *sins* has neither seen him nor known him (3:5b–6).

The audience hear the b) sub-element, "and you know that that one was manifested" (3:5a), as the unparalleled center of this chiastic sub-unit. The audience then experience a pivot of parallels from the a) sub-element (3:4) to the a') sub-element (3:5b–6) involving the only occurrences in this sub-unit of "everyone," "sin," and "is." "Everyone [πᾶς] who does sin [ἁμαρτίαν] also does lawlessness, indeed sin is [ἁμαρτία ἐστίν] lawlessness" (3:4) progresses to "he might take away sins [ἁμαρτίας], but sin [ἁμαρτία] is [ἔστιν] not in him" (3:5b), "everyone [πᾶς] ... does not sin [ἁμαρτάνει]" (3:6), and "everyone [πᾶς] who sins [ἁμαρτάνων]" (3:6).

"Everyone who does righteousness [πᾶς ὁ ποιῶν τὴν δικαιοσύνην] from him has been begotten" (2:29), so that he may become one of the children of God (3:1), as "one doing [ποιῶν] the will of God" and thus remaining forever (2:17). But "everyone who does sin [πᾶς ὁ ποιῶν τὴν ἁμαρτίαν] also does lawlessness [ἀνομίαν ποιεῖ], indeed sin is lawlessness" (3:4). That "sin is lawlessness [ἀνομία]" associates it with all "unrighteousness" (ἀδικίας) that needs to be cleansed and forgiven by God (1:9). In contrast to Jesus Christ as the one who "is" (ἐστιν) righteous (2:29) and who "is" (ἐστιν) pure (3:3), sin "is" (ἐστίν) lawlessness.[109]

---

109. "The word ἀνομία is a common word for sin in the OT (LXX). The word construction itself suggests the idea of law-breaking, transgressing the Law, which in a Jewish milieu is a typical description of sin" (Olsson, *Letters*, 164). "Very likely 'lawlessness' is understood as disregard for the commandments as set out in 1 John" (Painter, *1 John*, 222).

As "you" who "know [οἴδατε] the truth" (2:21) and "know [εἰδῆτε] that he is righteous" (2:29), the audience are "you" who "know [οἴδατε] that that one was manifested" (3:5a). "That one" (ἐκεῖνος) was manifested, that is, "that one" (ἐκεῖνος) who is pure (3:3), and "that one" (ἐκεῖνος) who "walked" just as we should "walk" (2:6)—in accord with the commandment to love one another (2:7-8).[110] Although there is a future time at his final coming when Jesus Christ will be "manifested [φανερωθῇ]" (2:28), that one was already "manifested" (ἐφανερώθη). And the life eternal that came to be in him was "manifested" (ἐφανερώθη), indeed it was "manifested" (ἐφανερώθη) to us (1:2).

Jesus Christ was manifested (3:5a), so that he might take away "sins [ἁμαρτίας]" (3:5b). But "sin" (ἁμαρτία), since "sin is" (ἁμαρτία ἐστίν) lawlessness (3:4), "is" (ἔστιν) not in him (3:5b), the one who "is" (ἔστιν) pure (3:3) and who "is" (ἔστιν) righteous (2:29). This recalls and reinforces that "sins" (ἁμαρτίαι) have been forgiven for the audience (2:12), that he is the expiation for our "sins [ἁμαρτιῶν]" (2:2), that he will forgive us the "sins" (ἁμαρτίας) we confess (1:9), and that the blood of Jesus cleanses us from all "sin [ἁμαρτίας]" (1:7).

Although "if we say that we have not sinned [οὐχ ἡμαρτήκαμεν], we make him a liar and his word is not in us" (1:10), the elder is writing that "you may not sin [μὴ ἁμάρτητε]" (2:1), and "everyone who in him remains does not sin [οὐχ ἁμαρτάνει]" (3:6a).[111] That everyone who "in him remains" (ἐν αὐτῷ μένων) does not sin reinforces the exhortations for the audience to "remain in him [μένετε ἐν αὐτῷ]" (2:27, 28). Indeed the one who "in him remains" (ἐν αὐτῷ μένειν) ought to "walk" as he "walked" (2:6) by practicing the commandment to love one another to live eternally (2:7-8).

---

110. "[T]he emphatic 'that one' (ἐκεῖνος) regularly introduces affirmations about Jesus (see 2:6)" (Lieu, *Commentary*, 126).

111. "The tension between 'now' and 'not yet' occurs throughout the letter, and in 1 John 2:28-3:10 the final destination of this temporal perspective comes very near. It is self-evident then that a child of God cannot sin. But as soon as the situation is viewed from the audience's own moment in time, it becomes clear that a child of God sometimes does sin. It is thus important to hold fast to public confession of sins and to God's forgiveness through Jesus Christ" (Olsson, *Letters*, 328). "Read within the context of the rest of the letter, it is clear that the writer does not necessarily expect a sinless life for those who 'remain in him.' He had made it clear in 2:1 that sin *may* occur in the believer's life" (Culy, *Handbook*, 73; emphasis original). See also Wallace, *Greek Grammar*, 525.

"Everyone [πᾶς] who does sin [ἁμαρτίαν] also does lawlessness" (3:4) and "everyone [πᾶς] who sins [ἁμαρτάνων]," especially by doing the lawlessness that fails to practice the commandment of loving one another, "has neither seen him nor known him" (3:6b). Although we hope that "we will see" (ὀψόμεθα) him just as he is (3:2), when he is manifested at his final coming (2:28), everyone who sins has not "seen" (ἑώρακεν) him as the one already manifested (3:5). This means that everyone who sins has not seen in him the life eternal that was manifested and that "we," the elder and his associates, "have seen [ἑωράκαμεν]" (1:1, 2, 3).

And that everyone who sins has not "known him [ἔγνωκεν αὐτόν]" (3:6b) means that such a person is not one of "you" who "know" (γινώσκετε) that everyone who does righteousness from him has been begotten (2:29) to become one of the children of God (3:1). Indeed "in this we know [γινώσκομεν] that we have known him [ἐγνώκαμεν αὐτόν], if we keep his commandments" (2:3). The one saying, "I have known him [ἔγνωκα αὐτόν]" but not keeping his commandments is a liar and the truth of living eternally by practicing the commandment of loving one another is not in this one (2:4). He is thus not a true worshiper of the Father in the Spirit of truth (John 4:23–24).[112]

Summary of 1 John 2:28–3:6

Having previously addressed his audience as his "little children" (2:1, 12), the elder again addresses them as "little children" with the exhortation for them to "remain in him" (2:28). This repeats and thus emphatically reinforces his preceding exhortation for them to "remain in him" (2:27), that is, in the Son Jesus Christ (2:6, 24). By remaining in him, we may have confidence and not be shamed away from him at his final coming, when he is "manifested" (2:28), as the one in whom life eternal was "manifested" (1:2), in contrast to those "manifested that they all are not from us" (2:19).

That those begotten from him (2:29) have been given the authority to become "children of God" (John 1:12) is confirmed as the elder declares, "See what sort of love the Father has given to us, that we may be called children of God, and indeed we are" (1 John 3:1a). This reinforces the exhortation for the audience not to love the world, since the "love of the Father" is not in anyone who loves the world (2:15). But whoever keeps his word, the commandment to love one another to live eternally, "truly in this one the love of God has been perfected" (2:5).

112. Keener, "Transformation," 13–22.

The elder emphatically underlines "the sort of love the Father has given us, that we may be called children of God, and indeed we are" (3:1a), with his address to the audience as "beloved, now we are children of God" (3:2a). They are children of God as the "beloved" who practice the commandment to love one another (2:7). "But it has not yet been manifested what we will be" (3:2b), when he is "manifested" (2:28). "We know that when it is manifested, we will be like him," as those who do righteousness, "because we will see him just as he is" (3:2b), that is, as the one whom "you know is" righteous (2:29).

Everyone who hopes to see Jesus Christ "just as he is" (3:2), as the one who "is" righteous (2:29), purifies himself, "just as that one is pure." This recalls and reinforces the assertion that "the one saying that he remains in him ought, just as that one walked, he himself thus to walk" (2:6). This means practicing the truth of the commandment (2:7–8) to love one another to live eternally as children of God, as true worshipers of God the Father in the Spirit of truth (John 4:23–24).

Although "if we say that we have not sinned, we make him a liar and his word is not in us" (1 John 1:10), the elder is writing that "you may not sin" (2:1), and "everyone who in him remains does not sin" (3:6a). That everyone who "in him remains" does not sin reinforces the exhortations for the audience to "remain in him" (2:27, 28). Indeed the one who "in him remains" ought to "walk" as he "walked" (2:6) by practicing the commandment to love one another to live eternally (2:7–8).

"Everyone who does sin also does lawlessness" (3:4) and "everyone who sins," especially by doing the lawlessness that fails to practice the commandment of loving one another, "has neither seen him nor known him" (3:6b). Although we hope that "we will see" him just as he is (3:2), when he is manifested at his final coming (2:28), everyone who sins has not "seen" him as the one already manifested (3:5). This means that everyone who sins has not seen in him the life eternal that was manifested and that "we," the elder and his associates, "have seen" (1:1, 2, 3).

And that one who sins has not "known him" (3:6b) means that such a person is not one of "you" who "knows" that everyone who does righteousness from him has been begotten (2:29) to become one of the children of God (3:1). Indeed "in this we know that we have known him, if we keep his commandments" (2:3). The one saying, "I have known him," but not keeping his commandments, is a liar and the truth of living eternally by practicing the commandment of loving one another is not in this one (2:4). Such a person is thus not a true worshiper of the Father in the Spirit of truth (John 4:23–24).

9

1 John 3:7–12
We Should Love One Another

The one not loving his brother is not from God

A   ⁷Little children, let no one deceive you. The one *doing righteousness* is *righteous*, just as that one is *righteous*. ⁸The one doing sin is from the devil, for *from the beginning* the devil has been sinning. For this the Son of God was manifested, so that he might destroy *the works* of the devil. ⁹Everyone who has been begotten *from God* does not do sin, because his seed remains in him, and thus he is not able to sin, because *from God* he has been begotten.

B   ¹⁰ᵃIn this is manifest *the children* of God

B'   ¹⁰ᵇand *the children* of the devil.

A'   ¹⁰ᶜEveryone who does not *do righteousness* is not *from God*, that is, the one not loving his brother. ¹¹For this is the message which you heard *from the beginning*, that we should love one another, ¹²not like Cain. He was from the evil one and slaughtered his brother. And why did he slaughter him? Because *his works* were evil but those of his brother *righteous*.[113]

---

113. For the establishment of 3:7–12 as a chiasm, see ch. 1.

3:7–9 (A): *The One Doing Righteousness Is Righteous Just as That One Is Righteous*

The audience hear the A element (3:7–9) of this chiastic unit as a chiastic pattern in itself:

- a) Little children, let no one deceive you. The one doing righteousness is righteous, just as that one is righteous. The one *doing sin* (3:7–8a)

  - b) is from the *devil*, for from the beginning the *devil* has been sinning (3:8b).

    - c) For this the Son of God was manifested (3:8c),

  - b') so that he might destroy the works of the *devil* (3:8d).

- a') Everyone who has been begotten from God does not *do sin*, because his seed remains in him, and thus he is not able to sin, because from God he has been begotten (3:9).

After the central and unparalleled c) sub-element, "for this the Son of God was manifested" (3:8c), the audience experience a pivot of parallels from the b) to the b') sub-element involving the only occurrences in this sub-unit of the term "devil." "From the devil [διαβόλου]" and "the devil [διάβολος] has been sinning" (3:8b) progress to "the works of the devil [διαβόλου]" (3:8d). The audience then hear a progession of parallels from the a) sub-element (3:7–8a) to the a') sub-element (3:9) involving the only occurrences in this sub-unit of the expression "to do sin." "The one doing sin [ποιῶν τὴν ἁμαρτίαν]" (3:8a) progresses to "does not do sin [ἁμαρτίαν οὐ ποιεῖ]" (3:9). In addition, when the audience hear the reference to "the one doing sin [ποιῶν τὴν ἁμαρτίαν]" (3:8a) near the beginning of this chiastic unit (3:7–12), they hear the expression that connects this unit to the preceding unit (2:28–3:6), whose conclusion begins with a reference to "everyone who does sin [ποιῶν τὴν ἁμαρτίαν]" (3:4).

And the audience hear the a') sub-element (3:9) of this chiastic sub-unit as yet another chiastic pattern in itself:

- (a) Everyone who *has been begotten* (3:9a)

  - (b) *from God* (3:9b)

    - (c) does not do *sin* (3:9c),

(d) because his seed remains in him (3:9d),

(c') and thus he is not able to *sin* (3:9e),

(b') because *from God* (3:9f)

(a') he *has been begotten* (3:9g).

After the central and unparalleled (d) sub-element, "because his seed remains in him" (3:9d), the audience experience a pivot of parallels from the (c) to the (c') sub-element involving the only occurrences in this sub-unit of expressions for "sin." "Does not do sin [ἁμαρτίαν]" (3:9c) progresses to "he is not able to sin [ἁμαρτάνειν]" (3:9e). The audience then hear a progression of parallels from the (b) to the (b') sub-element involving the only occurrences in this sub-unit of the phrase "from God." "From God [ἐκ τοῦ θεοῦ]" (3:9b) progresses to "because from God [ἐκ τοῦ θεοῦ]" (3:9f). Finally, the audience hear a progression of parallels from the (a) to the (a') sub-element involving the only occurrences in this sub-unit of the verb "begotten." "Everyone who has been begotten [γεγεννημένος]" (3:9a) progresses to "he has been begotten [γεγέννηται]" (3:9g).

Again addressing his audience as "little children [τεκνία]" in need of instruction (cf. 2:1, 12, 28), the elder exhorts them, "Let no one deceive [πλανάτω] you" (3:7a). This resonates with his assertion that he has written this letter concerning those "deceiving" (πλανώντων) them (2:26). It recalls that "many deceivers [πλάνοι] have gone out into the world, those not confessing Jesus Christ as coming in flesh. This is the deceiver [πλάνος] and the antichrist" (2 John 1:7).

The elder told his audience that "if you know that he is righteous [δίκαιός], you know that also everyone who does righteousness [ποιῶν τὴν δικαιοσύνην] from him has been begotten" (1 John 2:29) to be among the children of God (3:1-2). And now he tells them that "the one doing righteousness [ποιῶν τὴν δικαιοσύνην] is righteous [δίκαιός], just as that one is righteous [καθὼς ἐκεῖνος δίκαιός ἐστιν]" (3:7b). This reinforces the exhortation that everyone who has the hope of being like Jesus Christ, the "righteous one [δίκαιον]" (2:1), who is faithful and "righteous [δίκαιος]" (1:9), because we will see him just as he is (3:2), "purifies" himself ethically, "just as that one is pure [καθὼς ἐκεῖνος ἁγνός ἐστιν]" (3:3). This means "walking" ethically as he "walked" (2:6), namely by doing the commandment of loving one another (2:7–8) and thereby living eternally as children of God.

Everyone "who does sin" (ποιῶν τὴν ἁμαρτίαν) not only does lawlessness (3:4), but "the one doing sin [ποιῶν τὴν ἁμαρτίαν] is from the devil [ἐκ τοῦ διαβόλου], for from the beginning [ἀπ' ἀρχῆς] the devil [διάβολος] has been sinning" (3:8ab).[114] This recalls and resonates with Jesus' address to those trying to kill him (John 8:40): "You are from [ἐκ] your father the devil [διαβόλου] and the desires of your father you wish to do. That one was a murderer from the beginning [ἀπ' ἀρχῆς] and does not stand in the truth, because truth is not in him" (8:44). In contrast to the devil, who from the beginning "has been sinning" (ἁμαρτάνει), everyone who in Jesus Christ remains does not "sin [ἁμαρτάνει]" (1 John 3:6).

"For this the Son [υἱός] of God was manifested [ἐφανερώθη]," that is, "his Son [υἱοῦ] Jesus Christ" (1:3), "so that [ἵνα] he might destroy the works of the devil" (3:8cd). One of the ways he destroys the works of the devil, who from the beginning has been sinning (3:8b), is as the one who was "manifested [ἐφανερώθη], so that [ἵνα] he might take away sins" (3:5).[115] Whereas "everyone [πᾶς] who does righteousness from him has been begotten [γεγέννηται]" (2:29), "everyone [πᾶς] who has been begotten [γεγεννημένος] from God does not do sin" (3:9). And whereas "the one doing sin [ποιῶν τὴν ἁμαρτίαν] is from [ἐκ] the devil" (3:8ab), "everyone who has been begotten from [ἐκ] God does not do sin [ἁμαρτίαν οὐ ποιεῖ]."

The reason everyone who has been begotten from God does not do sin is "because his seed remains in him, and thus he is not able to sin, because from God he has been begotten" (3:9). That the seed of God "remains" (μένει) in the one begotten from God accords with the anointing that "remains" (μένει) in the audience and teaches them concerning all things (2:27). It recalls that if what the audience heard from the beginning "remains" (μείνῃ) in them, then they will "remain" (μενεῖτε) in the Son and in the Father (2:24). And it recalls that in the young men representative of the audience the word of God "remains" (μένει), so that

114. "As it has previously, the preposition ἐκ . . . specifies again both a 'coming from' and a 'belonging to'" (Schuchard, *1–3 John*, 333). The phrase "from the beginning" may refer to "the time covered in Genesis 1–4, a section that opens with the words 'in the beginning' (Gen 1:1)" (Olsson, *Letters*, 166). Or it may be "dealing more with character than chronology. However long he has been at work, nothing but malice and woe attends his activity" (Yarbrough, *1–3 John*, 188n30).

115. "Here 'the devil's works' are probably equivalent to 'the sins' in v. 5" (Olsson, *Letters*, 166).

they have conquered the evil one (2:14), that is, the devil, who from the beginning has been sinning (3:8). Consequently, not only does everyone begotten by the seed that is "from God" (ἐκ τοῦ θεοῦ) not sin, but he is not even able to sin, because, with an emphatic repetition, it is *"from God"* (ἐκ τοῦ θεοῦ) that he has been begotten (3:9).[116]

3:10a (B): In This Is Manifest the Children of God

The Son of God was "manifested" (ἐφανερώθη) to destroy the works of the devil (3:8). And in this is "manifest" (φανερά) the "children of God [τέκνα τοῦ θεοῦ]" (3:10a), the "children of God" (τέκνα θεοῦ) that we are now, although it has not yet been "manifested" (ἐφανερώθη) what we will be (3:2).

3:10b (B'): And the Children of the Devil

At this point the audience experience the pivot of parallels at the center of this chiastic unit. "The children [τὰ τέκνα] of God" in the B element (3:10a) progresses to "the children [τὰ τέκνα] of the devil" in the B' element (3:10b). The children of the "devil" (διαβόλου) include the one doing sin, who is "from the devil [διαβόλου]" (3:8ab). And that "the Son of God was manifested, so that he might destroy the works of the devil [ἔργα τοῦ διαβόλου]" (3:8cd), the "father" of the children of the devil, resonates with Jesus' accusation of those who were trying to kill him (John 8:40): "You are doing the works [ἔργα] of your father" (8:41) and "you are from your father the devil [διαβόλου]" (8:44).[117]

---

116. On the possible meanings of "seed" (σπέρμα) in 3:9, see de Waal Dryden, "Sense of σπέρμα," 85–100. "The 'seed' carries with it both a life principle and certain to-be inherited characteristics" (Schuchard, *1–3 John*, 336–37). "[T]he author is talking about a divine agency for begetting God's children, which not only brings us into being but also remains and keeps us His children" (Brown, *Epistles*, 411). "Being born from God means to continue to be vivified by God's creative power; such birth cannot be lost or abrogated" (Lieu, *Commentary*, 138). "The question of what 'his seed' (σπέρμα αὐτοῦ) denotes is debatable. There is a basic ambiguity about the referent. It could be some indwelling regenerative agent from God. . . . In that case, it is still unspecified if that agent is the Holy Spirit, the word of God, the *chrisma* mentioned in 2:27, or something else" (Jobes, *1, 2, & 3 John*, 148).

117. Nowhere does the elder "ever speak of a person being 'born' of the devil, for the devil neither creates nor begets; he only corrupts, destroys, and kills what is begotten of another" (Schuchard, *1–3 John*, 339). "There is no neutral ground; either one is

3:10c–12 (A'): Everyone Who Does Not Do Righteousness Is Not from God

The audience then hear a progression of parallels from the A (3:7–9) to the A' (3:10c–12) element of this chiastic unit: from "the one doing righteousness [ποιῶν τὴν δικαιοσύνην] is righteous [δίκαιός], just as that one is righteous [δίκαιός]" (3:7) to "everyone who does not do righteousness [ποιῶν δικαιοσύνην]" (3:10c) and "those [works] of his brother righteous [δίκαια]" (3:12); from "from the beginning [ἀπ' ἀρχῆς] the devil has been sinning" (3:8) to "the message which you heard from the beginning [ἀπ' ἀρχῆς]" (3:11); from "the works [ἔργα] of the devil" (3:8) to "his works [ἔργα] were evil" (3:12); from "everyone [πᾶς] who has been begotten" (3:9) to "everyone [πᾶς] who does not do righteousness" (3:10c); and from "begotten from God [ἐκ τοῦ θεοῦ]" as well as "from God [ἐκ τοῦ θεοῦ] he has been begotten" (3:9) to "is not from God [ἐκ τοῦ θεοῦ]" (3:10c).

The audience hear the A' element (3:10c–12) of this chiastic unit as a chiastic pattern in itself:

a) Everyone who does not do *righteousness* is not from God (3:10c),

   b) that is, the one not *loving his brother* (3:10d).

      c) For this is the message which you heard from the beginning (3:11a),

   b') that we should *love* one another, not like Cain. He was from the evil one and slaughtered *his brother*. And why did he slaughter him? Because his works were evil (3:11b–12a)

a') but those of his brother *righteous* (3:12b).

After the unparalleled c) sub-element at the center of this chiastic sub-unit, "for this is the message which you heard from the beginning" (3:11a), the audience experience a pivot of parallels from the b) sub-element (3:10d) to the b') sub-element (3:11b–12a) involving the only occurrences in this sub-unit of the verb "love" and of "his brother" in the accusative case. "The one not loving his brother [ἀγαπῶν τὸν ἀδελφὸν αὐτοῦ]" (3:10d) progresses to "we should love [ἀγαπῶμεν] one another" (3:11b) and "slaughtered his brother [τὸν ἀδελφὸν αὐτοῦ]" (3:12a). The audience then hear a progression of parallels from the a) to the a') sub-element involving the only occurrences in this sub-unit of "righteousness/

---

a child of God or one is a child of the devil!" (Jobes, *1, 2, & 3 John*, 146).

righteous." "Everyone who does not do righteousness [δικαιοσύνην]" (3:10c) progresses to "but those [works] of his brother righteous [δίκαια]" (3:12b).

Whereas "the one doing righteousness [ποιῶν τὴν δικαιοσύνην] is righteous [δίκαιός], just as that one [Jesus Christ; cf. 1:9; 2:1, 29] is righteous [δίκαιός]" (3:7), and "everyone [πᾶς] who has been begotten from God [ἐκ τοῦ θεοῦ] does not do sin" (3:9), "everyone who does not do righteousness [ποιῶν δικαιοσύνην] is not from God [ἐκ τοῦ θεοῦ]" (3:10c). This means that such a person is not among the children of God (3:10a). "Everyone who does not do righteousness" is then further specified as "the one not loving his brother [ἀγαπῶν τὸν ἀδελφὸν αὐτοῦ]" (3:10d). This recalls that "the one loving his brother [ἀγαπῶν τὸν ἀδελφὸν αὐτοῦ] remains in the light and there is no fault in him" (2:10).

The elder reminds his audience that, in contrast to "from the beginning [ἀπ' ἀρχῆς] the devil has been sinning" (3:8), "this is the message [ἀγγελία] which you heard from the beginning [ἀπ' ἀρχῆς], that we should love one another [ἵνα ἀγαπῶμεν ἀλλήλους]" (3:11). This recalls "the message [ἀγγελία] which we have heard from him and announce to you, that God is light and there is no darkness in him at all" (1:5).[118] And it recalls and resonates with what the elder told his audience previously, namely, that in this letter he is writing a commandment "which we have had from the beginning [ἀπ' ἀρχῆς], that we should love one another [ἵνα ἀγαπῶμεν ἀλλήλους]" (2 John 1:5).

The audience hear the remainder of the b') sub-element as yet another chiastic pattern in itself:

(a) not like Cain. He *was* from the *evil one* (3:12a)

(b) and *slaughtered* his brother (3:12b).

(b') And why did he *slaughter* him? (3:12c)

(a') Because his works *were evil* (3:12d).

At the center of this chiastic sub-unit the audience experience a pivot of parallels from the (b) to the (b') sub-element involving the only occurrences in 1 John of the verb "slaughter." "And slaughtered [ἔσφαξεν] his

---

118. "Just as for God to be light cannot be independent of the lives of those who confess him, so here the call to love one another is not based on a common humanity or on a shared set of ethical values but on an understanding of God" (Lieu, *Commentary*, 145).

brother" (3:12b) progresses to "and why did he slaughter [ἔσφαξεν] him?" (3:12c). The audience then hear a progression of parallels from the (a) to the (a') sub-element involving the only occurrences in this sub-unit of the verb "to be" and expressions for "evil." "He was [ἦν] from the evil one [πονηροῦ]" (3:12a) progresses to "because his works were evil [πονηρὰ ἦν]" (3:12d).

The audience should love one another and not become like Cain, who was "from the evil one [ἐκ τοῦ πονηροῦ]" (3:12a), likening him to the one doing sin, who is "from the devil [ἐκ τοῦ διαβόλου]" (3:8). Instead of loving "his brother [ἀδελφὸν αὐτοῦ]" (3:10c), in accord with the message that we should love one another (3:11), he slaughtered "his brother [ἀδελφὸν αὐτοῦ]" (3:12b), Abel (cf. Gen 4:8). The reason he slaughtered him was that, as one who "was from the evil one [ἐκ τοῦ πονηροῦ ἦν]" (3:12a), his "works were evil [ἔργα αὐτοῦ πονηρὰ ἦν]" (3:12d), associating them with the "works" (ἔργα) of the devil to be destroyed by the Son of God (3:8). But the works of his brother were "righteous [δίκαια]" (3:12e), associating him with the one doing "righteousness" (δικαιοσύνην), who is "righteous" (δίκαιός), just as Jesus Christ is "righteous [δίκαιός]" (3:7).[119] This reinforces the exhortation for the audience to do the righteousness of loving their brother (3:10c), their fellow believer, in accord with the truth that we should love one another to live the divine, eternal life as children of God (3:10a).

Summary of 1 John 3:7-12

The reason everyone who has been begotten from God does not do sin is "because his seed remains in him, and thus he is not able to sin, because from God he has been begotten" (3:9). That the seed of God "remains" in the one begotten from God accords with the anointing that "remains" in the audience and teaches them concerning all things (2:27). It recalls that if what the audience heard from the beginning "remains" in them, then they will "remain" in the Son and in the Father (2:24). And it recalls that in the young men representative of the audience the word of God "remains," so that they have conquered the evil one (2:14), that is, the

---

119. Byron, "Slaughter," 526-35. "Cain and Abel appear early on to have been interpreted as ethical examples on the basis of the division of humanity into 'the evil' and 'the righteous'" (Olsson, *Letters*, 330). "Cain's murder of his brother is . . . a summons to remain in solidarity with one another and as children of God" (Lieu, *Commentary*, 144-45).

devil, who from the beginning has been sinning (3:8). Consequently, not only does everyone begotten by the seed that is "from God" not sin, but he is not even able to sin, because, with an emphatic repetition, it is "*from God*" that he has been begotten (3:9).

Whereas "the one doing righteousness is righteous, just as that one [Jesus Christ; cf. 1:9; 2:1, 29] is righteous" (3:7), and "everyone who has been begotten from God does not do sin" (3:9), "everyone who does not do righteousness is not from God" (3:10c). This means that such a person is not among the children of God (3:10a). "Everyone who does not do righteousness" is then further specified as "the one not loving his brother" (3:10d). This recalls that "the one loving his brother remains in the light and there is no fault in him" (2:10).

The elder reminds his audience that, in contrast to "from the beginning the devil has been sinning" (3:8), "this is the message which you heard from the beginning, that we should love one another" (3:11). This recalls "the message which we have heard from him and announce to you, that God is light and there is no darkness in him at all" (1:5). And it recalls and resonates with what the elder told his audience previously, namely, that in this letter he is writing a commandment "which we have had from the beginning, that we should love one another" (2 John 1:5).

The audience should love one another and not become like Cain, who was "from the evil one" (1 John 3:12a), likening him to the one doing sin, who is "from the devil" (3:8). Instead of loving "his brother" (3:10c), in accord with the message that we should love one another (3:11), he slaughtered "his brother" (3:12b), Abel (cf. Gen 4:8). The reason he slaughtered him was that, as one who "was from the evil one" (3:12a), his "works were evil" (3:12d), associating them with the "works" of the devil to be destroyed by the Son of God (3:8). But the works of his brother were "righteous" (3:12e), associating him with the one doing "righteousness," who is "righteous," just as Jesus Christ is "righteous" (3:7). This reinforces the exhortation for the audience to do the righteousness of loving their brother (3:10c), their fellow believer, in accord with the truth that we should love one another to live the divine, eternal life as children of God (3:10a).

10

1 John 3:13–17
We Ought To Lay Down Our Lives for the Brothers

Whoever hates his brother does not have life eternal remaining in him

A   ¹³And do not be amazed, brothers, if the *world* hates you. ¹⁴We know that we have moved from death to life, because we love the brothers. The one not loving remains in death. ¹⁵Everyone who hates his brother is a murderer, and you know that every murderer does not *have* life eternal *in him remaining*.

B   ¹⁶ªIn this we have known love, that that one *for* us *laid down* his *life*;

B'   ¹⁶ᵇso we ourselves ought *for* the brothers to *lay down* our *lives*.

A'   ¹⁷But whoever *has* the livelihood of the *world* and observes his brother *having* a need and shuts off his compassion from him, how does the love of God *remain in him*?[120]

---

120. For the establishment of 3:13–17 as a chiasm, see ch. 1.

3:13–15 (A): Everyone Who Hates His Brother Does Not Have Life Eternal Remaining in Him

The audience hear the A element (3:13–15) of this chiastic unit as a chiastic pattern in itself:

a) And do not be amazed, brothers, if the world *hates* you. We *know* that we have moved from death to *life* (3:13–14a),

b) because we *love* the brothers (3:14b).

b') The one not *loving* remains in death (3:14c).

a') Everyone who *hates* his brother is a murderer, and you *know* that every murderer does not have *life* eternal in him remaining (3:15).

At the center of this chiastic sub-unit the audience experience a pivot of parallels from the b) to the b') sub-element involving the only occurrences in this sub-unit of the verb "love." "Because we love [ἀγαπῶμεν] the brothers" (3:14b) progresses to "the one not loving [ἀγαπῶν]" (3:14c). The audience then hear a progression of parallels from the a) sub-element (3:13–14a) to the a') sub-element (3:15) involving the only occurrences in this sub-unit of the verbs "hate" and "know" as well as the noun "life." "If the world hates [μισεῖ] you" (3:13) and "we know [οἴδαμεν] that we have moved from death to life [ζωήν]" (3:14a) progress to "everyone who hates [μισῶν] his brother ... you know [οἴδατε] ... does not have life [ζωήν] eternal" (3:15). In addition, when the audience are addressed as "brothers" (ἀδελφοί) at the beginning of this unit (3:13), they hear the transitional term that links this chiastic unit (3:13–17) to the preceding one (3:7–12), which concludes with a reference to the righteous works of Cain's "brother [ἀδελφοῦ]" (3:12).

Having heard that Cain slaughtered his "brother" (ἀδελφόν), although the works of his "brother" (ἀδελφοῦ) were righteous (3:12), the audience are addressed as those who are to relate properly to their fellow believers as "brothers [ἀδελφοί]" (3:13), in contrast to the way Cain treated his brother.[121] That they are not to be amazed if the "world" (κόσμος) hates them (3:13) recalls that the "world" (κόσμος) does not know them as children of God, because it did not know God himself

---

[121] "The address 'Brothers' is especially appropriate here where the author has just described how Cain killed his brother; it is part of the author's appeal to his adherents not to imitate Cain who killed his brother" (Brown, *Epistles*, 444).

(3:1). It reinforces the exhortation for the audience not to love the "world" (κόσμον) or the things in the "world" (κόσμῳ). Indeed, "if anyone loves the world [κόσμον], the love of the Father is not in him" (2:15).[122]

Jesus declared that the one who hears his word and believes in the one who sent him "has moved from death to life [μεταβέβηκεν ἐκ τοῦ θανάτου εἰς τὴν ζωήν]" and thus has life eternal (John 5:24). In development of this, "we," the elder, the audience, and all their fellow believing brothers, "know that we have moved from death to life [μεταβεβήκαμεν ἐκ τοῦ θανάτου εἰς τὴν ζωήν], because we love the brothers" (1 John 3:14a). That "we know that" (οἴδαμεν ὅτι) we have moved from death to life eternal, the divine life of God, resonates with the assertion that, as those who are already children of God, "we know that" (οἴδαμεν ὅτι) we will be like God (3:2). In accord with the message that "we should love [ἀγαπῶμεν] one another" (3:11), since one "loving [ἀγαπῶν] his brother [ἀδελφόν]" is among the children of God (3:10), we know that we have moved from death to the divine eternal life of God, because "we love the brothers" (ἀγαπῶμεν τοὺς ἀδελφούς). In contrast to the one "loving" (ἀγαπῶν) his brother, who "remains" (μένει) in the light of life eternal (2:10), "the one not loving remains [ἀγαπῶν μένει] in death" (3:14b).

That "everyone who hates his brother [ἀδελφόν] is a murderer [ἀνθρωποκτόνος], and you know that every murderer [ἀνθρωποκτόνος] does not have life eternal in him remaining" (3:15), likens such a person not only to the devil, who was a "murderer" (ἀνθρωποκτόνος) from the beginning (John 8:44), but to Cain, who "slaughtered his brother [ἀδελφόν]" (1 John 3:12).[123] That everyone who "hates his brother" (μισῶν τὸν ἀδελφὸν αὐτοῦ) does not have "life eternal" (ζωὴν αἰώνιον) resonates with the one "hating his brother" (μισῶν τὸν ἀδελφὸν αὐτοῦ) being in the darkness of death (2:11; cf. 2:9), rather than having the "life eternal" (ζωὴν τὴν αἰώνιον), which was with the Father (1:2) and promised to us (2:25). That "you know" (οἴδατε) that everyone who hates his brother does not have "life" (ζωήν) eternal accords with the assertion that "we know [οἴδαμεν] that we have moved from death to life [ζωήν], because

---

122. "'World' in 3:13 denotes the realm of the devil's influence and human opposition to God; it is not a denigration of the created order in toto" (Yarbrough, *1–3 John*, 199).

123. The elder is asserting that "all hatred is potentially, and may become in practice, murderous" (Smalley, *1 John*, 182). "[T]o hate someone because they are living rightly, and consequently pressuring them by example or teaching to live like the world, is a wish for their spiritual death and is, in effect, spiritual murder" (Jobes, *1, 2, & 3 John*, 157).

we love the brothers" (3:14ab). And that everyone who hates his brother does not have life eternal in him "remaining" (μένουσαν) reinforces the assertion that the one not loving "remains" (μένει) in death (3:14c).

3:16a (B): That One for Us Laid Down His Life

The elder told his audience that "in this we know [ἐν τούτῳ γινώσκομεν] that we have known [ἐγνώκαμεν] him" (2:3a), that is, Jesus Christ (2:1-2), "if we keep his commandements" (2:3b), preeminent of which is that we should love one another (3:11). He then declared that the "love" (ἀγάπη) of God has been perfected in the one who keeps his word, namely, his commandment that we should love one another, and "in this we know [ἐν τούτῳ γινώσκομεν] that we are in him" (2:5). And he now declares that "in this we have known love [ἐν τούτῳ ἐγνώκαμεν τὴν ἀγάπην]" (3:16a), preparing his audience for a further specification regarding the kind of love they are to have for one another as brothers.

The elder then specifies the kind of love we have known, namely, that "that one" (ἐκεῖνος), that is, "that one" (ἐκεῖνος) who is Jesus Christ (2:6; 3:3, 5, 7), "for us laid down his life [ὑπὲρ ἡμῶν τὴν ψυχὴν αὐτοῦ ἔθηκεν]" (3:16a). This recalls and resonates with Jesus' statement that "greater love than this no one has, that one lays down his life for his friends [τὴν ψυχὴν αὐτοῦ θῇ ὑπὲρ τῶν φίλων αὐτοῦ]" (John 15:13). And Jesus said this to further explain to his disciples what kind of love is involved in his commandment "that you love one another as I have loved you" (15:12).[124]

3:16b (B'): So We Ourselves Ought for the Brothers to Lay Down Our Lives

At this point the audience experience the pivot of parallels from the B to the B' element at the center of this chiastic unit. "For us laid down his life [ὑπὲρ ἡμῶν τὴν ψυχὴν αὐτοῦ ἔθηκεν]" (3:16a) progresses to "for the brothers to lay down our lives [ὑπὲρ τῶν ἀδελφῶν τὰς ψυχὰς θεῖναι]" (3:16b). That "we ourselves ought" (ἡμεῖς ὀφείλομεν) to lay down our lives for the brothers recalls that the one saying he remains in Jesus Christ "ought" (ὀφείλει) to "walk" just as he did (2:6), that is, according to the commandment (2:7-8) to love one another (3:11). It also recalls

---

[124]. "If hatred, the failure to love, is made concrete in the example of Cain, love is made concrete in the example of Jesus" (Lieu, *Commentary*, 149).

and resonates with Jesus' command to his disciples that "you yourselves ought" (ὑμεῖς ὀφείλετε) to wash the feet of one another (John 13:14) in accord with his commandment that "you love one another, just as I have loved you, so also you yourselves should love one another" (13:34). And that we ourselves ought to lay down our lives for the "brothers" (ἀδελφῶν) indicates how we are to love the "brothers" (ἀδελφούς), so that we know we have moved from death to life eternal (1 John 3:14).[125]

3:17 (A'): How Does the Love of God Remain in Him?

The audience then hear a progression of parallels from the A (3:13-15) to the A' (3:17) element of this chiastic unit: from "if the world [κόσμος] hates you" (3:13) to "livelihood of the world [κόσμου]" (3:17); from "does not have [ἔχει] life eternal" (3:15) to "has [ἔχῃ] the livelihood" and "having [ἔχοντα] a need" (3:17); and from "in him remaining [ἐν αὐτῷ μένουσαν]" (3:15) to "remain in him [μένει ἐν αὐτῷ]" (3:17).

Whoever "has" (ἔχῃ) the livelihood of the "world" (κόσμου), the "world" (κόσμος) that hates the brothers (3:13) who love one another (3:14), and observes his brother "having" (ἔχοντα) a need should have the compassion of using the livelihood to help the brother in need (3:17). Such a person will avoid being a "murderer," one who hates his brother and thus does not "have" (ἔχει) life eternal (3:15). In contrast to the "arrogance concerning the livelihood [βίου]" that is from the world (2:16), the audience are to use whatever "livelihood" (βίον) they have to show compassion for a "brother" (ἀδελφόν) in need as a way of laying down their lives in love for the "brothers [ἀδελφῶν]" (3:16).[126] For the audience to help a brother "having a need" (χρείαν ἔχοντα) accords with the assertion that "you do not have need [χρείαν ἔχετε] that anyone teach you" how to remain in Christ by loving one another (2:27).[127]

---

125. "The language of 'laying down (his) life' is exclusive to 1 John and the Fourth Gospel in the New Testament. Although the reference is clearly to Jesus' death, in other Greek usage the metaphor means to take a risk, to hazard one's life rather than actually to sacrifice it: to put oneself on the line" (Lieu, *Commentary*, 149).

126. "Those who work for a living spend their time (i.e., their lives) earning a livelihood. Sharing those earned resources with the vulnerable poor means that one is laying down one's life for the benefit of others" (Jobes, *1, 2, & 3 John*, 159).

127. The elder "moves quite understandably from the believer's need to give of himself as Jesus gave of himself to the need to give in everyday terms of one's everyday life" (Schuchard, *1-3 John*, 384).

But for one who shuts off his compassion from a brother in need, "how does the love of God [ἀγάπη τοῦ θεοῦ] remain in him?" (3:17).[128] Not to help a brother in need would contradict the divine "love" (ἀγάπην) we have known, as demonstrated by the Christ who for us laid down his life (3:16). Indeed, it is in the one who keeps the commandment that we should love one another that the "love of God [ἀγάπη τοῦ θεοῦ] has been perfected" (2:5). And if anyone loves the world rather than using the livelihood of the world to help a brother, "the love [ἀγάπη] of the Father is not in him" (2:15). That the love of God would not "remain in him [μένει ἐν αὐτῷ]" (3:17) means that such a person would in effect "hate" rather than help and love a brother in need and thus not have life eternal "in him remaining [ἐν αὐτῷ μένουσαν]" (3:15), for the one not loving "remains" (μένει) in death (3:14). This reinforces the letter's exhortation to live eternally by loving one another in accord with the assertion that we know that we have moved from death to life eternal, because we love the brothers (3:14).

Summary of 1 John 3:13–17

Having heard that Cain slaughtered his "brother," although the works of his "brother" were righteous (3:12), the audience are addressed as those who are to relate properly to their fellow believers as "brothers" (3:13), in contrast to the way Cain treated his brother. That they are not to be amazed if the "world" hates them (3:13) recalls that the "world" does not know them as children of God, because it did not know God himself (3:1). It reinforces the exhortation for the audience not to love the "world" or the things in the "world." Indeed, "if anyone loves the world, the love of the Father is not in him" (2:15).

That "everyone who hates his brother is a murderer, and you know that every murderer does not have life eternal in him remaining" (3:15), likens such a person not only to the devil, who was a "murderer" from the beginning (John 8:44), but to Cain, who "slaughtered his brother" (1 John 3:12). That everyone who "hates his brother" does not have "life eternal" resonates with the one "hating his brother" being in the darkness of death (2:11; cf. 2:9), rather than having the "life eternal," which was with the Father (1:2) and promised to us (2:25). That "you know" that everyone who hates his brother does not have "life" eternal accords with the assertion

---

128. "The circularity of God's love for believers and the believer's love for God mitigates the need to determine whether the genitive 'love of God' (ἡ ἀγάπη τοῦ θεοῦ) expresses love from God or love for God in this statement" (Jobes, *1, 2, & 3 John*, 159).

that "we know that we have moved from death to life, because we love the brothers" (3:14ab). And that everyone who hates his brother does not have life eternal in him "remaining" reinforces the assertion that the one not loving "remains" in death (3:14c).

That "we ourselves ought" to lay down our lives for the brothers (3:16) recalls that the one saying that he remains in Jesus Christ "ought" to "walk" just as he did (2:6), that is, according to the commandment (2:7–8) to love one another (3:11). It also recalls and resonates with Jesus' command to his disciples that "you yourselves ought" to wash the feet of one another (John 13:14) in accord with his commandment that "you love one another, just as I have loved you, so also you yourselves should love one another" (13:34). And that we ourselves ought to lay down our lives for the "brothers" indicates how we are to love the "brothers," so we know we have moved from death to life eternal (1 John 3:14).

Whoever "has" the livelihood of the "world," the "world" that hates the brothers (3:13) who love one another (3:14), and observes his brother "having" a need should have the compassion of using the livelihood to help the brother in need (3:17). Such a person will avoid being a "murderer," one who hates his brother and thus does not "have" life eternal (3:15). In contrast to the "arrogance concerning the livelihood" that is from the world (2:16), the audience are to use whatever "livelihood" they have to show compassion for a "brother" in need as a way of laying down their lives in love for the "brothers" (3:16). For the audience to help a brother "having a need" accords with the assertion that "you do not have need that anyone teach you" how to remain in Christ by loving one another (2:27).

But for one who shuts off his compassion from a brother in need, "how does the love of God remain in him?" (3:17). Not to help a brother in need would contradict the divine "love" we have known, as demonstrated by the Christ who for us laid down his life (3:16). Indeed, it is in the one who keeps the commandment that we should love one another that the "love of God has been perfected" (2:5). And if anyone loves the world rather than using the livelihood of the world to help a brother, "the love of the Father is not in him" (2:15). That the love of God would not "remain in him" (3:17) means that such a person would in effect "hate" rather than help and love a brother in need and thus not have life eternal "in him remaining" (3:15), for the one not loving "remains" in death (3:14). This reinforces the letter's exhortation to live eternally by loving one another in accord with the assertion that we know that we have moved from death to life eternal, because we love the brothers (3:14).

11

1 John 3:18–24

Believe in the Name of His Son Jesus Christ and Love One Another

If our heart does not condemn, we have confidence with God

A   [18]Little children, let us not *love* with word or with the tongue but in work and truth. [19a]And *in this we will know* that we are from the truth,

    B   [19b]and *before him* we will assure *our heart*, [20a]that if *our heart condemns*, that *God* is greater than *our heart*

        C   [20b]and knows all things.

    B'   [21]Beloved, if *our heart* does not *condemn*, we have confidence with *God* [22]and whatever we ask we receive from him, because we keep his commandments and do the things pleasing *before him*.

A'   [23]And this is his commandment, that we should believe in the name of his Son Jesus Christ and we should *love* one another, just as he gave the commandment to us. [24]And the one keeping *his* commandments in him remains and he in him. And *in this we know* that he remains in us, from the Spirit which to us he gave."[129]

The G unit (3:13-17) functions as the unparalleled central and pivotal unit within the macrochiastic structure of 1 John. In this unit the audience heard that "we know that we have moved from death to life, because we love the brothers" (3:14) and "in this we have known love, that that one for us laid down his life; so we ourselves ought for the brothers to lay down our lives" (3:16). These unique assertions at the center of 1 John provide the pivot from the F (3:7-12) to the F' (3:18-24) unit for the first two occurrences in 1 John of the exhortation that "we should love one another [ἀγαπῶμεν ἀλλήλους]" (3:11, 23). In addition, with the exhortation, "let us not love [ἀγαπῶμεν] in word" (3:18), at the beginning of the F' unit the audience hear the transitional term linking this unit to the G unit, which concluded with a reference to "the love [ἀγάπη] of God" (3:17).

3:18-19a (A): Let Us Love in Work and Truth

Again addressing the audience as "little children [τεκνία]" (cf. 2:1, 12, 28; 3:7), and recalling that "we love" (ἀγαπῶμεν) the brothers (3:14), as "we should love" (ἀγαπῶμεν) one another (3:11), the elder exhorts them, "Let us not love [ἀγαπῶμεν] with word or with tongue but in work and truth [ἀληθείᾳ]" (3:18).[130] In other words, we are not just to talk about loving one another but actually to practice it. This reinforces the exhortation that "we do the truth [ἀλήθειαν]" (1:6), the "truth" (ἀλήθεια) that entails keeping his commandments (2:4), preeminent of which is that "we should love [ἀγαπῶμεν] one another" (2 John 1:5; 1 John 3:11) to live eternally.[131] Becoming "coworkers" (συνεργοί) with the elder and Gaius to the "truth" (ἀληθείᾳ) by supporting those brothers who have gone out as missionaries (3 John 1:8) exemplifies for the audience what it means to love in "work [ἔργῳ] and truth [ἀληθείᾳ]."

---

129. For the establishment of 3:18-24 as a chiasm, see ch. 1.

130. "That they are to love 'in action' or 'deed (ἔργον)' recalls the evil deeds of Cain and the just deeds of his brother, as well as the deeds of the devil destroyed by the Son of God (1 John 3:8, 12)" (Lieu, *Commentary*, 152).

131. "The love they are called to is not only expressed in action and integrity, but characterizes those who belong to the sphere of life and not of death" (Lieu, *Commentary*, 152).

Previously the elder told the audience that "in this we know [ἐν τούτῳ γινώσκομεν] that we have known him, if we keep his commandments" (1 John 2:3), especially the commandment to love one another. Indeed, "in this we know [ἐν τούτῳ γινώσκομεν] that we are in him" (2:5). And now, having exhorted the audience to love "in work and truth [ἀληθείᾳ]" (3:18), he tells them that "in this we will know [ἐν τούτῳ γνωσόμεθα] that we are from the truth [ἐκ τῆς ἀληθείας]" (3:19a). He thus reinforces his assertion that "I have written to you not because you do not know the truth [ἀλήθειαν], but because you know it, and because every lie is not from the truth [ἐκ τῆς ἀληθείας]" (2:21).

3:19b–20a (B): If Our Heart Condemns, God Is Greater than Our Heart

If we love one another not merely with word or tongue but in work and truth (3:18), we will know that we are from the truth (3:19a), and "before him," that is, before God, we will assure our "heart," that is, our conscience (3:19b).[132] But if our heart or conscience "condemns" (καταγινώσκῃ), that is, contradicts or raises uncertainty that "we will know" (γνωσόμεθα) that we are from the truth, "God is greater than our heart" (3:20a).[133] That God is greater than our heart or conscience thus reinforces the promise that before God we will assure our heart, if there is any doubt that we have really loved one another in work and truth.

3:20b (C): And Knows All Things

God is greater than our heart or conscience that might "condemn" (καταγινώσκῃ) or contradict and make uncertain (3:20a) our knowledge that we are from the truth (3:19a), since God "knows [γινώσκει] all things" (3:20b). This implies that God knows whether we have actually loved one another in work and truth (3:18), so that before the God who knows all things we will assure our heart (3:19b).[134] Although the world

---

132. "In Hebrew thought the heart is tantamount to the conscience, there being no separate word in Hebrew for 'conscience'" (Marshall, *Epistles*, 198n5).

133. Note the wordplay between "we will know [γνωσόμεθα]" (3:19a) and "condemns [καταγινώσκῃ]" (3:20a), literally to "know" or "make known" (γινώσκῃ) "against" (κατα).

134. Jung, "1 John 3:19-20," 97–111.

does not "know" (γινώσκει) us as children of God, because it did not "know" (ἔγνω) God (3:1), God "knows" (γινώσκει) all things, including whether we are children of God who love one another in work and truth.

3:21-22 (B'): If Our Heart Does Not Condemn, We Have Confidence with God

After the unparalleled and central C element, "and knows all things" (3:20b), the audience experience a pivot of parallels from the B (3:19b-20a) to the B' (3:21-22) element of this chiastic unit. "Before him [ἔμπροσθεν αὐτοῦ] we will assure our heart [καρδίαν ἡμῶν]" (3:19b), "if our heart condemns [καταγινώσκῃ ἡμῶν ἡ καρδία]" (3:20a), and "God [θεός] is greater than our heart [καρδίας ἡμῶν]" (3:20a) occur in the B element. These progress, via the chiastic parallels, to "if our heart [ἡ καρδία ἡμῶν] does not condemn [καταγινώσκῃ], we have confidence with God [θεόν]" (3:21), and "do the things pleasing before him [ἐνώπιον αὐτοῦ]" (3:22).

The elder again addresses his audience as "beloved [ἀγαπητοί]" (3:21; cf. 2:7; 3:2), connoting that they are loved by both God and the elder as those who love one another. He asserts that "if our heart does not condemn" (3:21), that is, does not contradict or render uncertain our knowledge that we are from the truth (3:19a), as those who love one another in work and truth (3:18), then we have confidence with God (3:21), the God who is greater than our heart (3:20a). That "we have confidence with God" (παρρησίαν ἔχομεν πρὸς τὸν θεόν) by loving one another in work and truth reinforces the exhortation for the audience "to remain in him [Jesus Christ], so that when he is manifested we may have confidence [σχῶμεν παρρησίαν] and not be shamed away from him at his coming" (2:28). And it resonates with the assurance that "if anyone sins, we have an advocate with the Father [παράκλητον ἔχομεν πρὸς τὸν πατέρα], Jesus Christ the righteous one" (2:1).[135]

The elder then assures the audience that "whatever we ask [αἰτῶμεν]" (3:22) the God with whom we have confidence (3:21) "we receive [λαμβάνομεν] from him" (3:22). This assurance regarding the effectiveness of the prayers offered in liturgical worship recalls and resonates with Jesus' farewell instruction that his disciples are to "ask and you will receive [αἰτεῖτε καὶ λήμψεσθε]" (John 16:24), after repeatedly urging

---

135. The elder's "primary point is that Christian believers can have confidence before God even when their inner voice accuses them" (Jobes, *1, 2, & 3 John*, 167).

them to ask the Father in his name for whatever they need (14:13, 14; 15:7, 16; 16:23; cf. 16:26). We will receive whatever we ask from him, "because we keep his commandments [ἐντολὰς αὐτοῦ τηροῦμεν]" (1 John 3:22). This further reinforces that we will know that we are from the truth (3:19a), as those who love in work and truth (3:18), as it recalls that "in this we know that we have known him [Jesus Christ], if we keep his commandments [ἐντολὰς αὐτοῦ τηρῶμεν]" (2:3). Indeed, the truth is not in one not "keeping [τηρῶν] his commandments [ἐντολὰς αὐτοῦ]" (2:4).

Whatever we ask in our prayerful worship we receive from God, because we keep his commandments "and do the things pleasing before him [ἐνώπιον αὐτοῦ]" (3:22).[136] This further reinforces the exhortation that "before him [ἔμπροσθεν αὐτοῦ] we will assure our heart" (3:19b) by keeping the commandment to love one another in work and truth (3:18).[137] That "we do the things pleasing before him [τὰ ἀρεστὰ ἐνώπιον αὐτοῦ ποιοῦμεν]" means that we offer the ethical worship that pleases God by loving one another in work and truth. Jesus himself provided the model for this when he declared emphatically that "I always do what is pleasing to him [ἐγὼ τὰ ἀρεστὰ αὐτῷ ποιῶ πάντοτε]," to the God who sent him and who is with him (John 8:29). The liturgical worship of praying for what we need is thus complemented by the ethical worship of pleasing God by keeping the divine commandment that we should love one another.

3:23-24 (A'): We Should Love One Another

At this point the audience hear a progression of parallels from the A (3:18-19a) to the A' (3:23-24) element of this chiastic unit. "Let us not love [ἀγαπῶμεν] with word or with tongue" (3:18) and "in this we will know [ἐν τούτῳ γνωσόμεθα] that we are from the truth" (3:19a) occur in the A element. These progress, via the chiastic parallels, to "we should love [ἀγαπῶμεν] one another" (3:23) and "in this we know [ἐν τούτῳ γινώσκομεν] that he remains in us" (3:24) in the A' element.

---

136. "Although this may sound like a quid pro quo deal—we do something for God and he repays us by granting something we ask for—it is nothing of the kind. It is another way of saying that people who keep God's command and do what pleases him *know* God's will. As a result, they will ask only what is consistent with what they know of God, for they are his children" (Jobes, *1, 2, & 3 John*, 168; emphasis original).

137. The variation between each of these prepositions meaning "before" (ἔμπροσθεν and ἐνώπιον) here "is purely stylistic" (Brown, *Epistles*, 455).

1 JOHN 3:18–24

The audience hear the A' element (3:23–24) of this chiastic unit as a chiastic pattern in itself:

a) And this is his *commandment* (3:23a),

   b) that *we should believe* in the name of his Son Jesus Christ (3:23b)

   b') and *we should love* one another (3:23c),

a') just as he gave the *commandment* to us. And the one keeping his *commandments* in him remains and he in him. And in this we know that he remains in us, from the Spirit which to us he gave (3:23d–24).

At the center of this chiastic sub-unit the audience experience a pivot of parallels from the b) to the b') sub-element involving the only occurrences in this sub-unit of subjunctive first person plural verbs. "That we should believe [πιστεύσωμεν]" (3:23b) progresses to "we should love [ἀγαπῶμεν]" (3:23c). The audiences then hear a progression of parallels from the a) sub-element (3:23a) to the a') sub-element (3:23d–34) involving the only occurrences in his sub-unit of the term "commandment." "This is his commandment [ἐντολή]" (3:23a) progresses to "he gave the commandment [ἐντολήν] to us" (3:23d) and "the one keeping his commandments [ἐντολάς]" (3:24).

And the audience hear the a') sub-element (3:23d–24) of this chiastic sub-unit as yet another chiastic pattern in itself:

(a) just as *he gave* the commandment to us (3:23d).

   (b) And the one keeping his commandments in him *remains* and he in him (3:24a).

   (b') And in this we know that he *remains* in us (3:24b),

(a') from the Spirit which to us *he gave* (3:24c).

At the center of this chiastic sub-unit the audience experience a pivot of parallels from the (b) to the (b') sub-element involving the only occurrences in this sub-unit of the verb "remain." "In him remains [μένει]" (3:24a) progresses to "he remains [μένει] in us" (3:24b). The audience then hear a progression of parallels from the (a) to the (a') sub-element involving the only occurences in this sub-unit of the verb "he gave." "He gave [ἔδωκεν] the commandment to us" (3:23d) progresses to "the Spirit which to us he gave [ἔδωκεν]" (3:24c).

That "this is his commandment [αὕτη ἐστὶν ἡ ἐντολὴ αὐτοῦ]" (3:23a) resonates with the "commandment" (ἐντολή), which is both old and new, that the elder is now writing to the audience in this letter (2:7–8). It recalls that "this is the commandment [αὕτη ἡ ἐντολή ἐστιν]" (2 John 1:6), the "commandment" (ἐντολήν) "which we had from the beginning, that we should love one another" (1:5), a "commandment" (ἐντολήν) we received from the Father (1:4). The commandment "that we should believe [πιστεύσωμεν] in the name [ὀνόματι] of his Son [υἱοῦ] Jesus Christ" (1 John 3:23b) recalls and resonates with the stated purpose of the Gospel of John: "These things are written that you may believe [πιστεύητε] that Jesus is the Christ, the Son [υἱός] of God, and that believing [πιστεύοντες], you may have life in his name [ὀνόματι]" (John 20:31).

But this "commandment [ἐντολή]" (1 John 3:23a) includes that "we should love one another [ἀγαπῶμεν ἀλλήλους]" (3:23c), "just as he gave [ἔδωκεν] the commandment [ἐντολήν] to us" (3:23d). This recalls the message and commandment the audience heard from the beginning, that "we should love one another [ἀγαπῶμεν ἀλλήλους]" (3:11; 2 John 1:5). And it recalls that the Father "gave" (δέδωκεν) this "commandment" (ἐντολήν) to Jesus (John 12:49), the "commandment" (ἐντολή) that is eternal life (12:50). And Jesus, in turn, declared to his disciples, "A new commandment [ἐντολήν] I give [δίδωμι] you, that you love one another [ἀγαπᾶτε ἀλλήλους], as I have loved you, you also should love one another [ἀγαπᾶτε ἀλλήλους]" (13:34). Thus, Jesus gave to us the commandment the Father gave to him, that we should love one another to live eternally.

The "one keeping his commandments [τηρῶν τὰς ἐντολὰς αὐτοῦ] in him remains and he in him [ἐν αὐτῷ μένει καὶ αὐτὸς ἐν αὐτῷ]" (1 John 3:24). This recalls that the "one saying that he remains in him [ἐν αὐτῷ μένειν]," that is, in Jesus, ought to walk as he walked (2:6), namely, by "keeping [τηρῶν] his commandments [τὰς ἐντολὰς αὐτοῦ]" (2:4), particularly that we should love one another. And it recalls Jesus' exhortation to his disciples, "Remain in me, and I in you [μείνατε ἐν ἐμοί, κἀγὼ ἐν ὑμῖν]" (John 15:4). The "one remaining in me and I in him [μένων ἐν ἐμοὶ κἀγὼ ἐν αὐτῷ]—this one bears much fruit" (15:5).

That "in this we know [ἐν τούτῳ γινώσκομεν] that he remains in us [ὅτι μένει ἐν ἡμῖν]" (1 John 3:24) resonates with "in this we know [ἐν τούτῳ γινώσκομεν] that we are in him [ὅτι ἐν αὐτῷ ἐσμεν]" (2:5), as "one is to remain in him [ἐν αὐτῷ μένειν]" (2:6), by keeping his word, his commandment, that we should love one another (2:5; 3:11). And that "in this we know that he remains in us, from the Spirit [ἐκ τοῦ πνεύματος]," which emphatically "*to us* [ἡμῖν] he gave [ἔδωκεν]" (3:24), reinforces that "in this we will know [ἐν τούτῳ γνωσόμεθα] that we are from the truth [ἐκ τῆς ἀληθείας]" (3:19a). It recalls Jesus' promise that the Father "will give [δώσει]" (John 14:16) his disciples "the Spirit of truth [τὸ πνεῦμα τῆς ἀληθείας]" (14:17; 15:26; 16:13; cf. 20:22). This will enable them to worship the Father "in Spirit and truth [πνεύματι καὶ ἀληθείᾳ]" (4:23-24) in accord with the truth of the commandment "he gave" (ἔδωκεν) to us, that we should love one another (1 John 3:23) to live eternally, as the commandment of love the Father "gave" (δέδωκεν) to Jesus (John 12:49) is life eternal (12:50).[138]

Summary of 1 John 3:18–24

The elder again addresses his audience as "beloved" (3:21; cf. 2:7; 3:2), connoting that they are loved by both God and the elder as those who love one another. He asserts that "if our heart does not condemn" (3:21), that is, does not contradict or render uncertain our knowledge that we are from the truth (3:19a), as those who love one another in work and truth (3:18), then we have confidence with God (3:21), the God who is greater than our heart (3:20a). That "we have confidence with God" by loving one another in work and truth reinforces the exhortation for the audience "to remain in him [Jesus Christ], so that when he is manifested we may have confidence and not be shamed away from him at his coming" (2:28). And it resonates with the assurance that "if anyone sins, we have an advocate with the Father, Jesus Christ the righteous one" (2:1).

Whatever we ask in our prayerful worship we receive from God, because we keep his commandments "and do the things pleasing before him" (3:22). This further reinforces the exhortation that "before him we will assure our heart" (3:19b) by keeping the commandment to love one another in work and truth (3:18). That "we do the things pleasing before him" means we offer the ethical worship that pleases God by loving one another in work and truth. Jesus himself provided the model for this when he declared emphatically that "I always do what is pleasing to him," to the God who sent him and who is with him (John 8:29). The

---

138. "The spirit in 1 John comes close to the concept of the spirit of truth, the Helper, as it is presented in John 14–16" (Olsson, *Letters*, 184).

liturgical worship of praying for what we need is thus complemented by the ethical worship of pleasing God by keeping the divine commandment to love one another.

That "this is his commandment" (1 John 3:23a) resonates with the "commandment," which is both old and new, that the elder is now writing to the audience in this letter (2:7-8). It recalls that "this is the commandment" (2 John 1:6), the "commandment which we had from the beginning, that we should love one another" (1:5), a "commandment" we received from the Father (1:4). The commandment "that we should believe in the name of his Son Jesus Christ" (1 John 3:23b) recalls and resonates with the stated purpose of the Gospel of John: "These things are written that you may believe that Jesus is the Christ, the Son of God, and that believing, you may have life in his name" (John 20:31).

But this "commandment" (1 John 3:23a) includes that "we should love one another" (3:23c), "just as he gave the commandment to us" (3:23d). This recalls the message and commandment the audience heard from the beginning, that "we should love one another" (3:11; 2 John 1:5). And it recalls that the Father "gave" this "commandment" to Jesus (John 12:49), the "commandment" that is life eternal (12:50). And Jesus, in turn, declared to his disciples, "A new commandment I give you, that you love one another, as I have loved you, you also should love one another" (13:34). Thus, Jesus gave to us the commandment the Father gave to him, that we should love one another to live eternally.

That "in this we know that he remains in us" (1 John 3:24) resonates with "in this we know that we are in him" (2:5), as "one is to remain in him" (2:6), by keeping his word, his commandment, that we should love one another (2:5; 3:11). And that "in this we know that he remains in us, from the Spirit" that emphatically "*to us* he gave" (3:24), reinforces that "in this we will know that we are from the truth" (3:19a). It recalls Jesus' promise that the Father "will give" (John 14:16) his disciples "the Spirit of truth" (14:17; 15:26; 16:13; cf. 20:22). This will enable them to worship the Father "in Spirit and truth" (4:23-24) in accord with the truth of the commandment "he gave" to us, that we should love one another (1 John 3:23) to live eternally, as the commandment of love the Father "gave" to Jesus (John 12:49) is life eternal (12:50).

12

1 John 4:1–6

In This You Know the Spirit of God

The one knowing God hears us

A   ⁴:¹Beloved, do not believe every *spirit* but test whether the *spirits* are *from God*, because many false prophets have gone out into the world. ²In *this* you *know* the *Spirit* of God. Every *spirit* that confesses Jesus Christ as having come in flesh is *from God*, ³ᵃbut every *spirit* that does not confess Jesus is not *from God*. ³ᵇAnd *this* is that of the antichrist, which you have *heard* that he is coming,

B   ³ᶜbut now is already *in the world*.

    C   ⁴ᵃYou are from God, little children, and you have conquered them,

B'   ⁴ᵇbecause the one in you is greater than the one *in the world*.

A'   ⁵They are from the world, on account of *this* from the world they speak and the world *hears* them. ⁶We are *from God*, the one *knowing* God *hears* us, whoever is not *from God* does not *hear* us. From *this* we *know* the *Spirit* of truth and the *spirit* of deceit.[139]

---

139. For the establishment of 4:1–6 as a chiasm, see ch. 1.

At this point the audience hear a progression, via the macrochiastic parallels, from the E (2:28–3:6) to the E' (4:1–6) unit involving the only occurrences in 1 John of the second person plural present active indicative of the verb "to know." "You know [γινώσκετε] that also everyone who does righteousness from him has been begotten" (2:29) progresses to "in this you know [γινώσκετε] the Spirit of God" (4:2). In addition, when the audience hear the term "spirit [πνεύματι]" (4:1) at the beginning of the E' unit, they hear the transitional term that links this unit to the preceding F' unit (3:18–24), which ends with the clause, "from the Spirit [πνεύματος] which to us he gave" (3:24).

4:1–3b (A): Every Spirit Confessing Jesus Christ as Having Come in Flesh Is from God

The audience hear the A element (4:1–3b) of this chiastic unit as a chiastic pattern in itself:

a) Beloved, do not believe every spirit but test whether the spirits are from God, because many false prophets have gone out into the world. ² In *this* you know the Spirit of God (4:1–2a).

  b) *Every spirit* that confesses Jesus Christ as having come in flesh is from God (4:2b),

  b') but *every spirit* that does not confess Jesus is not from God (4:3a).

a') And *this* is that of the antichrist, which you have heard that he is coming (4:3b).

At the center of this chiastic sub-unit the audience experience a pivot of parallels from the b) to the b') sub-element involving the only occurrences in 1 John of the expression "every spirit" in the nominative case. "Every spirit [πᾶν πνεῦμα] that confesses Jesus" (4:2b) progresses to "every spirit [πᾶν πνεῦμα] that does not confess Jesus" (4:3a). The audience then hear a progression of parallels from the a) sub-element (4:1–2a) to the a') sub-element (4:3b) involving the only occurrences in this sub-unit of the demonstrative pronoun "this." "In this [τούτῳ] you know the Spirit of God" (4:2a) progresses to "this [τοῦτό] is that of the antichrist" (4:3b).

And the audience hear the a) sub-element (4:1–2a) of this chiastic sub-unit as yet another chiastic pattern in itself:

(a) Beloved, do not believe every *spirit* but test whether the *spirits* are from *God* (4:1a),

    (b) because many false prophets have gone out into the world (4:1b).

(a') In this you know the *Spirit* of *God* (4:2a).

At the center of this chiastic sub-unit the audience hear the unparalleled (b) sub-element, "because many false prophets have gone out into the world" (4:1b). The audience then experience a pivot of parallels from the (a) to the (a') sub-element involving the only occurrences in this sub-unit of the terms "spirit" and "God." "Do not believe every spirit [πνεύματι] but test whether the spirits [πνεύματα] are from God [θεοῦ]" (4:1a) progresses to "in this you know the Spirit [πνεῦμα] of God [θεοῦ]" (4:2a).

The elder again addresses his audience as "beloved [ἀγαπητοί]" (4:1a; cf. 2:7; 3:2, 21), reminding them they are loved by God, by the elder, and by one another. The audience were just reminded that "we should believe [πιστεύσωμεν] in the name of his Son Jesus Christ" (3:23). And now the elder exhorts them not to "believe [πιστεύετε] every spirit but test whether the spirits are from God" (4:1a). As those among whom Jesus Christ gave the divine "Spirit" (πνεύματος) from which we know that he remains in us (3:24), the audience are not to believe every human "spirit" (πνεύματι) but test whether the human "spirits" (πνεύματα) are "from God" (ἐκ τοῦ θεοῦ).[140] They are to determine whether a "spirit," that is, a human being who claims to pronounce a prophecy inspired by the divine Spirit in the worshiping assembly, is actually begotten "from God" (ἐκ τοῦ θεοῦ) so as to be among the children of God (3:9). If such a person does not love his brother, then he is not "from God [ἐκ τοῦ θεοῦ]" (3:10).[141]

The elder had already alerted the audience that from their midst "many deceivers have gone out into the world [πολλοὶ πλάνοι ἐξῆλθον

---

140. The elder's "urging of his own *not* to believe in any and every spirit complements his prior exhortation to believe in Jesus through the Spirit that Jesus gives (3:23–24)" (Schuchard, *1–3 John*, 417; emphasis original).

141. "The term πνεῦμα, 'spirit,' signifies a human person who is inspired by the spirit of truth or the spirit of error" (Smalley, *1 John*, 207). See also Moberly, "'Test the Spirits,'" 296–307.

εἰς τὸν κόσμον]" (2 John 1:7a). They collectively represent "the deceiver and the antichrist" (1:7c). He then reminded the audience that just as they heard "that the antichrist is coming, so now many [πολλοί] antichrists have appeared" (1 John 2:18). "From us they have gone out [ἐξῆλθαν]," although they were not really from us (2:19). And now the elder exhorts the audience to test every "spirit" (4:1a), everyone who claims to pronounce true prophecy inspired by the Spirit of God, because, as he emphatically reinforces with the perfect tense verb, "many false prophets have gone out into the world [πολλοὶ ψευδοπροφῆται ἐξεληλύθασιν εἰς τὸν κόσμον]" (4:1b).[142]

The many deceivers, antichrists, and false prophets have gone out into the "world [κόσμον]" (4:1b), the "world" (κόσμος) that hates the audience (3:13), and the "world" (κόσμος) that does not know the audience as children of God, because it did not know God (3:1). The audience are not to love the "world" (κόσμον) or the things in the "world" (κόσμῳ). If anyone loves the "world" (κόσμον), the love of the Father is not in him (2:15), because all that is in the "world" (κόσμῳ) is not from the Father but is from the "world [κόσμου]" (2:16). Although the "world" (κόσμος) is passing away, the one doing the will of God to love one another remains forever as one living eternally (2:17).

The way the audience may know the "Spirit" (πνεῦμα) of God (4:2a), and thus whether "every spirit" (παντὶ πνεύματι) who pronounces a prophecy is "from God [ἐκ τοῦ θεοῦ ἐστιν]" (4:1a), is that "every spirit" (πᾶν πνεῦμα) "confesses [ὁμολογεῖ] Jesus Christ as having come in flesh is from God [ἐν σαρκὶ ἐληλυθότα ἐκ τοῦ θεοῦ ἐστιν]" (4:2b). But "every spirit" (πᾶν πνεῦμα) that "does not confess [μὴ ὁμολογεῖ] Jesus is not from God [ἐκ τοῦ θεοῦ οὐκ]" (4:3a). This assertion emphatically reinforces, with the perfect participle "having come" (ἐληλυθότα), that the many false prophets are the same as the many deceivers "not confessing [μὴ ὁμολογοῦντες] Jesus Christ as coming in flesh [ἐρχόμενον ἐν σαρκί]" (2 John 1:7).[143]

Such a deceiving spirit is not that of a true prophet but that of the "antichrist" (ἀντιχρίστου), which "you have heard that he is coming

---

142. "The false prophets, like the deceivers and antichrists, are described as 'many,' which underscores the general situation and its seriousness" (Olsson, *Letters*, 198).

143. "The perfect participle ἐληλυθότα points to a settled staus: Christ did not merely make an appearance in a fleshly guise but fully assumed the bodily existence common to humanity" (Yarbrough, *1–3 John*, 223). "Yet to acknowledge Jesus Christ as having come in flesh is not merely another way of saying that he has come into the world. 'In flesh' signals not destination but mode and location: the means by which and wherein his presence is known" (Lieu, *Commentary*, 167).

[ἀκηκόατε ὅτι ἔρχεται]" (1 John 4:3b). This recalls that "just as you heard that the antichrist is coming [ἠκούσατε ὅτι ἀντίχριστος ἔρχεται], so now many antichrists [ἀντίχριστοι] have appeared" (2:18). They collectively represent *the* "antichrist" (ἀντίχριστος) as the one who denies that Jesus is the Christ (2:22). And this is *the* "antichrist [ἀντίχριστος]" (2 John 1:7) who does not remain in the teaching of the Christ (1:9) that we should love one another in order to live eternally.[144]

4:3c (B): But Now the Antichrist Is Already in the World

The antichrist the audience heard is coming (1 John 4:3b) "is now already in the world [ἐν τῷ κόσμῳ]" (4:3c). This reinforces the exhortation for the audience not to love the world or the things "in the world [ἐν τῷ κόσμῳ]" (2:15a). Indeed, if anyone loves the world, the love of the Father is not in him (2:15b), because all that is "in the world" (ἐν τῷ κόσμῳ) is not from the Father but is from the world (2:16).

4:4a (C): You Are from God

Whereas every spirit that does not confess Jesus is not "from God [ἐκ τοῦ θεοῦ]" (4:3a), the elder assures the audience, with an emphatic use of the personal pronoun, that "*you* [ὑμεῖς] are from God [ἐκ τοῦ θεοῦ]" (4:4a). They are thus among those who confess Jesus Christ as having come in flesh so that they are "from God [ἐκ τοῦ θεοῦ]" (4:2b). The elder again addresses his audience as "little children [τεκνία]" (4:4a; cf. 2:1, 12, 28; 3:7, 18), reminding them that, as those who are from God, they are "children" (τέκνα) of God (3:1, 2, 10). He then assures them that "you have conquered [νενικήκατε] them" (4:4a), that is, the antichrists and false prophets who are in the world (4:1–3). This extends and develops what the elder told the "young men" of the audience previously, namely, that "you have conquered [νενικήκατε] the evil one" (2:13, 14).[145]

---

144. The false prophets/deceivers/antichrists "apparently disputed the claim that the locus of true knowledge about God, and thus possession of eternal life, is centered in the historical incarnation of the Son of God in Jesus Christ" (Jobes, *1, 2, & 3 John*, 179).

145. "By not being swayed by those who left, those who remain in the Johannine church(es) have overcome whatever appeal the false teaching may have had" (Jobes, *1, 2, & 3 John*, 182).

4:4b (B'): The One in You Is Greater than the One in the World

The audience hear the elder's assurance that "you are from God, little children, and you have conquered them" (4:4a) as the unparalleled C element at the center of this chiastic unit. The audience then experience a pivot of chiastic parallels from the B to the B' element. "But now is already in the world [ἐν τῷ κόσμῳ]" (4:3c) progresses to "because the one in you is greater than the one in the world [ἐν τῷ κόσμῳ]" (4:4b).

As those from God, the audience have conquered the antichrist (4:4a), who is already in the world (4:3c). This is "because the one in you is greater [μείζων ἐστίν]" (4:4b), that is "the God who is greater [μείζων ἐστίν] than our heart and knows all things" (3:20), "than the one in the world" (4:4b).[146] God is the one "in you" (ἐν ὑμῖν) in the form of the divine anointing that the audience received from God and that remains "in you" (ἐν ὑμῖν), so that they do not have need for anyone to teach them, but just as it has taught them, they are to remain in him (2:27). The audience are to let the promise of life eternal that he himself promised to us (2:25), as they heard from the beginning, to remain "in you" (ἐν ὑμῖν), and if "in you" (ἐν ὑμῖν) it remains, they will remain in the Son and in the Father (2:24). They have conquered the evil one because the word of God "in you" (ἐν ὑμῖν) remains (2:14). This includes the word of the new commandment, which is true "in you" (ἐν ὑμῖν) and in him (2:8), that we should love one another (3:11, 23) in order to live eternally (1:2; 2:25; 3:15).

4:5–6 (A'): We Are from God But Whoever Is Not from God Does Not Hear Us

At this point the audience hear a progression of parallels from the A (4:1–3b) to the A' (4:5–6) element of this chiastic unit. The expressions "spirit [πνεῦμα]" (4:1[2x], 2[2x], 3a), "from God [ἐκ τοῦ θεοῦ]" (4:1, 3a), "in this [τούτῳ]" (4:2), "this [τοῦτό]" (4:3), "you know [γινώσκετε]" (4:2), and "you have heard [ἀκηκόατε]" (4:3b) occur in the A element. These progress to the expressions "on account of this [τοῦτο]" (4:5), "hears [ἀκούει]" (4:5, 6[2x]), "from God [ἐκ τοῦ θεοῦ]" (4:6[2x]), "knowing

---

146. "The one who is in them is presumably either God (cf. 3:20) or Jesus—the author would have seen even less reason here than elsewhere to belabor the distinction" (Lieu, *Commentary*, 171).

[γινώσκων]" (4:6), "from this [τούτου] we know [γινώσκομεν]" (4:6), and "spirit [πνεῦμα]" (4:6[2x]) in the A' element.

The audience hear the A' element (4:5-6) of this chiastic unit as a chiastic pattern in itself:

a) They are from the world, on account of *this* from the world they speak (4:5abc)

  b) and the world *hears* them. We are from God (4:5d-6a),

  b') the one knowing God *hears us*, whoever is not from God does not *hear us* (4:6b).

a') From *this* we know the Spirit of truth and the spirit of deceit (4:6c).

At the center of this chiastic sub-unit the audience experience a pivot of parallels from the b) sub-element (4:5d-6a) to the b') sub-element (4:6b) involving the only occurrences in this sub-unit of the verb "hear," the first person plural pronoun, and the term "God." "The world hears [ἀκούει] them" (4:5d) and "we [ἡμεῖς] are from God [θεοῦ]" (4:6a) progress to "the one knowing God hears us [θεὸν ἀκούει ἡμῶν], whoever is not from God [θεοῦ] does not hear us [ἀκούει ἡμῶν]" (4:6b). The audience then hear a progression of parallels from the a) to the a') sub-element involving the only occurrences in this sub-unit of the demonstrative pronoun "this." "On account of this [τοῦτο]" (4:5b) progresses to "from this [τούτου]" (4:6c).

And the audience hear the a) sub-element (4:5abc) of this chiastic sub-unit as yet another chiastic pattern in itself:

(a) They are *from the world* (4:5a),

  (b) on account of this (4:5b)

(a') *from the world* they speak (4:5c).

The audience hear the expression "on account of this" (4:5b) as the central and unparalleled (b) sub-element of this chiastic sub-unit. The audience then experience a pivot of parallels from the (a) to the (a') sub-element involving the only occurrences in this sub-unit of the phrase "from the world." "They are from the world [ἐκ τοῦ κόσμου]" (4:5a) progresses to "from the world [ἐκ τοῦ κόσμου] they speak" (4:5c).

"They" (αὐτοί), the emphatic use of the personal pronoun to refer to the false prophets (4:1) who collectively represent the antichrist (4:3b), "are from the world [ἐκ τοῦ κόσμου], on account of this, from the world [ἐκ τοῦ κόσμου] they speak" (4:5abc). This means that they speak about all "that is in the world—the desire of the flesh and the desire of the eyes and the arrogance concerning the livelihood" (2:16ab). All of this "is not from the Father but is from the world [ἐκ τοῦ κόσμου]" (2:16c). Although "the world hears [ἀκούει] them" (4:5d), the elder has assured the audience that they have conquered (4:4) the antichrist that "you have heard" (ἀκηκόατε) is coming and now indeed is already in the world (4:3).

Having assured the audience that "*you* are from God [ὑμεῖς ἐκ τοῦ θεοῦ ἐστε]" (4:4a), the elder expands this to include himself and all believers, as he declares, with another emphatic use of the personal pronoun, that "*we* are from God [ἡμεῖς ἐκ τοῦ θεοῦ ἐσμεν]" (4:6a).[147] Although the world "hears" (ἀκούει) the false prophets as the antichrist (4:5d), the one "knowing" (γινώσκων) God "hears" (ἀκούει) us (4:6b), because the one who has "known" (ἔγνω) God "knows" (γινώσκει) that we are children of God (3:1). "Whoever is not from God [οὐκ ἔστιν ἐκ τοῦ θεοῦ]" (4:6b), and "every spirit that does not confess Jesus is not from God [ἐκ τοῦ θεοῦ οὐκ ἔστιν]" (4:3a), "does not hear us" (4:6b).

The elder then concludes by summing up that "*from this* we know the Spirit [ἐκ τούτου γινώσκομεν τὸ πνεῦμα] of truth and the spirit [πνεῦμα] of deceit" (4:6c).[148] As he stated, "every spirit [πνεῦμα] that does not confess Jesus is not from God" (4:3a), and is thus the spirit of deceit. He likewise stated that "in this you know the Spirit [ἐν τούτῳ γινώσκετε τὸ πνεῦμα] of God. Every spirit [πνεῦμα] that confesses Jesus Christ as having come in flesh is from God" (4:2), and is thus the Spirit of truth. We know the "Spirit of truth" (πνεῦμα τῆς ἀληθείας) "from the Spirit [πνεύματος] which to us he gave" (3:24). And we know the Spirit of truth as those who are from the "truth [ἀληθείας]" (3:19), which includes that Jesus has come in the flesh to give us the new commandment to love one another (3:11, 23) to live eternally (1:1–2; 2:25; 3:14–15). This is the promised "Spirit of truth [πνεῦμα τῆς ἀληθείας]" (John 14:17; 15:26;

---

147. "'*We*' is emphatic (as were '*you*,' 4:4a; and '*they*,' 4:5a), highlighting in summary terms the contrast between those who are 'of the world' (4:5a, 5b) and those who are 'of God'" (Schuchard, *1–3 John*, 430; emphases original).

148. "The fronted and emphatic prepositional phrase ἐκ τούτου, 'by this,' a phrase that appears only here in John's Epistles, is retrospective" (Schuchard, *1–3 John*, 431–32).

16:13) by which we may become true worshipers who worship the Father in "Spirit and truth [πνεύματι καὶ ἀληθείᾳ]" (4:23–24).

Summary of 1 John 4:1–6

The way the audience may know the "Spirit" of God (4:2a), and thus whether "every spirit" who pronounces a prophecy is "from God" (4:1a), is that "every spirit" that "confesses Jesus Christ as having come in flesh is from God" (4:2b). But "every spirit" that "does not confess Jesus is not from God" (4:3a). This assertion emphatically reinforces, with the perfect participle "having come," that the many false prophets are the same as the many deceivers "not confessing Jesus Christ as coming in flesh" (2 John 1:7).

Such a deceiving spirit is not that of a true prophet but that of the "antichrist," which "you have heard that he is coming" (1 John 4:3b). This recalls that "just as you heard that the antichrist is coming, so now many antichrists have appeared" (2:18). They collectively represent *the* "antichrist" as the one who denies Jesus is the Christ (2:22). And this is *the* "antichrist" (2 John 1:7) who does not remain in the teaching of the Christ (1:9) to love one another in order to live eternally.

As those who are from God, the audience have conquered the antichrist (4:4a), who is already in the world (4:3c). This is "because the one in you is greater" (4:4b), that is "the God who is greater than our heart and knows all things" (3:20), "than the one in the world" (4:4b). God is the one "in you" in the form of the divine anointing that the audience received from God and that remains "in you," so that they do not have need for anyone to teach them, but just as it has taught them, they are to remain in him (2:27). The audience are to let the promise of life eternal that he himself promised to us (2:25), as they heard from the beginning, to remain "in you," and if "in you" it remains, they will remain in the Son and in the Father (2:24). They have conquered the evil one because the word of God "in you" remains (2:14). This includes the word of the new commandment, which is true "in you" and in him (2:8), that we should love one another (3:11, 23) in order to live eternally (1:2; 2:25; 3:15).

Having assured the audience that "*you* are from God" (4:4a), the elder expands this to include himself and all believers, as he declares, with another emphatic use of the personal pronoun, that "*we* are from God" (4:6a). Although the world "hears" the false prophets as the antichrist (4:5d), the one "knowing" God "hears" us (4:6b), because the one who has "known" God "knows" we are children of God (3:1). "Whoever is not from God" (4:6b), and "every spirit that does not confess Jesus is not from God" (4:3a), "does not hear us" (4:6b).

The elder concludes by summing up that *"from this* we know the Spirit of truth and the spirit of deceit" (4:6c). As he stated, "every spirit that does not confess Jesus is not from God" (4:3a), and is thus the spirit of deceit. He likewise stated that "in this you know the Spirit of God. Every spirit that confesses Jesus Christ as having come in flesh is from God" (4:2), and is thus the Spirit of truth. We know the "Spirit of truth" "from the Spirit which to us he gave" (3:24). And we know the Spirit of truth as those who are from the "truth" (3:19), which includes that Jesus has come in the flesh to give us the new commandment to love one another (3:11, 23) to live eternally (1:1-2; 2:25; 3:14-15). This is the promised "Spirit of truth" (John 14:17; 15:26; 16:13) by which we may become true worshipers who worship the Father in "Spirit and truth" (4:23-24).

13

1 John 4:7–12
God Has Sent His Son so that We Might Live through Him

> If we love one another, God remains
> in us and his love is perfected in us

A   ⁷*Beloved, let us love one another*, because love is from God, and everyone who loves from God has been begotten and knows God. ⁸The one not loving does not know God, because God is love.

    B   ⁹ᵃ*In this* the love of God was manifested in us, because *his* Son, the unique one, God has *sent* into the world

        C   ⁹ᵇso that we might live through him.

    B'   ¹⁰*In this* is love, not that we have loved God but that he loved us and *sent his Son* as expiation for our sins.

A'   ¹¹*Beloved*, if God so loved us, then we ourselves ought to *love one another*. ¹²No one has ever observed God. If *we love one another*, God remains in us and his love is perfected in us.[149]

At this point the audience hear a progression, via the macrochiastic parallels, from the D (2:18–27) to the D' (4:7–12) unit involving

---

149. For the establishment of 4:7–12 as a chiasm, see ch. 1.

successive occurrences in 1 John of the term "son" in the accusative case. "The one who denies the Father and the Son [τὸν υἱόν]" (2:22), "everyone who denies the Son [τὸν υἱόν]" (2:23), and "the one confessing the Son [τὸν υἱόν]" (2:23) progress to God has sent "his Son [τὸν υἱόν], the unique one" (4:9), and "sent his Son [τὸν υἱόν] as expiation for our sins" (4:10). In addition, when the audience hear the statement that "love is from God [ἐκ τοῦ θεοῦ]" (4:7) at the beginning of the D' unit, it hears the transitional phrase that links this unit to the preceding E' unit (4:1–6), which concludes with a reference to "whoever is not from God [ἐκ τοῦ θεοῦ]" (4:6).

4:7–8 (A): Beloved, Let Us Love One Another

The audience hear the A element (4:7–8) of this chiastic unit as a chiastic pattern in itself:

- a) Beloved, let us love one another, because *love is* from God, and everyone who loves from God has been begotten (4:7a)

  - b) and *knows God* (4:7b).

    - c) The one not loving (4:8a)

  - b') does not *know God* (4:8b),

- a') because God *is love* (4:8c).

The audience hear "the one not loving" (4:8a) as the unparalleled and central c) sub-element of this chiastic sub-unit. The audience then experience a pivot of parallels from the b) to the b') sub-element involving the only occurrences in this sub-unit of the expression "know God." "Knows God [γινώσκει τὸν θεόν]" (4:7b) progresses to "does not know God [ἔγνω τὸν θεόν]" (4:8b). The audience then hear a progression of parallels from the a) to the a') sub-element involving the only occurences in this sub-unit of the noun "love" together with the verb "to be." "Love [ἀγάπη] is [ἐστιν] from God" (4:7a) progresses to "God is love [ἀγάπη ἐστίν]" (4:8c).

The elder again addresses his audience as "beloved [ἀγαπητοί]" (4:7a; cf. 2:7; 3:2, 21; 4:1), reminding them that they are loved by both God and the elder, and thus appropriately exhorts them, "let us love one another [ἀγαπῶμεν ἀλλήλους]" (4:7a). This reinforces the previous exhortation that "we should love one another" (ἀγαπῶμεν ἀλλήλους) in accord with the commandment Jesus Christ gave to us (3:23). And that "we should love one another" (ἀγαπῶμεν ἀλλήλους) is the message the audience heard from the beginning (3:11). The emphatic assertions both that "*you* are from God [ἐκ τοῦ θεοῦ]" (4:4) and "*we* are from God [ἐκ τοῦ θεοῦ]" (4:6) have made it all the more fitting for the audience to love one another, "because love is from God [ἐκ τοῦ θεοῦ]" (4:7a).

"Everyone who loves from God has been begotten [ἐκ τοῦ θεοῦ γεγέννηται]" (4:7a). This resonates with "everyone who has been begotten from God [γεγεννημένος ἐκ τοῦ θεοῦ] does not do sin" (3:9a) by failing to do the righteousness (3:10) that we should love one another (3:11), "because from God he has been begotten [ἐκ τοῦ θεοῦ γεγέννηται]" (3:9b; cf. 2:29). The world does not "know" (γινώσκει) us as children of God, because it did not "know" (ἔγνω) God (3:1). But everyone who loves from God has been begotten as a child of God and thus "knows" (γινώσκει) God in the sense of experiencing who and what God is all about (4:7b), as the God who "knows" (γινώσκει) all things (3:20). The one "not loving" (μὴ ἀγαπῶν) his brother is not from God (3:10). The one "not loving" (μὴ ἀγαπῶν) remains in death (3:14) and does not have eternal life in him (3:15). And the one "not loving [μὴ ἀγαπῶν]" (4:8a) "does not know" (οὐκ ἔγνω) God (4:8b), just as the world "does not know" (οὐκ ἔγνω) him (3:1), because not only "is" (ἐστιν) "love" (ἀγάπη) from God (4:7a), but God himself "is love [ἀγάπη ἐστίν]" (4:8c).[150]

4:9a (B): His Son, the Unique One, God Has Sent into the World

"In this the love [ἀγάπη] of God," the "love" (ἀγάπη) that is not only from God (4:7a) but the "love" (ἀγάπη) that is God (4:8c), "was manifested [ἐφανερώθη] in us [ἐν ἡμῖν], because his Son, the unique one, God has sent into the world" (4:9a). This recalls and resonates with the assertion that "the life was manifested [ἐφανερώθη]" (1:2a), "the life eternal which was with the Father and manifested to us [ἐφανερώθη ἡμῖν]" (1:2c). And the close connection between eternal life and love was indicated in the statement that "we know that we have moved from death to life, because

---

150. "No other biblical writing makes this explicit assertion [God is love], but the claim is strongly implied in both John's Gospel and throughout the OT wherever God's steadfast covenant love is mentioned" (Yarbrough, *1–3 John*, 236).

we love the brothers. The one not loving remains in death," rather than living eternally (3:14).

His "Son" (υἱόν), "the unique one" (μονογενῆ), God has "sent" (ἀπέσταλκεν) "into the world [εἰς τὸν κόσμον]" (4:9a). This recalls and resonates with the proclamation that God so loved the world that he gave the "Son" (υἱόν), "the unique one [μονογενῆ]" (John 3:16a; cf. 1:14, 18; 3:18).[151] And God did not "send" (ἀπέστειλεν) the "Son" (υἱόν) "into the world" (εἰς τὸν κόσμον) to condemn the world, but that the world might be saved through him (3:17). This implies that there is still hope for the salvation of the false prophets, deceivers, and antichrists, who have gone out "into the world [εἰς τὸν κόσμον]" (1 John 4:1), the world loved by God.

4:9b (C): So that We Might Live through Him

The love of God was manifested in us, because God sent his Son, the unique one, into the world (4:9a), "so that we might live through him [ἵνα ζήσωμεν δι' αὐτοῦ]" (4:9b). This recalls and resonates with the purpose for which God loved the world and gave his Son, the unique one, "so that [ἵνα] everyone who believes in him might not perish but might have life eternal [ζωὴν αἰώνιον]" (John 3:16).[152] Indeed, God sent his Son into the world, "so that the world might be saved through him [δι' αὐτοῦ]" (3:17). That we might be saved and live through him thus means that we might have the "life eternal" (ζωὴν τὴν αἰώνιον) that was declared and manifested to us (1 John 1:2), the "life eternal" (ζωὴν τὴν αἰώνιον) that he himself promised to us (2:25), and the "life eternal" (ζωὴν αἰώνιον) one may have in him (3:15), "because we love the brothers" (3:14).[153]

---

151. Morgen, "Le (Fils) *monogène*," 165–83. On the meaning of "unique" for μονογενῆ, see BDAG, 658. "God has many children, both sons and daughters throughout history, but Jesus is not just one of them. He is unique, the μονογενής Son, who was with God and was God (John 1:1)" (Jobes, *1, 2, & 3 John*, 192).

152. Frick, "Johannine Soteriology," 415–21.

153. "[T]he verb 'to live' appears only here in 1 John, but even, as here, without the adjective 'eternal' (2:25) the noun has been used of the life that belongs to God's realm (1:2; 3:14)" (Lieu, *Commentary*, 180).

4:10 (B'): God Loved Us and Sent His Son as Expiation for Our Sins

The audience hear the statement, "so that we might live through him" (4:9b), as the unparalleled and central C element of this chiastic unit. The audience then experience a pivot of parallels from the B (4:9a) to the B' (4:10) element. "In this" (ἐν τούτῳ), "his Son" (υἱὸν αὐτοῦ) and God has "sent [ἀπέσταλκεν]" (4:9a) progress to "in this" (ἐν τούτῳ) and God "sent his Son [ἀπέστειλεν τὸν υἱὸν αὐτοῦ]" (4:10).

In this is "love [ἀγάπη]" (4:10a), the "love" (ἀγάπη) whose origin is from God (4:7), the "love" (ἀγάπη) that God is (4:8), and the "love" (ἀγάπη) of God that was manifested in us (4:9a).[154] It is not that "*we* [ἡμεῖς]," with an emphatic use of the personal pronoun, in the first instance have loved God but that "*he* [αὐτός]," with a corresponding emphatic use of the personal pronoun, "loved" (ἠγάπησεν) us (4:10b), again recalling how God so "loved" (ἠγάπησεν) the world (John 3:16).[155] And out of this love God "sent his Son [ἀπέστειλεν τὸν υἱὸν αὐτοῦ] as expiation for our sins [ἱλασμὸν περὶ τῶν ἁμαρτιῶν ἡμῶν]" (1 John 4:10c). This recalls and reinforces that Jesus Christ himself "is the expiation for our sins [ἱλασμός ἐστιν περὶ τῶν ἁμαρτιῶν ἡμῶν], not for ours only but for the whole world" (2:2). And it accords with the fact that God "sent" (ἀπέστειλεν) "the Son" (τὸν υἱόν) into the world, so that the world might be saved through him (John 3:17).

4:11–12 (A'): Beloved, We Ought to Love One Another

At this point the audience experience a progression of parallels from the A (4:7–8) to the A' (4:11–12) element of this chiastic unit. "Beloved, let us love one another [ἀγαπητοί, ἀγαπῶμεν ἀλλήλους]" (4:7) occurs in the A element. This progresses to "beloved [ἀγαπητοί]" (4:11), "we ourselves ought to love one another [ἀλλήλους ἀγαπᾶν]" (4:11), and "if we love one another [ἀγαπῶμεν ἀλλήλους]" (4:12) in the A' element.

---

154. The elder "does not say that love is God, a statement found nowhere in Scripture.... To do so would be to replace a living, personal, and active God with an intellectual, ethical, volitional, or emotional abstraction" (Yarbrough, *1–3 John*, 237).

155. "A right understanding of love begins not with the question of our love for God but with his for us" (Schuchard, *1–3 John*, 449). The elder "emphasizes both 'we' and 'he' by employing the pronouns, which strengthens the contrast" (Olsson, *Letters*, 211).

The audience experience the A' element (4:11-12) of this chiastic unit as a chiastic pattern in itself:

a) Beloved, if *God* so loved us (4:11a),

   b) then we ourselves ought to *love one another* (4:11b).

      c) No one has ever observed God (4:12a).

   b') If we *love one another* (4:12b),

a') *God* remains in us and his love is perfected in us (4:12c).

The audience hear "no one has ever observed God" (4:12a) as the unparalleled and central c) sub-element of this chiastic sub-unit. The audience then experience a pivot of parallels from the b) to the b') sub-element involving the only occurences in this sub-unit of expressions for loving one another. "We ourselves ought to love one another [ἀλλήλους ἀγαπᾶν]" (4:11b) progresses to "if we love one another [ἀγαπῶμεν ἀλλήλους]" (4:12b). They then hear a progression of parallels from the a) to the a') sub-element involving the only occurrences in this sub-unit of the term for "God" in the nominative case. "If God [θεός] so loved us" (4:11a) progresses to "God [θεός] remains in us" (4:12c).

The elder began this unit with the exhortation, "beloved, let us love one another" (4:7a). And now he elaborates and reiterates with the exhortation, "beloved, if God so loved [οὕτως ὁ θεὸς ἠγάπησεν] us, then we ourselves ought to love one another" (4:11), again recalling "for God so loved [οὕτως γὰρ ἠγάπησεν ὁ θεός] the world" (John 3:16). That "*we ourselves* ought [καὶ ἡμεῖς ὀφείλομεν] to love one another" (1 John 4:11), intensified by an emphatic use of the personal pronoun, reinforces the exhortation that "*we ourselves* ought [καὶ ἡμεῖς ὀφείλομεν] for the brothers to lay down our lives" (3:16).

That "no one has ever observed God [θεὸν οὐδεὶς πώποτε τεθέαται]" (4:12a) recalls that "no one has ever seen God [θεὸν οὐδεὶς ἑώρακεν πώποτε]," but "the unique one [μονογενής], God, who is in the bosom of the Father, that one made known" the unseen God (John 1:18). He made God known as his Son, the "unique one" (μονογενῆ), whom God sent into the world as a manifestation of his love, so that we might live eternally through him (1 John 4:9). But "if we love one another" (4:12b), as those who ought "to love one another" (4:11b), reinforcing the exhortation, "let us love one another" (4:7a), then "God remains in us [ἐν ἡμῖν μένει] and his love is perfected in us" (4:12c). This recalls that the one keeping his commandments, especially that we should love one another, "in him remains [μένει] and he in him. And in this we know that he remains in us [μένει ἐν ἡμῖν], from the Spirit which to us he gave" (3:24).

Previously the elder exhorted his audience that whoever keeps his word—the commandment to love one another (3:11, 23), "truly in this one the love [ἀγάπη] of God has been perfected [τετελείωται]" (2:5). And now he exhorts them that "if we love one another, God remains in us and his love [ἀγάπη] is perfected [τετελειωμένη] in us [ἐν ἡμῖν]" (4:12).[156] This is "the love of God that was manifested in us [ἐν ἡμῖν]," because he sent his Son into the world so that we might live eternally through him (4:9). This further supports the letter's concerted and overall exhortation for believers to live eternally as true worshipers who love God and one another.[157]

Summary of 1 John 4:7–12

"Everyone who loves from God has been begotten" (4:7a). This resonates with "everyone who has been begotten from God does not do sin" (3:9a) by failing to do the righteousness (3:10) that we should love one another (3:11), "because from God he has been begotten" (3:9b; cf. 2:29). The world does not "know" us as children of God, because it did not "know" God (3:1). But everyone who loves from God has been begotten as a child of God and thus "knows" God in the sense of experiencing who and what God is all about (4:7b), as the God who "knows" all things (3:20). The one "not loving" his brother is not from God (3:10). The one "not loving" remains in death (3:14) and does not have eternal life in him (3:15). And the one "not loving" (4:8a) "does not know" God (4:8b), just as the world "does not know" him (3:1), because not only "is love" from God (4:7a), but God himself "is love" (4:8c).

The love of God was manifested in us, because God sent his Son, the unique one, into the world (4:9a), "so that we might live through him" (4:9b). This recalls and resonates with the purpose for which God loved the world and gave his Son, the unique one, "so that everyone who

---

156. "The root of the perfect participle τετελειωμένη means 'to finish, complete, or bring to the desired outcome'" (Yarbrough, *1–3 John*, 245).

157. "[W]e love because God first loved us. But God has deemed it necessary that we express our love for him in the act of loving other human beings with a love that derives from the kind of love he has shown for us in Christ" (Jobes, *1, 2, & 3 John*, 195).

believes in him might not perish but might have life eternal" (John 3:16). Indeed, God sent his Son into the world, "so that the world might be saved through him" (3:17). That we might be saved and live through him thus means that we might have the "life eternal" that was declared and manifested to us (1 John 1:2), the "life eternal" that he himself promised to us (2:25), and the "life eternal" one may have in him (3:15), "because we love the brothers" (3:14).

In this is "love" (4:10a), the "love" whose origin is from God (4:7), the "love" that God is (4:8), and the "love" of God that was manifested in us (4:9a). It is not that "*we*," with an emphatic use of the personal pronoun, in the first instance have loved God but that "*he*," with a corresponding emphatic use of the personal pronoun, "loved" us (4:10b), again recalling how God so "loved" the world (John 3:16). And out of this love God "sent his Son as expiation for our sins" (1 John 4:10c). This recalls and reinforces that Jesus Christ himself "is the expiation for our sins, not for ours only but for the whole world" (2:2). And it accords with the fact that God "sent the Son" into the world, so that the world might be saved through him (John 3:17).

That "no one has ever observed God" (1 John 4:12a) recalls that "no one has ever seen God," but "the unique one, God, who is in the bosom of the Father, that one made known" the unseen God (John 1:18). He made God known as his Son, the "unique one," whom God sent into the world as a manifestation of his love, so that we might live eternally through him (1 John 4:9). But "if we love one another" (4:12b), as those who ought "to love one another" (4:11b), reinforcing the exhortation, "let us love one another" (4:7a), then "God remains in us and his love is perfected in us" (4:12c). This recalls that the one keeping his commandments, especially that we should love one another, "in him remains and he in him. And in this we know that he remains in us, from the Spirit which to us he gave" (3:24).

Previously the elder exhorted his audience that whoever keeps his word—the commandment to love one another (3:11, 23), "truly in this one the love of God has been perfected" (2:5). And now he exhorts them that "if we love one another, God remains in us and his love is perfected in us" (4:12). This is "the love of God that was manifested in us," because he sent his Son into the world so that we might live eternally through him (4:9). This further supports the letter's concerted and overall exhortation for believers to live eternally as true worshipers who love God and one another.

14

1 John 4:13—5:2

Just as That One Is so We Are in This World

The one loving God should love also his brother

A   ¹³*In this we know* that in him we remain and he in us, because he has given us from his Spirit. ¹⁴And we ourselves have observed and testify that the Father sent the Son as savior of the world. ¹⁵Whoever confesses that Jesus is the Son of *God*, *God* in him remains and he in *God*. ¹⁶And we ourselves have known and *believed* the love which *God* has in us. *God* is love, and the one remaining in love in *God* remains and *God* in him remains.

B   ¹⁷In this has love been *perfected* with us, so that we may have confidence on the day of judgment, because just as that one is so we ourselves are in this world. ¹⁸ᵃThere is no *fear* in love but *perfect* love drives out *fear*,

B   ¹⁸ᵇbecause *fear* has to do with punishment, and one *fearing* has not been *perfected* in love.

A   ¹⁹ We ourselves love, because he first loved us. ²⁰If anyone says "I love *God*," but hates his brother, he is a liar. For the one not loving his brother whom he has seen, is not able to love *God* whom he has not seen. ²¹And this commandment we have from him, that the one loving *God* should love also his brother. ⁵:¹Everyone who *believes* that Jesus is the Christ, from *God* has been begotten, and everyone who loves the one begetting loves also the one begotten from him. ²*In this we know* that we love the children of *God*, whenever we love *God* and do his commandments.¹⁵⁸

At this point the audience hear a progression, via the macrochiastic parallels, from the C (2:15–17) to the C' (4:13–5:2) unit involving the initial and final occurrences in 1 John of the phrase "in the/this world."¹⁵⁹ "The things in the world [ἐν τῷ κόσμῳ]" (2:15) and "all that is in the world [ἐν τῷ κόσμῳ]" (2:16) progress to "we ourselves are in this world [ἐν τῷ κόσμῳ τούτῳ]" (4:17). In addition, when the audience hear "that in him we remain [μένομεν]" (4:13) at the beginning of the C' unit, they hear the transitional term that links this unit to the preceding D' unit (4:7–12) whose final verse states that "God remains [μένει] in us" (4:12).

4:13–16 (A): *The One Remaining in Love in God Remains and God in Him Remains*

The audience hear the A element (4:13–16) of this chiastic unit as a chiastic pattern in itself:

a) In this we know that in him we *remain* and he in us, because he has given us from his Spirit (4:13).

   b) *And we ourselves* have observed and testify that the Father sent the Son as savior of the world (4:14).

      c) Whoever confesses that Jesus is the Son of God, God in him remains and he in God (4:15).

   b') *And we ourselves* have known and believed the love which God has in us. God is love (4:16abcde),

a') and the one *remaining* in love in God *remains* and God in him *remains* (4:16f).

---

158. For the establishment of 4:13–5:2 as a chiasm, see ch. 1.
159. The phrase "in the world" also occurs in 4:3, 4.

The audience hear the statement, "whoever confesses that Jesus is the Son of God, God in him remains and he in God" (4:15), as the central c) sub-element of this chiastic sub-unit. They then experience a pivot of parallels from the b) sub-element (4:14) to the b') sub-element (4:16abcde) involving the only occurrences in this sub-unit of the phrase "and we ourselves." "And we ourselves [καὶ ἡμεῖς] have observed" (4:14) progresses to "and we ourselves [καὶ ἡμεῖς] have known" (4:16a). And the audience hear a progression of parallels from the a) to the c) to the a') sub-element involving the only occurrences in this sub-unit of the verb "remain." "In him we remain [μένομεν]" (4:13) progresses first to "God in him remains [μένει]" (4:15) and then to "the one remaining [μένων] in love in God remains [μένει] and God in him remains [μένει]" (4:16f).

And the audience hear the b') sub-element (4:16abcde) as yet another chiastic pattern in itself:

(a) And we ourselves have known and believed the *love* (4:16a)

  (b) which *God* has (4:16b)

    (c) in us (4:16c).

  (b') *God* (4:16d)

(a') is *love* (4:16e).

The audience hear the phrase "in us" (4:16c) as the central and unparalleled (c) sub-element of this chiastic sub-unit. The audience then experience a pivot of parallels from the (b) to the (b') sub-element involving the only occurrences in this sub-unit of the term "God." "Which God [θεός] has" (4:16b) progresses to "God [θεός]" (4:16d). And the audience hear a progression of parallels from the (a) to the (a') sub-element involving the only occurrences in this sub-unit of the term "love." "Believed the love [ἀγάπην]" (4:16a) progresses to "is love [ἀγάπη]" (4:16e).

"In this we know [ἐν τούτῳ γινώσκομεν] that in him we remain and he in us [ἐν αὐτῷ μένομεν καὶ αὐτὸς ἐν ἡμῖν], because he has given us [δέδωκεν ἡμῖν] from his Spirit [πνεύματος]" (4:13). This recalls that the one keeping God's commandments "in him remains and he in him [ἐν αὐτῷ μένει καὶ αὐτὸς ἐν αὐτῷ]. And in this we know [ἐν τούτῳ γινώσκομεν] that he remains in us [μένει ἐν ἡμῖν], from the Spirit [πνεύματος] which to us he gave [ἡμῖν ἔδωκεν]" (3:24). This refers to the "Spirit [πνεῦμα] of truth" (4:6) from which God "has given and continues to give" (δέδωκεν;

perfect tense) in accord with Jesus' promise that God "will give [δώσει]" (John 14:16) "the Spirit [πνεῦμα] of truth" to guide "in all the truth" (16:13) that includes keeping the commandment to love one another (13:34) to live eternally (12:50). This reinforces the exhortation that if we love one another, God "remains in us [ἐν ἡμῖν μένει] and his love is perfected in us" (1 John 4:12), so that we might live eternally (4:9), as true worshipers of God "in Spirit [πνεύματι] and truth" (John 4:23-24).

"And we ourselves have observed [τεθεάμεθα] and testify [μαρτυροῦμεν] that the Father [πατήρ] sent the Son as savior of the world" (1 John 4:14). This recalls "what we observed [ἐθεασάμεθα] and our hands touched concerning the word of life" (1:1) and "we have seen and testify [μαρτυροῦμεν] and declare to you the life eternal which was with the Father [πατέρα] and manifested to us" (1:2). That the Father "sent the Son [ἀπέσταλκεν τὸν υἱὸν] as savior of the world [κόσμου]" recalls that "his Son" (τὸν υἱὸν αὐτοῦ) God "sent [ἀπέσταλκεν] into the world [κόσμον]," so that we might live eternally through him (4:9), and that God loved us and "sent his Son [ἀπέστειλεν τὸν υἱὸν αὐτοῦ] as expiation for our sins" (4:10). And that the Father sent his Son as "savior of the world" (σωτῆρα τοῦ κόσμου) resonates with the Samaritans' confession that Jesus "is truly the savior of the world [σωτὴρ τοῦ κόσμου]" (John 4:42). Indeed, God "sent [ἀπέστειλεν] the Son [τὸν υἱόν] into the world [κόσμον]" so that "the world might be saved [σωθῇ ὁ κόσμος] through him" (3:17) and thus have life eternal (3:16).

The elder then further assures his audience, who know that "in him we remain [ἐν αὐτῷ μένομεν] and he in us [αὐτὸς ἐν ἡμῖν]" (1 John 4:13), that "whoever confesses that Jesus is the Son of God, God in him remains [ἐν αὐτῷ μένει] and he in God [αὐτὸς ἐν τῷ θεῷ]" (4:15). "Whoever confesses [ὁμολογήσῃ] that Jesus is the Son [υἱός] of God" recalls that "the one confessing [ὁμολογῶν] the Son [υἱόν] also has the Father" (2:23). This reinforces the exhortation for the audience to "let remain" (μενέτω) in them what they heard from the beginning, for "if in you remains [μείνῃ] what you heard from the beginning" (2:24a), namely, the commandment to love one another (2:7; 2 John 1:5-6), then "you also will remain [μενεῖτε] in the Son and in the Father" (2:24b). And such "remaining" in the commandment to love one another carries with it the promise of life eternal (2:25).

"We ourselves" (ἡμεῖς) not only "have observed and testify that the Father sent the Son as savior of the world" (4:14), but "we ourselves [ἡμεῖς] have known and believed the love which God has in us" (4:16).[160] "And we ourselves have known and believed [καὶ ἡμεῖς ἐγνώκαμεν καὶ πεπιστεύκαμεν] the love which God has in us" recalls and resonates with Peter's confession of Jesus as the one who has the words of life eternal (John 6:68): "And we ourselves have believed and known [καὶ ἡμεῖς πεπιστεύκαμεν καὶ ἐγνώκαμεν] that you are the holy one of God!" (6:69). "And we ourselves have known" (καὶ ἡμεῖς ἐγνώκαμεν) "the love" (τὴν ἀγάπην) which God, as the God who remains "in us [ἐν ἡμῖν]" (1 John 4:13), has "in us [ἐν ἡμῖν]" (4:16). This reinforces the exhortation that "in this we have known love [ἐγνώκαμεν τὴν ἀγάπην], that that one for us laid down his life; so we ourselves [καὶ ἡμεῖς] ought for the brothers to lay down our lives" (3:16). The one having such love for one another assures that the "love" (ἀγάπη) of God remains in him (3:17).

That "God is love [θεὸς ἀγάπη ἐστίν]" (4:16) reinforces the exhortation that we should love one another (4:7) to truly know God, because "God is love [θεὸς ἀγάπη ἐστίν]" (4:8).[161] "The one remaining [μένων] in love in God remains [μένει] and God in him remains [θεὸς ἐν αὐτῷ μένει]" (4:16f) complements "whoever confesses that Jesus is the Son of God, God in him remains [θεὸς ἐν αὐτῷ μένει] and he in God" (4:15) and further assures that "in him we remain [μένομεν] and he in us" (4:13). This accords with the complementarity between believing and loving expressed in God's dual commandment "that we should believe in the name of his Son Jesus Christ and we should love one another" (3:23). Indeed, the one keeping these commandments of God "in him remains [μένει] and he in him" (3:24).

4:17-18a (B): Perfect Love Drives Out Fear

The audience hear the B element (4:17-18a) of this chiastic unit as a chiastic pattern in itself:

a) In this has *love* been *perfected* with us (4:17a),

---

160. "Herein is fulfilled Jesus' prayer for future believers in John 17:26: 'And to them I made known Your name; and I will continue to make it known, so that the love You had for me may be *in them*, and I may be in them'" (Brown *Epistles*, 559-60; emphasis original). "Everything favors taking 'know' and 'believe' as two ways of describing the same relation, put together here in order to strengthen the expression" (Olsson, *Letters*, 212).

161. Carson, "God Is Love," 131-42.

b) so that *we may have* confidence on the day of the judgment (4:17b),

b′) because just as that one is so *we ourselves are* in this world (4:17c).

a′) There is no fear in *love* but *perfect love* drives out fear (4:18a).

At the center of this chiastic sub-unit the audience experience a pivot of parallels from the b) to the b′) sub-element involving the only occurrences in this sub-unit of first person plural verbs. "So that we may have [ἔχωμεν] confidence" (4:17b) progresses to "so we ourselves are [ἐσμεν] in this world" (4:17c). The audience then hear a progression of parallels from the a) to the a′) sub-element involving the only occurrences in this sub-unit of expressions for "love" and "perfection." "In this has love [ἀγάπη] been perfected [τετελείωται]" (4:17a) progresses to "there is no fear in love [ἀγάπη] but perfect love [τελεία ἀγάπη] drives out fear" (4:18a).

The elder assured his audience that "whoever keeps his word" (2:5a), namely, that we should love one another (3:11, 23), "truly in this one the love [ἀγάπη] of God has been perfected [τετελείωται]" (2:5b). He then assured them that "if we love one another, God remains in us and his love [ἀγάπη] is perfected [τετελειωμένη] in us" (4:12). And now, after assuring them that "God is love [ἀγάπη], and the one remaining in love [ἀγάπη] in God remains and God in him remains" (4:16), he asserts that "in this has love [ἀγάπη] been perfected [τετελείωται] with us" (4:17a). In a marked contrast to the antichrists, who have not "remained" (μεμενήκεισαν) "with us [μεθ' ἡμῶν]" (2:19), God "remains" (μένει) in us and the love of God has been perfected "with us" (μεθ' ἡμῶν).[162]

The elder exhorted his audience to "remain in him, so that when he is manifested we may have confidence [σχῶμεν παρρησίαν] and not be shamed away from him at his coming" (2:28), that is, at the final coming of Jesus for judgment. He then assured them that "if our heart does not condemn, we have confidence [παρρησίαν ἔχομεν] with God" (3:21). And now he further assures them that because love has been perfected with us (4:17a), "we may have confidence [παρρησίαν ἔχωμεν] on the day of the judgment" (4:17b).

---

162. That these are successive and the final occurrences in 1 John of the phrase "with us" (μεθ' ἡμῶν) enhances this connection. The elder "writes 'with us' (μεθ' ἡμῶν) in keeping with his awareness from the previous verse that God is abidingly present" (Yarbrough, *1–3 John*, 259).

The reason "we may have" (ἔχωμεν) confidence on the day of the judgment (4:17b) is that "just as that one is so we ourselves [ἐσμεν] are in this world" (4:17c). "Just as that one is" (καθὼς ἐκεῖνός ἐστιν) recalls the exhortation to be righteous by doing righteousness "just as that one" (καθὼς ἐκεῖνός), that is, Jesus, "is [ἐστιν] righteous" (3:7), as "that one" (ἐκεῖνος) who "was manifested, so that he might take away sins, but sin is [ἔστιν] not in him" (3:5). It recalls the exhortation to purify oneself "just as that one" (καθὼς ἐκεῖνος) "is [ἐστιν] pure" (3:3), and to walk "just as that one" (καθὼς ἐκεῖνος) walked (2:6). And Jesus "walked" or conducted himself in love for the other as "that one" (ἐκεῖνος) who "for us laid down his life; so we ourselves ought for the brothers to lay down our lives" (3:16) in love for one another.

"Just as that one is so we ourselves are in this world [ἐν τῷ κόσμῳ τούτῳ]" (4:17c) reminds the audience that they have conquered the false prophets and antichrists, because the one in them, as those who are children of God, "is greater than the one in the world [ἐν τῷ κόσμῳ]" (4:4), that is, the antichrist, who "now is already in the world [ἐν τῷ κόσμῳ]" (4:3). It reminds them that all that is "in the world" (ἐν τῷ κόσμῳ) "is not from the Father but is from the world [κόσμου]" (2:16). They are thus not to love the "world" (κόσμον) or the things "in the world" (ἐν τῷ κόσμῳ), because "if anyone loves the world [κόσμον], the love of the Father is not in him" (2:15). But, as those who are in this world, the audience may have hope of eternal life not only for themselves but for the whole world, since "the Father sent the Son as savior of the world [κόσμου]" (4:14), indeed, as the expiation for the sins of "the whole world [κόσμου]" (2:2).

"There is no fear in love [ἐν τῇ ἀγάπῃ]" (4:18a), because "the one remaining in love [ἐν τῇ ἀγάπῃ] in God remains and God in him remains" (4:16). Indeed, "perfect love [τελεία ἀγάπη] drives out fear" (4:18a), that is, the "love" (ἀγάπη) that "has been perfected [τετελείωται] with us" (4:17a). This reminds the audience of Jesus' exhortation for his disciples to "remain in my love [ἐν τῇ ἀγάπῃ τῇ ἐμῇ]" (John 15:9). If they keep his commandments, preeminently that we should love one another, they will remain "in the love" (ἐν τῇ ἀγάπῃ) of Jesus, "just as I myself have kept the commandments of my Father and remain in his love [αὐτοῦ ἐν τῇ ἀγάπῃ]" (15:10).[163]

---

163. "Therefore, he who loves, because his is the promise of a God of love, because his is a relationship of love with the God and Father of our Lord Jesus Christ, fears not. He who fears loves not" (Schuchard, *1–3 John*, 489).

4:18b (B'): One Fearing Has Not Been Perfected in Love

At this point the audience experience a pivot of parallels from the B (4:17-18a) to the B' (4:18b) element at the center of this chiastic unit. "Love has been perfected [τετελείωται]" (4:17) and "there is no fear [φόβος] in love but perfect [τελεία] love drives out fear [φόβον]" (4:18a) occur in the B element. These progress to "because fear [φόβος] has to do with punishment, and one fearing [φοβούμενος] has not been perfected [τετελείωται] in love" (4:18b) in the B' element.

The elder continues the focus on love as he notes that "fear has to do with punishment, and the one fearing has not been perfected in love [ἀγάπη]" (4:18b). But he assures the audience that they need not have fear of punishment on the day of the judgment, but may rather have confidence, because "love" (ἀγάπη) has been perfected with them (4:17). And "there is no fear in love [ἀγάπη] but perfect love [ἀγάπη] drives out fear" (4:18a).

4:19-5:2 (A'): The One Loving God Should Love also His Brother

The audience hear the A' element (4:19-5:2) of this chiastic unit as a chiastic pattern in itself:

a) *We* ourselves *love*, because he first loved us. If anyone says, "I love God," but hates his brother, he *is* a liar (4:19-20a).

    b) For the one not loving his brother whom he has *seen* (4:20b),

    b') is not able to love God whom he has not *seen* (4:20c).

a') And this commandment we have from him, that the one loving God should love also his brother. Everyone who believes that Jesus *is* the Christ, from God has been begotten, and everyone who loves the one begetting loves also the one begotten from him. In this we know that *we love* the children of God, whenever *we love* God and do his commandments (4:21-5:2).

At the center of this chiastic sub-unit the audience experience a pivot of parallels from the b) to the b') sub-element involving the only occurrences in this sub-unit of the verb "see." "His brother whom he has seen [ἑώρακεν]" (4:20b) progresses to "God whom he has not seen [ἑώρακεν]" (4:20c). The audience then hear a progression of parallels from the a) sub-element (4:19–20a) to the a') sub-element (4:21–5:2) involving the only occurrences in this sub-unit of the verbs "we love" and "is." "We ourselves love [ἀγαπῶμεν]" (4:19) and "he is [ἐστίν] a liar" (4:20a) progress to "Jesus is [ἐστιν] the Christ" (5:1) and "we love [ἀγαπῶμεν] the children of God whenever we love [ἀγαπῶμεν] God" (5:2).

The audience then hear the a') sub-element (4:21–5:2) of this chiastic sub-unit as yet another chiastic pattern in itself:

(a) And this *commandment* we have from him (4:21a),

    (b) that the one *loving God* should love also his brother (4:21b).

        (c) *Everyone* who believes that Jesus is the Christ, from God has been *begotten* (5:1a),

        (c') and *everyone* who loves the one *begetting* loves also the one *begotten* from him (5:1b).

    (b') In this we know that we love the children of God, whenever *we love God* (5:2a)

(a') and do his *commandments* (5:2b).

At the center of this chiastic sub-unit the audience experience a pivot of parallels from the (c) to the (c') sub-element involving the only occurrences in this sub-unit of the expression "everyone" and the verb "beget." "Everyone" (πᾶς) and "from God has been begotten [γεγέννηται]" (5:1a) progress to "everyone" (πᾶς), "the one begetting [γεννήσαντα]," and "the one begotten [γεγεννημένον]" (5:1b). The audience then hear a progression of parallels from the (b) to the (b') sub-element involving the only occurrences in this sub-unit of expressions for "loving God." "The one loving God [ἀγαπῶν τὸν θεόν]" (4:21b) progresses to "whenever we love God [θεὸν ἀγαπῶμεν]" (5:2a). Finally, the audience hear a progression of parallels from the (a) to the (a') sub-element involving the only occurrences in this sub-unit of the term "commandment." "This commandment [ἐντολήν]" (4:21a) progresses to "his commandments [ἐντολάς]" (5:2b).

With an emphatic use of pronouns the elder asserts that "*we ourselves* [ἡμεῖς] love, because *he* [αὐτός] first loved us" (4:19). That "we ourselves love [ἀγαπῶμεν]" recalls that because "we love" (ἀγαπῶμεν) the brothers, we know that we have moved from death to life eternal (3:14). "Because he [αὐτός] first loved us [ἠγάπησεν ἡμᾶς]" recalls and resonates with the assertion that "in this is love, not that we have loved God but that he loved us [αὐτὸς ἠγάπησεν ἡμᾶς] and sent his Son as expiation for our sins" (4:10). It reinforces the exhortation that "if God so loved us [ἠγάπησεν ἡμᾶς], then we ourselves ought to love one another" (4:11) in order to live eternally.

"If anyone says, 'I love God,' but hates his brother [ἀδελφὸν αὐτοῦ μισῇ]" (4:20a) recalls that "the one saying that he is in the light but hating his brother [ἀδελφὸν αὐτοῦ μισῶν] is still in darkness" (2:9).[164] Whereas the one loving his brother remains in the light (2:10), "the one hating his brother [μισῶν τὸν ἀδελφὸν αὐτοῦ] is in the darkness that is associated with death rather than life eternal. This was confirmed as the audience heard that "the one not loving remains in death" (3:14). Indeed, "everyone who hates his brother [μισῶν τὸν ἀδελφὸν αὐτοῦ] is a murderer," who does not have life eternal remaining in him (3:15). That anyone who claims to love God while hating his brother "is a liar [ψεύστης ἐστίν]" (4:20a) recalls that "the liar is" (ἐστιν ὁ ψεύστης) the one who denies that Jesus is the Christ (2:22). And "the one saying, 'I have known him,' but not keeping his commandments," preeminent of which is that we should love one another (3:11, 23), "is a liar [ψεύστης ἐστίν]" (2:4).

"For the one not loving his brother [μὴ ἀγαπῶν τὸν ἀδελφὸν αὐτοῦ] whom he has seen [ἑώρακεν], is not able to love God whom he has not seen [ἑώρακεν]" (4:20bc). This recalls and resonates with "the one not loving [μὴ ἀγαπῶν] does not know God, because God is love" (4:8), "the one not loving [μὴ ἀγαπῶν] remains in death" (3:14), and "the one not loving his brother" (μὴ ἀγαπῶν τὸν ἀδελφὸν αὐτοῦ) is not from God (3:10). It recalls that "everyone who sins has neither seen [ἑώρακεν] him nor known him" (3:6). Whereas everyone who has been begotten from God "is not able [οὐ δύναται] to sin" (3:9), the one not loving his brother "is not able [οὐ δύναται] to love God" (4:20c).

"And this commandment [ταύτην τὴν ἐντολήν] we have from him, that the one loving God should love [ἀγαπᾷ] also his brother" (4:21). This recalls that "this [αὕτη] is his commandment [ἐντολή], that we should believe in the name of his Son Jesus Christ and we should love [ἀγαπῶμεν] one another, just as he gave the commandment [ἐντολήν] to us" (3:23). Whereas anyone who says, "I love God [ἀγαπῶ τὸν θεόν]," but hates his brother is a liar, and the one not "loving his brother" (ἀγαπῶν

---

164. "This is the first time the letter has spoken explicitly of someone loving God, although it is implicit in at least some occurrences of the ambiguous 'love of God' [2:5; 3:17; cf. 2:15]" (Lieu, *Commentary*, 198).

τὸν ἀδελφὸν αὐτοῦ) is not able "to love [ἀγαπᾶν] God [τὸν θεόν]" (4:20), "the one loving God [ἀγαπῶν τὸν θεόν] should love [ἀγαπᾷ] also his brother [τὸν ἀδελφὸν αὐτοῦ]" (4:21b). Indeed, the "love of God" (ἀγάπη τοῦ θεοῦ) does not remain in one who "observes his brother [τὸν ἀδελφὸν αὐτοῦ] having a need and shuts off his compassion from him" (3:17).

"We ourselves have known [ἐγνώκαμεν] and believed [πεπιστεύκαμεν] the love [ἀγάπην] which God has in us" (4:16) and "everyone [πᾶς] who believes [πιστεύων] that Jesus is the Christ, from God has been begotten [ἐκ τοῦ θεοῦ γεγέννηται]" (5:1a). These assertions resonate with "everyone [πᾶς] who loves [ἀγαπῶν] from God has been begotten [ἐκ τοῦ θεοῦ γεγέννηται] and knows [γινώσκει] God" (4:7). And the audience have already heard of the complementarity between believing and loving in the commandment that "we should believe [πιστεύσωμεν] in the name of his Son Jesus Christ and we should love [ἀγαπῶμεν] one another" (3:23). Accordingly, just as "everyone who believes that Jesus is the Christ, from God has been begotten" (5:1a), so "everyone [πᾶς] who loves [ἀγαπῶν] the one begetting [γεννήσαντα]" (5:1b), that is, "the one loving [ἀγαπῶν] God" (4:21), "loves also [ἀγαπᾷ καί] the one begotten [γεγεννημένον] from him" (5:1b), that is, his brother whom "he should love also [ἀγαπᾷ καί]" (4:21).[165]

"In this [ἐν τούτῳ] we know that we love the children of God [ἀγαπῶμεν τὰ τέκνα τοῦ θεοῦ], whenever we love God and do his commandments" (5:2). This recalls and resonates with "in this [ἐν τούτῳ] is manifest the children of God [τὰ τέκνα τοῦ θεοῦ]" (3:10a). They include everyone who is from God, as one "loving [ἀγαπῶν] his brother" (3:10c) as a fellow child of God. We know that we love the children of God, our fellow brothers, "whenever we love God [τὸν θεὸν ἀγαπῶμεν] and do his commandments [ἐντολάς]" (5:2), since the "commandment [ἐντολήν] we have from him" is "that the one loving God [ἀγαπῶν τὸν θεὸν] should love [ἀγαπᾷ] also his brother" (4:21).[166]

"In this we know that [ἐν τούτῳ γινώσκομεν ὅτι] we love the children of God, whenever we love God and do his commandments" (5:2) complements "in this we know that [ἐν τούτῳ γινώσκομεν ὅτι] in him we remain

---

165. "The argument might appear to run that anyone who loves God necessarily loves a God who begets offspring; love of those others who like oneself are begotten by God follows inescapably. To fail in this would be to fail in love of God as the begetter even of oneself" (Lieu, *Commentary*, 200).

166. "The two loves are inseparable (4:12); we are to love others in God and God in others" (Smalley, *1 John*, 255–56).

and he in us, because he has given us of his Spirit" (4:13). This is the Spirit of truth that guides us in all the truth (John 16:13; cf. 14:17; 15:26), which includes doing the commandment to love one another (13:34)—our fellow brothers and children of God—to live eternally (12:50). It is the Spirit of truth that thus enables us to become true worshipers of God (4:23-24) by doing his commandments, that is, by practicing the worship that consists of loving God and one another to live eternally.

Summary of 1 John 4:13-5:2

"In this we know that in him we remain and he in us, because he has given us from his Spirit" (4:13). This recalls that the one keeping God's commandments "in him remains and he in him. And in this we know that he remains in us, from the Spirit which to us he gave" (3:24). This refers to the "Spirit of truth" (4:6) from which God "has given and continues to give" (perfect tense) in accord with Jesus' promise that God "will give" (John 14:16) "the Spirit of truth" to guide "in all the truth" (16:13) that includes keeping the commandment to love one another (13:34) to live eternally (12:50). This reinforces the exhortation that if we love one another, God "remains in us and his love is perfected in us" (1 John 4:12), so that we might live eternally (4:9), as true worshipers of God "in Spirit and truth" (John 4:23-24).

"And we ourselves have observed and testify that the Father sent the Son as savior of the world" (1 John 4:14). This recalls "what we observed and our hands touched concerning the word of life" (1:1) and "we have seen and testify and declare to you the life eternal which was with the Father and manifested to us" (1:2). That the Father "sent the Son as savior of the world" recalls that "his Son" God "sent into the world," so that we might live eternally through him (4:9), and that God loved us and "sent his Son as expiation for our sins" (4:10). And that the Father sent his Son as "savior of the world" resonates with the Samaritans' confession that Jesus "is truly the savior of the world" (John 4:42). Indeed, God "sent the Son into the world" so that "the world might be saved through him" (3:17) and thus have life eternal (3:16).

The elder then further assures his audience, who know that "in him we remain and he in us" (1 John 4:13), that "whoever confesses that Jesus is the Son of God, God in him remains and he in God" (4:15). "Whoever confesses that Jesus is the Son of God" recalls that "the one confessing the

Son also has the Father" (2:23). This reinforces the exhortation for the audience to "let remain" in them what they heard from the beginning, for "if in you remains what you heard from the beginning" (2:24a), namely, the commandment that we should love one another (2:7; 2 John 1:5–6), then "you also will remain in the Son and in the Father" (2:24b). And such "remaining" in the commandment to love one another carries with it the promise of life eternal (2:25).

"And we ourselves have known and believed the love which God has in us" (4:16) recalls and resonates with Peter's confession of Jesus as the one who has the words of life eternal (John 6:68): "And we ourselves have believed and known that you are the holy one of God!" (6:69). It reinforces the exhortation that "in this we have known love, that that one for us laid down his life; so we ourselves ought for the brothers to lay down our lives" (1 John 3:16). The one having such love for one another assures that the "love" of God remains in him (3:17).

The elder assured his audience that "whoever keeps his word" (2:5a), namely, that we should love one another (3:11, 23), "truly in this one the love of God has been perfected " (2:5b). He then assured them that "if we love one another, God remains in us and his love is perfected in us" (4:12). And now, after assuring them that "God is love, and the one remaining in love in God remains and God in him remains" (4:16), he asserts that "in this has love been perfected with us" (4:17a). In a marked contrast to the antichrists, who have not "remained with us" (2:19), God "remains" in us and the love of God has been perfected "with us."

"Just as that one is so we ourselves are in this world" (4:17c) reminds the audience that they have conquered the false prophets and antichrists, because the one in them, as those who are children of God, "is greater than the one in the world" (4:4), that is, the antichrist, who "now is already in the world" (4:3). It reminds them that all that is "in the world is not from the Father but is from the world" (2:16). They are thus not to love the "world" or the things "in the world," because "if anyone loves the world, the love of the Father is not in him" (2:15). But, as those who are in this world, the audience may have hope of eternal life not only for themselves but for the whole world, since "the Father sent the Son as savior of the world" (4:14), indeed, as the expiation for the sins of "the whole world" (2:2).

The elder continues the focus on love as he notes that "fear has to do with punishment, and the one fearing has not been perfected in love" (4:18b). But he assures the audience that they need not have fear of punishment on the day of the judgment, but may rather have confidence, because "love" has been perfected with them (4:17). And "there is no fear in love but perfect love drives out fear" (4:18a).

With an emphatic use of pronouns the elder asserts that "*we ourselves* love, because *he* first loved us" (4:19). That "we ourselves love" recalls that because "we love" the brothers, we know that we have moved from death to life eternal (3:14). "Because he first loved us" recalls and resonates with the assertion that "in this is love, not that we have loved God but that he loved us and sent his Son as expiation for our sins" (4:10). It reinforces the exhortation that "if God so loved us, then we ourselves ought to love one another" (4:11) in order to live eternally.

"If anyone says, 'I love God,' but hates his brother " (4:20a) recalls that "the one saying that he is in the light but hating his brother is still in darkness" (2:9). Whereas the one loving his brother remains in the light (2:10), "the one hating his brother is in the darkness that is associated with death rather than life eternal. This was confirmed as the audience heard that "the one not loving remains in death" (3:14). Indeed, "everyone who hates his brother is a murderer," who does not have life eternal remaining in him (3:15).

"And this commandment we have from him, that the one loving God should love also his brother" (4:21). This recalls that "this is his commandment, that we should believe in the name of his Son Jesus Christ and we should love one another, just as he gave the commandment to us" (3:23). Whereas anyone who says, "I love God," but hates his brother is a liar, and the one not "loving his brother" is not able "to love God" (4:20), "the one loving God should love also his brother" (4:21b). Indeed, the "love of God" does not remain in one who "observes his brother having a need and shuts off his compassion from him" (3:17).

"We ourselves have known and believed the love which God has in us" (4:16) and "everyone who believes that Jesus is the Christ, from God has been begotten" (5:1a). These assertions resonate with "everyone who loves from God has been begotten and knows God" (4:7). And the audience have already heard of the complementarity between believing and loving in the commandment that "we should believe in the name of his Son Jesus Christ and we should love one another" (3:23). Accordingly, just as "everyone who believes that Jesus is the Christ, from God has been begotten" (5:1a), so "everyone who loves the one begetting" (5:1b), that is, "the one loving God" (4:21), "loves also the one begotten from him" (5:1b), that is, his brother whom "he should love also" (4:21).

"In this we know that we love the children of God, whenever we love God and do his commandments" (5:2) complements "in this we know that in him we remain and he in us, because he has given us of his Spirit" (4:13). This is the Spirit of truth that guides us in all the truth (John 16:13; cf. 14:17; 15:26) that includes the commandment to love one another (13:34)—our fellow brothers and children of God—to live eternally (12:50). It is the Spirit of truth that thus enables us to become true worshipers of God (4:23–24) by doing his commandments, that is, by practicing the worship of loving God and one another to live eternally.

15

1 John 5:3–12
This Is the Love of God that We Keep His Commandments

Life eternal God has given to us,
and this life is in his Son

A   ³For *this* is the love of *God*, that we keep his commandments, and his commandments are not burdensome, ⁴because everyone begotten from *God* conquers the world. And *this* is the conquering power that conquers the world—our *faith*. ⁵Who is the one conquering the world except the one *believing* that Jesus is the *Son* of *God*? ⁶ᵃThis is the one who came through *water* and *blood*, Jesus Christ, not in the *water* only but in the *water* and in the *blood*.

B   ⁶ᵇAnd *the Spirit is* the one who testifies,

B'   ⁶ᶜbecause *the Spirit is* the truth.

A'   ⁷For three are they who are testifying, ⁸the Spirit and the *water* and the *blood*, and the three are as the one. ⁹If we receive the testimony of human beings, the testimony of *God* is greater, because *this* is the testimony of *God* that he has testified concerning his *Son*. ¹⁰The one *believing* in the *Son* of *God* has the testimony in himself, the one not *believing God* has made him a liar, because he has not *believed* in the testimony which *God* has testified concerning his *Son*. ¹¹And *this* is the testimony, that life eternal *God* has given us, and *this* life is in his *Son*. ¹²The one having the *Son* has the life. The one not having the *Son* of *God* does not have the life.¹⁶⁷

At this point the audience hear a progression, via the macrochiastic parallels, from the B (2:1–14) to the B' (5:3–12) unit involving the first and final occurrences in 1 John of the phrase "love of God" as well as the only occurrences in 1 John of the expression "we keep his commandments."¹⁶⁸ "In this we know that we have known him, if we keep his commandments [τὰς ἐντολὰς αὐτοῦ τηρῶμεν]" (2:3) and "truly in this one the love of God [ἡ ἀγάπη τοῦ θεοῦ] has been perfected" (2:5) progress to "for this is the love of God [ἡ ἀγάπη τοῦ θεοῦ], that we keep his commandments [τὰς ἐντολὰς αὐτοῦ τηρῶμεν]" (5:3). In addition, when the audience hear the phrase "love [ἀγάπη] of God [θεοῦ]" (5:3) at the beginning of the B' unit, they hear the transitional terms that link this unit to the preceding C' unit (4:13–5:2), which concluded with "whenever we love God [θεὸν ἀγαπῶμεν] and do his commandments" (5:2).

5:3–6a (A): Not by the Water Only but by the Water and by the Blood

The audience hear the A element (5:3–6a) of this chiastic unit as a chiastic pattern in itself:

a) For this is the love of *God*, that we keep his commandments, and his commandments are not burdensome, because everyone begotten from *God* (5:3–4a)

    b) *conquers the world.* And this is the *conquering power* that *conquers the world*—our *faith* (5:4b).

    b') Who is the one *conquering the world* except the one *believing* (5:5a)

a') that Jesus is the Son of *God*? This is the one who came through water and blood, Jesus Christ, not in the water only but in the water and in the blood (5:5b–6a).

---

167. For the establishment of 5:3–12 as a chiasm, see ch. 1.
168. The phrase "love of God" occurs also in 3:17 and 4:9.

At the center of this chiastic sub-unit the audience experience a pivot of parallels from the b) to the b') sub-element involving the only occurrences in this sub-unit of expressions for conquering the world and believing. "Conquers the world [νικᾷ τὸν κόσμον]. And this is the conquering power that conquers the world [ἡ νίκη ἡ νικήσασα τὸν κόσμον]—our faith [πίστις]" (5:4b) progresses to "who is the one conquering the world [νικῶν τὸν κόσμον] except the one believing [πιστεύων]" (5:5a). The audience then hear a progression of parallels from the a) sub-element (5:3-4a) to the a') sub-element (5:5b-6a) involving the only occurrences in this sub-unit of the term "God." "The love of God [θεοῦ]" (5:3) and "begotten from God [θεοῦ]" (5:4a) progress to "the Son of God [θεοῦ]" (5:5b).

And the audience hear the a) sub-element (5:3-4a) of this chiastic sub-unit as yet another chiastic pattern in itself:

(a) For this is the love of *God* (5:3a),

    (b) that we keep *his commandments* (5:3b),

    (b') and *his commandments* are not burdensome (5:3c),

(a') because everyone begotten from *God* (5:4a).

At the center of this chiastic sub-unit the audience experience a pivot of parallels from the (b) to the (b') sub-element involving the only occurrences in this sub-unit of the expression "his commandments." "That we keep his commandments [τὰς ἐντολὰς αὐτοῦ]" (5:3b) progresses to "his commandments [αἱ ἐντολαὶ αὐτοῦ] are not burdensome" (5:3c). The audience then hear a progression of parallels from the (a) to the (a') sub-element involving the only occurrences in this sub-unit of the term "God." "The love of God [θεοῦ]" (5:3a) progresses to "begotten from God [θεοῦ]" (5:4a).

The elder asserted that whoever keeps God's word, his commandment to love one another (3:11, 23), "truly in this one the love of God [ἡ ἀγάπη τοῦ θεοῦ] has been perfected" (2:5)—both God's love for us and our love for God. He questioned how "the love of God" (ἡ ἀγάπη τοῦ θεοῦ)—both God's love for us and our love for God—can remain in one who "observes his brother having a need and shuts off his compassion from him" (3:17). He declared that "in this the love of God [ἡ ἀγάπη τοῦ θεοῦ] was manifested in us" (4:9a), referring both to our love for God as demonstrated in our love for one another (4:7) and to God's love for us as demonstrated in his sending his Son into the world so that we might live eternally through him (4:9ab). And now he asserts that "this is the love of God [ἡ ἀγάπη τοῦ θεοῦ], that we keep his commandments, and his commandments are not burdensome" (5:3). In other words, the goal of God's love for us is that we keep his commandments, especially that we should love one another, and thereby demonstrate our love for God (5:2).

"For this is the love of God, that we keep his commandments [τὰς ἐντολὰς αὐτοῦ τηρῶμεν]" (5:3) recalls that "the one keeping his commandments" (τηρῶν τὰς ἐντολὰς αὐτοῦ) in God remains and God in him (3:24). "And whatever we ask we receive from him, because we keep his commandments [τὰς ἐντολὰς αὐτοῦ τηροῦμεν]" (3:22). We know that we have known God, "if we keep his commandments [τὰς ἐντολὰς αὐτοῦ τηρῶμεν]" (2:3). The one "not keeping his comandments [τὰς ἐντολὰς αὐτοῦ μὴ τηρῶν] is a liar and the truth is not in this one" (2:4). But whoever "keeps" (τηρῇ) God's word, his commandment that we should love one another (3:11, 23), "truly in this one the love of God has been perfected" (2:5).

God's commandments are not burdensome (5:3), "because everyone begotten from God [πᾶν τὸ γεγεννημένον ἐκ τοῦ θεοῦ] conquers the world" (5:4).[169] This recalls that "everyone [πᾶς] who believes that Jesus is the Christ, from God has been begotten [ἐκ τοῦ θεοῦ γεγέννηται]" (5:1), as well as that "everyone [πᾶς] who loves from God has been begotten [ἐκ τοῦ θεοῦ γεγέννηται]" (4:7). And "everyone who has been begotten from God [πᾶς ὁ γεγεννημένος ἐκ τοῦ θεοῦ] does not do sin" (3:9a); indeed, "he is not able to sin, because from God he has been begotten [ἐκ τοῦ θεοῦ γεγέννηται]" (3:9c). Furthermore "everyone [πᾶς] who does righteousness," especially the righteousness of loving one's brother (3:7, 10), "from him has been begotten [ἐξ αὐτοῦ γεγέννηται]" (2:29). And so everyone begotten from God "conquers the world [κόσμον]" (5:4), the "world" (κόσμος) that does not know us as children of God, because it did not know God (3:1).

Everyone begotten from God "conquers the world [νικᾷ τὸν κόσμον]. And this is the conquering power [νίκη] that conquers the world [νικήσασα τὸν κόσμον]—our faith. Who is the one conquering the world [νικῶν τὸν κόσμον] except the one believing that Jesus is the

---

169. The elder "deliberately uses the neuter πᾶν, 'everyone' (as opposed to the masculine πᾶς, 'everyone,' in v 1) to generalize the reference" (Smalley, *1 John*, 257-58). "The neuter is sometimes used with reference to persons if it is not the individuals but a general quality that is to be emphasized" (BDF, § 138).

Son of God?" (5:4-5). This recalls and resonates with the assurance that "*you* are from God, little children, and you have conquered [νενικήκατε] them" (4:4a), that is, the false prophets who "have gone out into the world [κόσμον]" (4:1) and the antichrist who is "in the world [κόσμῳ]" (4:3). This accords with the assurance to the young men in the audience that "you have conquered [νενικήκατε] the evil one" (2:13, 14). And it recalls that the basis for this power that conquers the world was indicated in Jesus' declaration that "*I myself* have conquered the world [ἐγὼ νενίκηκα τὸν κόσμον]" (John 16:33).

Accordingly, the power that conquers the world is "our faith [πίστις]" (1 John 5:4), the faith of "one believing [πιστεύων] that Jesus is the Son of God" (5:5). This recalls and resonates with the assertion that "everyone who believes [πιστεύων] that Jesus is the Christ, from God has been begotten" (5:1). And this is God's commandment, "that we should believe [πιστεύσωμεν] in the name of his Son Jesus Christ and we should love one another" (3:23).

"The one conquering the world [κόσμον]" is "the one believing that Jesus is the Son [υἱός] of God" (5:5), that is, the "Son" (υἱόν) God sent as savior of the "world [κόσμου]" (4:14), the "Son" (υἱόν) he sent "as expiation for our sins" (4:10), the "Son" (υἱόν) he "sent into the world [κόσμον] so that we might live through him" (4:9). And we might live eternally "through him" (δι' αὐτοῦ) because he came as the Son of God "through water and blood [δι' ὕδατος καὶ αἵματος], Jesus Christ, not in the water only but in the water and in the blood" (5:6a).[170] This emphasis on both the water and the blood recalls that out of the pierced side of the dead Jesus there came out both "blood and water [αἷμα καὶ ὕδωρ]" (John 19:34) as the dual source of life eternal.[171] It reinforces how "the blood [αἷμα] of Jesus his Son [υἱοῦ] cleanses us from all sin" (1 John 1:7), so that we may

---

170. "If the use of the verb 'come' (ἔρχομαι) here carries the connotation of Christ's salvific mission, as argued in our comments on 4:2, then the prepositional phrases 'in the water' and 'in the blood' in 5:6c (ἐν τῷ ὕδατι and ἐν τῷ αἵματι) are instrumental datives adverbially modifying the elided verb 'come' (ἐλθών), which suggests that the salvific mission of Jesus was achieved *both* by water and by blood, not by water alone" (Jobes, *1, 2, & 3 John*, 219; emphasis original).

171. The life-giving water that follows the blood out of the pierced side of the dead Jesus gives to the blood its cleansing (John 1:26, 31, 33; 3:23; 5:7; 13:5) and thirst-quenching (2:7, 9; 4:7-15; 7:37-38) properties, so that the blood, together with the water, provides the drink that quenches the thirst for life eternal (6:53-56 and 4:7-15) and "cleanses us from all sin" (1 John 1:7), "so that we might live through him" (4:9). See Heil, *Blood and Water*, 105-9. See also Carnazzo, *Seeing Blood and Water*; Thatcher, "Water and Blood," 235-48.

share the fellowship of life eternal (1:2) "that is ours with the Father and with his Son [υἱοῦ] Jesus Christ" (1:3).[172] The water and blood together thus allude to both the baptismal and eucharistic dimensions key to sharing the fellowship of life eternal.[173]

5:6b (B): And the Spirit Is the One Who Testifies

That "the Spirit [πνεῦμά] is the one who testifies [μαρτυροῦν]" (5:6b) recalls Jesus' promise that he will send his disciples "the Spirit [πνεῦμα] of truth" and "that one will testify [μαρτυρήσει] concerning me" (John 15:26). The elder has assured the audience that we know that God remains in us "from the Spirit [πνεύματος] which to us he gave" (1 John 3:24). And since God "has given us from his Spirit [πνεύματος]" (4:13), as the one who testifies concerning Jesus, "we testify [μαρτυροῦμεν] that the Father sent the Son as savior of the world" (4:14). The Spirit as the one who testifies, then, has provided the basis for the elder's assertion that "we testify [μαρτυροῦμεν] and declare to you the life eternal which was with the Father and manifested to us" (1:2).[174]

5:6c (B'): Because the Spirit Is the Truth

At this point the audience experience a pivot of parallels from the B to the B' element at the center of this chiastic unit. "The Spirit is [πνεῦμά ἐστιν] the one who testifies" (5:6b) progresses to "because the Spirit is [πνεῦμά ἐστιν] the truth" (5:6c).

The "Spirit [πνεῦμά] is the truth [ἀλήθεια]" (5:6c) as the "Spirit of truth [πνεῦμα τῆς ἀληθείας]" (4:6), which inspires "every spirit [πνεῦμα] that confesses Jesus as having come in flesh" (4:2). This is the "Spirit of truth" (πνεῦμα τῆς ἀληθείας) that, according to the promise of Jesus, will guide his disciples "in all the truth [ἀληθείᾳ]" (John 16:13; cf. 14:17;

---

172. "To confess Jesus as the Son of God is to affirm as Son of God the one who so came, and whose coming brings the benefits of his death" (Lieu, *Commentary*, 213).

173. "The blood and water that flows from the death of Jesus fortifies the community of believers, by washing away their sin of unbelief in baptism and quenching their thirst for eternal life in the eucharist, to love one another as Jesus loved them [John 13:34-35; 15:12-13]" (Heil, *Blood and Water*, 109).

174. "By stating that the Spirit is the one who testifies (pres. tense), the author indicates that he does not think of the Spirit's testimony purely as a past phenomenon. It continues in the testimony of the 'we' . . . (I John 1:2)" (Brown, *Epistles*, 580).

15:26).[175] Thus, the Spirit is the one who testifies (1 John 5:6b) to the "truth" (ἀλήθεια) that is not in one who does not keep God's commandments (2:4), the "truth" (ἀληθείᾳ) in which we are to walk in accord with God's commandment (2 John 1:4). And in the "truth [ἀληθείᾳ]" (1 John 3:18) of God's commandment we, as those who are "from the truth [ἀληθείας]" (3:19; cf. 1:6, 8; 2:21), should love one another (2 John 1:5; 1 John 3:11, 23), and thus love God himself (4:20–5:2), to have life eternal (2:25; 3:14–15). We thereby become "true" (ἀληθινοί) worshipers who worship in "Spirit and truth [πνεύματι καὶ ἀληθείᾳ]" (John 4:23–24) by loving God and one another to live eternally.

5:7–12 (A'): The Spirit and the Water and the Blood

At this point the audience hear a progression of parallels from the A (5:3–6a) to the A' (5:7–12) element of this chiastic unit. "Of God [θεοῦ]" (5:3), "everyone begotten from God [θεοῦ]" (5:4), "our faith [πίστις]" (5:4), "the one believing [πιστεύων] that Jesus is the Son [υἱός] of God [θεοῦ]" (5:5), "through water and blood [ὕδατος καὶ αἵματος]" (5:6a), and "not in the water [ὕδατι] only but in the water [ὕδατι] and in the blood [αἵματι]" (5:6a) occur in the A element. These progress to "the water [ὕδωρ] and the blood [αἷμα]" (5:8), "of God [θεοῦ]" (5:9 [2x]), "his Son [υἱοῦ]" (5:9), "believing [πιστεύων] in the Son [υἱόν] of God [θεοῦ]" (5:10), "not believing [πιστεύων] God [θεῷ]" (5:10), "not believed [πεπίστευκεν] . . . God [θεός] . . . his Son [υἱοῦ]" (5:10), "God [θεός]" (5:11), "his Son [υἱῷ]" (5:11), "the Son [υἱόν]" (5:12), and "Son [υἱόν] of God [θεοῦ]" (5:12) in the A' element.

The audience hear the A' element (5:7–12) of this chiastic unit as a chiastic pattern in itself:

a) For three are they who are testifying, the Spirit and the water and the blood, and the three are as the one. If we receive the testimony of human beings, the testimony of God is greater, because *this is the testimony* of God (5:7–9b)

b) that he *has testified concerning his Son* (5:9c).

---

175. "Because the Spirit *is*, like Jesus (Jn 14:6), 'the truth,' the Spirit is 'the Spirit of Truth' (4:6; see also Jn 14:16–17; 15:26; cf. Jn 15:27)" (Schuchard, *1–3 John*, 533; emphasis original).

1 JOHN 5:3-12

> c) The one *believing* in the Son of God has the testimony in himself (5:10a),
>
> c') the one not *believing* God has made him a liar, because he has not *believed* in the testimony (5:10b).
>
> b') which God *has testified concerning his Son* (5:10c).
>
> a') And *this is the testimony*, that life eternal God has given us, and this life is in his Son. The one having the Son has the life. The one not having the Son of God does not have the life (5:11-12).

At the center of this chiastic sub-unit the audience experience a pivot of parallels from the c) to the c') sub-element involving the only occurrences in this sub-unit of the verb "believe." "The one believing [πιστεύων]" (5:10a) progresses to "the one not believing [πιστεύων]" and "has not believed [πεπίστευκεν]" (5:10b). The audience then hear a progression of parallels from the b) to the b') sub-element involving the only occurrences in 1 John of "has testified concerning his Son." "He has testified concerning his Son [μεμαρτύρηκεν περὶ τοῦ υἱοῦ αὐτοῦ]" (5:9c) progresses to "God has testified [μεμαρτύρηκεν] concerning his Son [περὶ τοῦ υἱοῦ αὐτοῦ]" (5:10c). Finally, the audience hear a progression of parallels from the a) sub-element (5:7-9b) to the a') sub-element (5:11-12) involving the only occurrences in 1 John of "this is the testimony." "This is the testimony [αὕτη ἐστὶν ἡ μαρτυρία] of God" (5:9b) progresses to "and this is the testimony [αὕτη ἐστὶν ἡ μαρτυρία]" (5:11).

The audience hear the a) sub-element (5:7-9b) of the A' element (5:7-12) as a yet another chiastic pattern in itself:

> (a) For three *are* they who are testifying, the Spirit and the water and the blood, and the three *are* as the one (5:7-8).
>
> > (b) If we receive the testimony of human beings (5:9a),
>
> (a') the testimony of God *is* greater, because this *is* the testimony of God (5:9b).

After hearing the unparalleled (b) sub-element, "if we receive the testimony of humans" (5:9a), at the center of this chiastic sub-unit, the audience experience a pivot of parallels from the (a) to the (a') sub-element involving the only occurrences in this sub-unit of the verb "to be." "Three are [εἰσιν] they who are testifying" (5:7) and "the three are [εἰσιν] as the one" (5:8) progress to "the testimony of God is [ἐστίν] greater, because this is [ἐστίν] the testimony of God" (5:9b).

And the audience hear the a') sub-element (5:11–12) of the A' element of this chiastic unit as yet another chiastic pattern in itself:

(a) *And this is* the testimony (5:11a),

  (b) that life eternal God has given us (5:11b),

(a') *and this* life *is* in his Son. The one having the Son has the life. The one not having the Son of God does not have the life (5:11c–12).

After hearing the unparalleled (b) sub-element, "that life eternal God has given us" (5:11b), at the center of this chiastic sub-unit, the audience experience a pivot of parallels from the (a) sub-element (5:11a) to the (a') sub-element (5:11c–12) involving the only occurrences in this sub-unit of "and this" and "is." "And this is [καὶ αὕτη ἐστίν] the testimony" (5:11a) progresses to "and this [καὶ αὕτη] life is [ἐστίν] in his Son" (5:11c).

The Spirit is not alone as the one who testifies (5:6b). "For three are they who are testifying" (5:7), "the Spirit and the water and the blood [τὸ ὕδωρ καὶ τὸ αἷμα]" (5:8a), that is, the "water and blood" (ὕδατος καὶ αἵματος) through which Jesus Christ came (5:6a) as the Son of God (5:5).[176] And these three are as "the one [τὸ ἕν]" (5:8b), that is, as "the Spirit" (τὸ πνεῦμά) as "the one who testifies [τὸ μαρτυροῦν]" (5:6b). This recalls the close association Jesus made between the Spirit and both the water and the blood as sources of eternal life. Following the unbelief after Jesus' declaration that "the one who eats my flesh and drinks my blood [αἷμα] has life eternal" (John 6:54), he asserted that "the Spirit [πνεῦμά] is the one who gives life" (6:63). After Jesus' declaration that, in accord with the Scripture, "rivers of living water [ὕδατος] will flow from his stomach" (7:38), the evangelist added that "he said this about the Spirit [πνεύματος]" (7:39). And so out of the pierced side of the dead Jesus came not only "blood" (αἷμα) but "water" (ὕδωρ) as a symbol of the Spirit that makes both blood and water sources of life eternal (19:34).[177]

"If we receive the testimony of human beings, the testimony of God is greater, because this is the testimony of God that he has testified

---

176. "[T]he emphasis lies upon 'three'" (Olsson, *Letters*, 227).

177. "Spirit, water, and blood inform, then, not just the life that was given by him, but the life that is now ours through him—through the water and the blood—that is now ours to live from him, for him, like him, for others, as did he himself in his living and loving, in his suffering and dying, for all" (Schuchard, *1–3 John*, 535).

[μεμαρτύρηκεν] concerning his Son" (1 John 5:9). This means that the testimony of the three who are "testifying [μαρτυροῦντες]" (5:7) as one, the Spirit and the water and the blood (5:8), amounts to the testimony of God himself.[178] That the testimony of God is "greater" (μείζων) than that of human beings recalls not only that God is "greater" (μείζων) than the antichrist in the world (4:4), but that "God is greater [μείζων] than our heart and knows all things" (3:20). And the "testimony [μαρτυρία] of God that he has testified concerning his Son [μεμαρτύρηκεν περὶ τοῦ υἱοῦ αὐτοῦ]" recalls Jesus' assertion that he has a "testimony greater [μαρτυρίαν μείζω] than that from John" (John 5:36), the testimony of the Father who sent him and "has testified concerning me [μεμαρτύρηκεν περὶ ἐμοῦ]" (5:37).[179]

Not only is "the one believing [πιστεύων] that Jesus is the Son of God [υἱὸς τοῦ θεοῦ]" one who is conquering the world (1 John 5:5), but the "one believing [πιστεύων] in the Son of God [υἱὸν τοῦ θεοῦ] has the testimony [μαρτυρίαν] in himself" (5:10a). This is "the testimony [μαρτυρία] of God" (5:9), which is the testimony of the life-giving Spirit and the water and the blood (5:8). And this accords with our knowing that the Son Jesus Christ (3:23) "remains in us, from the Spirit which to us he gave" (3:24). But "the one not believing God [πιστεύων τῷ θεῷ] has made him a liar [ψεύστην πεποίηκεν αὐτόν], because he has not believed [πεπίστευκεν] in the testimony which God has testified concerning his Son" (5:10b). This recalls that "if we say that we have not sinned" (1:10a), and thus not in need of the life-giving blood of Jesus his Son that cleanses us from all sin (1:7), "we make him a liar [ψεύστην ποιοῦμεν αὐτόν] and his word is not in us" (1:10b).

"And this is the testimony [μαρτυρία], that life eternal [ζωὴν αἰώνιον] God has given us, and this life is in his Son [υἱῷ]" (5:11). This confirms that the "testimony [μαρτυρία] of God" (5:9) is that of the Spirit of truth who testifies to the water and the blood (5:6) as the sources of life eternal, the water and the blood through which Jesus as the "Son [υἱός] of God" came (5:5). This recalls and reinforces the proclamation that "we have seen and testify [μαρτυροῦμεν] and declare to you the life eternal

---

178. "The witness of the Spirit, the water, and the blood are all integrally a part of God's testimony." (Jobes, *1, 2, & 3 John*, 224). "God, through his Spirit and ultimately also through the water and blood mentioned in 1 John 5:6-8, has registered eloquent testimony" (Yarbrough, *1-3 John*, 286).

179. The elder "interprets the blood and water from Jesus' side at the crucifixion as a kind of 'testimony' (μαρτυρία), comparable to the well-known 'testimony that God testified about his Son' at Jesus' baptism" (Michaels, "By Water and Blood," 159).

[ζωὴν τὴν αἰώνιον] that was with the Father and manifested to us" (1:2), the "life eternal" (ζωὴν τὴν αἰώνιον) divinely promised to us (2:25). It reinforces the exhortation for everyone in the audience to love his brother in order to "have life eternal [ζωὴν αἰώνιον] in him remaining" (3:15).

"The one having [ἔχων] the Son [υἱόν] has [ἔχει] the life [ζωήν]. The one not having [ἔχων] the Son of God [υἱὸν τοῦ θεοῦ] does not have [ἔχει] the life [ζωήν]" (5:12).[180] This reaffirms that "the one believing in the Son of God [υἱὸν τοῦ θεοῦ] has [ἔχει] the testimony in himself" (5:10), "the testimony, that life [ζωήν] eternal God has given us, and this life [ζωή] is in his Son [υἱῷ]" (5:11).[181] It reasserts that Jesus came as the "Son of God [υἱὸς τοῦ θεοῦ]" (5:5) through water and blood (5:6) as sources for the "life" (ζωήν) eternal that remains in one who loves his brother (3:15). It reinforces the exhortation that, since Jesus for us laid down his life in the sacrificial death that produced the life-giving water and blood, "we ourselves ought for the brothers to lay down our lives" (3:16) in our love for one another. This unit (5:3–12) thus further bolsters the concerted exhortation of 1 John for the audience to become true worshipers who worship in Spirit and truth (John 4:23–24; 1 John 5:6), that is, worship by loving God and one another to live eternally.

Summary of 1 John 5:3–12

The elder asserted that whoever keeps God's word, his commandment that we should love one another (3:11, 23), "truly in this one the love of God has been perfected" (2:5)—both God's love for us and our love for God. He questioned how "the love of God"—both God's love for us and our love for God—can remain in one who "observes his brother having a need and shuts off his compassion from him" (3:17). He declared that "in this the love of God was manifested in us" (4:9a), referring both to our love for God as demonstrated in our love for one another (4:7) and to

---

180. "When the author chooses to say 'the Son of God' in the second clause, instead of 'the Son,' the second clause takes on a greater weight" (Olsson, *Letters*, 228).

181. "Although the idea of 'eternal life' has its roots in the hope of an age to come, it is here, as regularly in the Johannine tradition, a present possession because it is the inevitable corollary of a present relationship. That relationship with the Son is expressed with the verb 'to have,' which is also used, more naturally, for the possession of life and, in verse 10, of the testimony. With a personal object the formula is unusual, but the author has already used it in 2:23, where 'to have' the Father is contingent upon confession of the Son" (Lieu, *Commentary*, 219).

God's love for us as demonstrated in his sending his Son into the world so that we might live eternally through him (4:9ab). And now he asserts that "this is the love of God, that we keep his commandments, and his commandments are not burdensome" (5:3). In other words, the goal of God's love for us is that we keep his commandments, especially that we should love one another, and thereby demonstrate our love for God (5:2).

"For this is the love of God, that we keep his commandments" (5:3) recalls that "the one keeping his commandments" in God remains and God in him (3:24). "And whatever we ask we receive from him, because we keep his commandments" (3:22). We know that we have known God, "if we keep his commandments" (2:3). The one "not keeping his comandments is a liar and the truth is not in this one" (2:4). But whoever "keeps" God's word, his commandment to love one another (3:11, 23), "truly in this one the love of God has been perfected" (2:5).

God's commandments are not burdensome (5:3), "because everyone begotten from God conquers the world" (5:4). This recalls that "everyone who believes that Jesus is the Christ, from God has been begotten" (5:1), as well as that "everyone who loves from God has been begotten" (4:7). And "everyone who has been begotten from God does not do sin" (3:9a); indeed, "he is not able to sin, because from God he has been begotten" (3:9c). Furthermore "everyone who does righteousness," especially the righteousness of loving one's brother (3:7, 10), "from him has been begotten" (2:29). And so everyone begotten from God "conquers the world" (5:4), the "world" that does not know us as children of God, because it did not know God (3:1).

Everyone begotten from God "conquers the world. And this is the conquering power that conquers the world—our faith. Who is the one conquering the world except the one believing that Jesus is the Son of God?" (5:4–5). This recalls and resonates with the assurance that "*you* are from God, little children, and you have conquered them" (4:4a), that is, the false prophets who "have gone out into the world" (4:1) and the antichrist who is "in the world" (4:3). This accords with the assurance to the young men in the audience that "you have conquered the evil one" (2:13, 14). And it recalls that the basis for this power that conquers the world was indicated in Jesus' declaration that "*I myself* have conquered the world" (John 16:33).

Accordingly, the power that conquers the world is "our faith" (1 John 5:4), the faith of "one believing that Jesus is the Son of God" (5:5). This recalls and resonates with the assertion that "everyone who believes that Jesus is the Christ, from God has been begotten" (5:1). And this is God's commandment, "that we should believe in the name of his Son Jesus Christ and we should love one another" (3:23).

"The one conquering the world" is "the one believing that Jesus is the Son of God" (5:5), that is, the "Son" God sent as savior of the "world" (4:14), the "Son" he sent "as expiation for our sins" (4:10), the "Son" he "sent into the world so that we might live through him" (4:9). And we might live eternally "through him" because he came as the Son of God "through water and blood, Jesus Christ, not in the water only but in the water and in the blood" (5:6a). This emphasis on both the water and the blood recalls that out of the pierced side of the dead Jesus there came out both "blood and water" (John 19:34) as the dual source of life eternal. It reinforces how "the blood of Jesus his Son cleanses us from all sin" (1 John 1:7), so that we may share the fellowship of life eternal (1:2) "that is ours with the Father and with his Son Jesus Christ" (1:3). The water and blood together thus allude to both the baptismal and eucharistic dimensions key to sharing the fellowship of life eternal.

The "Spirit is the truth" (5:6c) as the "Spirit of truth" (4:6) which inspires "every spirit that confesses Jesus as having come in flesh" (4:2). This is the "Spirit of truth" that, according to the promise of Jesus, will guide his disciples "in all the truth" (John 16:13; cf. 14:17; 15:26). Thus, the Spirit is the one who testifies (1 John 5:6b) to the "truth" that is not in one who does not keep God's commandments (2:4), the "truth" in which we are to walk in accord with God's commandment (2 John 1:4). And in the "truth" (1 John 3:18) of God's commandment we, as those who are "from the truth" (3:19; cf. 1:6, 8; 2:21), should love one another (2 John 1:5; 1 John 3:11, 23), and thus love God himself (4:20—5:2), to have life eternal (2:25; 3:14-15). We thereby become "true" worshipers who worship in "Spirit and truth" (John 4:23-24) by loving God and one another to live eternally.

The Spirit is not alone as the one who testifies (1 John 5:6b). "For three are they who are testifying" (5:7), "the Spirit and the water and the blood" (5:8a), that is, the "water and blood" through which Jesus Christ came (5:6a) as the Son of God (5:5). And these three are as "the one" (5:8b), that is, as "the Spirit" as "the one who testifies" (5:6b). This recalls the close association Jesus made between the Spirit and both the water and the blood as sources of eternal life. Following the unbelief after Jesus' declaration that "the one who eats my flesh and drinks my blood has life eternal" (John 6:54), he asserted that "the Spirit is the one who gives life" (6:63). After Jesus' declaration that, in accord with the Scripture, "rivers of living water will flow from his stomach" (7:38), the evangelist added that "he said this about the Spirit" (7:39). And so out of the pierced side of the dead Jesus came not only "blood" but "water" as a symbol of the Spirit that makes both blood and water sources of life eternal (19:34).

Not only is "the one believing that Jesus is the Son of God" one who is conquering the world (1 John 5:5), but the "one believing in the Son of God has the testimony in himself" (5:10a). This is "the testimony of God" (5:9), which is the testimony of the life-giving Spirit and the water and the blood (5:8). And this accords with our knowing that the Son Jesus Christ (3:23) "remains in us, from the Spirit which to us he gave" (3:24). But "the one not believing God has made him a liar, because he has not believed in the testimony which God has testified concerning his Son" (5:10b). This recalls that "if we say that we have not sinned" (1:10a), and thus not in need of the life-giving blood of Jesus his Son that cleanses us from all sin (1:7), "we make him a liar and his word is not in us" (1:10b).

"The one having the Son has the life. The one not having the Son of God does not have the life" (5:12). This reaffirms that "the one believing in the Son of God has the testimony in himself" (5:10), "the testimony, that life eternal God has given us, and this life is in his Son" (5:11). It reasserts that Jesus came as the "Son of God" (5:5) through water and blood (5:6) as sources for the "life" eternal that remains in one who loves his brother (3:15). It reinforces the exhortation that, since Jesus for us laid down his life in the sacrificial death that produced the life-giving water and blood, "we ourselves ought for the brothers to lay down our lives" (3:16) in our love for one another. This unit (5:3–12) thus further bolsters the concerted exhortation of 1 John for the audience to become true worshipers who worship in Spirit and truth (John 4:23-24; 1 John 5:6), that is, worship by loving God and one another to live eternally.

16

1 John 5:13–21
All Unrighteousness Is Sin

Guard yourselves from the idols

A   ¹³These things I have written to you so that you may *know that* you have *life eternal*, you who believe in the name of *the Son of God*. ¹⁴And this is the confidence which we have with him that if we ask anything according to his will, he hears us. ¹⁵And if we *know that* he hears us in regard to whatever we ask, we *know that* we have the requests which we asked *from* him.

    B   ^{16abc}If anyone sees his brother sinning a *sin* not *resulting in death*, he should ask and he will give him life, to those sinning not *resulting in death*.

    B'   ^{16de}There is a *sin resulting in death*. Not concerning that do I say that he should request. ¹⁷All unrighteousness is *sin*, but there is a *sin* not *resulting in death*.

A'   ¹⁸We *know that* everyone who has been begotten from God does not sin, but the one begotten from God, he keeps him, and the evil one does not touch him. ¹⁹We *know that* we are from God but the whole world lies in the evil one. ²⁰And we *know that the Son of God* has come and has given us understanding so that we might know the true one, and we are in the true one, in his Son

Jesus Christ. This one is the true God and *life eternal*. ²¹Little children, guard yourselves *from* the idols.[182]

At this point the audience hear a progression, via the macrochiastic parallels, from the A (1:1–10) to the A' (5:13–21) unit involving the only occurrences in 1 John of the phrase "all unrighteousness." "He will cleanse us from all unrighteousness [πάσης ἀδικίας]" (1:9) progresses to "all unrighteousness [πᾶσα ἀδικία] is sin" (5:17). In addition, when the audience hear "that you have life [ζωήν] eternal" (5:13) at the beginning of the A' unit, they hear the transitional term that links this unit to the preceding B' unit (5:3–12) that concludes by advising that "the one not having the Son of God does not have the life [ζωήν]" (5:12).

5:13–15 (A): So that You May Know that You Have Life Eternal

The audience hear the A element (5:13–15) of this chiastic unit as a chiastic pattern in itself:

a) These things I have written to you so that you may know that you *have* life eternal, you who believe in the name of the Son of God. And this is the confidence which we *have* with him (5:13–14a)

  b) that *if we ask* anything according to his will (5:14b),

    c) *he hears us* (5:14c).

      d) And if we know (5:15a)

    c') that *he hears us* (5:15b)

  b') with regard to *whatever we ask* (5:15c),

a') we know that we *have* the requests which we asked from him (5:15d).

After hearing the unparalleled d) sub-element, "and if we know" (5:15a), at the center of this chiastic sub-unit, the audience experience a pivot of parallels from the c) to the c') sub-element involving the only occurrences in this sub-unit of "he hears us." "He hears us [ἀκούει

---

182. For the establishment of 5:13–21 as a chiasm, see ch. 1.

ἡμῶν]" (5:14c) progresses to "that he hears us [ἀκούει ἡμῶν]" (5:15b). The audience then hear a progression of parallels from the b) to the b') sub-element involving the only occurrences in 1 John of "if/whatever we ask." "If [ἐάν] we ask [αἰτώμεθα] anything according to his will" (5:14b) progresses to "with regard to whatever we ask [ἐὰν αἰτώμεθα]" (5:15c). Finally, the audience hear a progression of parallels from the a) to the a') sub-element involving the only occurrences in this sub-unit of the verb "to have." "That you have [ἔχετε] life eternal" (5:13) and "the confidence which we have [ἔχομεν] with him" (5:14a) progress to "we know that we have [ἔχομεν] the requests" (5:15d).

The elder told the audience that "these things I have written to you [ταῦτα ἔγραψα ὑμῖν] concerning those deceiving you" (2:26), with the implication that the audience risk being deceived from attaining "the promise that he promised to us—life eternal [ζωὴν τὴν αἰώνιον]" (2:25). But now the elder reassures them that "these things I have written to you [ταῦτα ἔγραψα ὑμῖν] so that you may know that you have life eternal [ζωὴν ἔχετε αἰώνιον]" (5:13a). The audience, you who "may know" (εἰδῆτε) that Christ is righteous (2:29), are now told that "you may know [εἰδῆτε] that you have life eternal, you who believe in the name of the Son of God [πιστεύουσιν εἰς τὸ ὄνομα τοῦ υἱοῦ τοῦ θεοῦ]" (5:13).[183]

This implies the audience may know they have life eternal as those who have kept God's commandment "that we should believe in the name of his Son [πιστεύσωμεν τῷ ὀνόματι τοῦ υἱοῦ αὐτοῦ] Jesus Christ and we should love one another" (3:23). What the elder tells the audience here (5:13) thus resonates with the stated purpose of the Gospel of John: "These things have been written so that you may believe [ταῦτα δὲ γέγραπται ἵνα πιστεύητε] that Jesus is the Christ, the Son of God [ὁ υἱὸς τοῦ θεοῦ], and that, believing, you may have life in his name [πιστεύοντες ζωὴν ἔχητε ἐν τῷ ὀνόματι αὐτοῦ]" (John 20:31; cf. 1:12; 3:18).

"And this is the confidence [παρρησία] which we have with him [ἔχομεν πρὸς αὐτόν] that if we ask anything [ἐάν τι αἰτώμεθα] according to his will, he hears us" (1 John 5:14). This recalls that "if our heart does not condemn, we have confidence with God [παρρησίαν ἔχομεν πρὸς τὸν θεόν]" (3:21). And "whatever we ask [ὃ ἐὰν αἰτῶμεν] we receive from him" (3:22a).[184] And this is because we keep his commandments (3:22b), particularly that we believe in the name of God's Son and love one an-

---

183. "The name is tantamount to the fullness of his being, work, and word" (Yarbrough, *1–3 John*, 297).

184. See also John 14:13–14; 15:7, 16; 16:23–24.

other (3:23). That if we ask anything according to his "will" (θέλημα), as those who have "life eternal [αἰώνιον]" (5:13) resonates with "the one doing the will [θέλημα] of God remains forever [αἰῶνα]" (2:17). The elder asserted that "we are from God, the one knowing God hears us [ἀκούει ἡμῶν], whoever is not from God does not hear us [ἀκούει ἡμῶν]" (4:6). And now he assures the audience, as among those who have confidence with God, that God himself "hears us" (ἀκούει ἡμῶν), if we ask anything according to his will.[185]

The elder assured the audience "that you may know [εἰδῆτε] that you have [ἔχετε] life [ζωήν] eternal," as among those who believe in the name of the Son of God (5:13). And he further assures them that "if we know [οἴδαμεν] that he hears us in regard to whatever we ask, we know [οἴδαμεν] that we have [ἔχομεν] the requests which we asked from him" (5:15). This recalls the elder's assurance regarding the possession of life eternal for those who not only believe but also love one another (3:23), when he asserted that "we know [οἴδαμεν] that we have moved from death to life [ζωήν], because we love the brothers" (3:14a). Indeed, "the one not loving remains in death" (3:14b). And "that we have [ἔχομεν] the requests which we asked [ᾐτήκαμεν] from him [ἀπ' αὐτοῦ]" (5:15) further recalls that "whatever we ask [αἰτῶμεν] we receive from him [ἀπ' αὐτοῦ], because we keep his commandments" (3:22). "And this commandment we have [ἔχομεν] from him [ἀπ' αὐτοῦ], that the one loving God should love also his brother" (4:21).

5:16abc (B): A Sin Not Resulting in Death

The audience hear the B element (5:16abc) of this chiastic unit as a chiastic pattern in itself:

a) If anyone sees his brother *sinning* a sin *not resulting in death* (5:16a),

b) he should ask and he will give him life (5:16b),

a') to those *sinning not resulting in death* (5:16c).

After hearing the unparalleled b) sub-element, "he should ask and he will give him life" (5:16b), at the center of this chiastic sub-unit, the

---

185. See also John 9:31. "It is God's will, not the believer's whim, that is the cardinal criterion of prayer that God honors" (Yarbrough, *1–3 John*, 300).

audience experience a pivot of parallels from the a) to the a') sub-element involving the only occurrences in this sub-unit of the verb "to sin" and the expression "not resulting in death." "Sinning [ἁμαρτάνοντα] a sin not resulting in death [μὴ πρὸς θάνατον]" (5:16a) progresses to "those sinning not resulting in death [ἁμαρτάνουσιν μὴ πρὸς θάνατον]" (5:16c).

"If anyone sees his brother [ἀδελφόν] sinning a sin not resulting in death [θάνατον]" (5:16a) recalls that "we know that we have moved from death [θανάτου] to life, because we love the brothers [ἀδελφούς]. The one not loving remains in death [θανάτῳ]" (3:14). Furthermore, "everyone who hates his brother [ἀδελφόν] is a murderer, and you know that every murderer does not have life eternal in him remaining" (3:15). This suggests that "a sin not resulting in death" is one that does not involve the failure to love, which amounts to hating/murdering one's brother, a fellow believer, since such a sin deprives one of life eternal.[186]

Anyone in the audience who sees a fellow member "sinning a sin not resulting in death" (5:16a) "should ask" (αἰτήσει) and God "will give him life" (5:16b). This would be an instance of the confidence we have with God "that if we ask [αἰτώμεθα] anything according to his will, he hears us" (5:14). Indeed, "if we know that he hears us in regard to whatever we ask [αἰτώμεθα], we know that we have the requests which we asked [ᾐτήκαμεν] from him" (5:15). That God "will give him life" (δώσει αὐτῷ ζωήν) in answer to the prayerful request accords with the assertion "that life eternal God has given us [ζωὴν αἰώνιον ἔδωκεν ἡμῖν ὁ θεός], and this life [ζωή] is in his Son" (5:11). The elder then generalizes this instruction for a prayer for a "brother sinning [ἁμαρτάνοντα] a sin not resulting in death [μὴ πρὸς θάνατον]" to all "those sinning not resulting in death [ἁμαρτάνουσιν μὴ πρὸς θάνατον]" (5:16c).[187]

---

186. "Because death is separation from God, 'death' is in opposition to eternal life here, and so it refers to what happens beyond physical death" (Jobes, *1, 2, & 3 John*, 234).

187. For a similar use of the phrase πρὸς θάνατον, see John 11:4, where Jesus tells his disciples that the illness of Lazarus "is not to result in death [πρὸς θάνατον]," referring not to the physical but the eternal death of Lazarus. "Though plural, 'those who sin' stands in apposition to the prior and singular 'him'" (Schuchard, *1–3 John*, 576). "There is a sin that does not irrevocably separate the believer from God—it does not lead to spiritual death" (Yarbrough, *1–3 John*, 308).

5:16de–17 (B'): There Is a Sin Resulting in Death

At this point the audience experience a pivot of parallels from the B (5:16abc) to the B' (5:16de–17) element at the center of this chiastic unit. "A sin [ἁμαρτίαν] not resulting in death [πρὸς θάνατον]" (5:16a) and "those sinning not resulting in death [πρὸς θάνατον]" (5:16c) progress to "there is a sin resulting in death [ἁμαρτία πρὸς θάνατον]" (5:16d) and "all unrighteousness is sin [ἁμαρτία], but there is a sin [ἁμαρτία] not resulting in death [πρὸς θάνατον]" (5:17).

The audience hear the B' element (5:16de–17) of this chiastic unit as a chiastic pattern in itself:

a) there *is a sin resulting in death* (5:16d).

b) Not concerning that do I say that he should request (5:16e).

a') All unrighteousness *is sin*, but there *is a sin* not *resulting in death* (5:17).

After the unparalleled b) sub-element, "not concerning that do I say that he should request" (5:16e), at the center of this chiastic sub-unit, the audience experience a pivot of parallels from the a) to the a') sub-element involving the only occurrences in this sub-unit of "is," "sin," and "resulting in death." "There is a sin resulting in death [ἔστιν ἁμαρτία πρὸς θάνατον]" (5:16d) progresses to "all unrighteousness is sin [ἁμαρτία ἐστίν], but there is a sin [ἔστιν ἁμαρτία] not resulting in death [πρὸς θάνατον]" (5:17).

"There is a sin resulting in death [θάνατον]" (5:16d), namely, the sin of not loving one's fellow believer and thus remaining in "death [θανάτῳ]" (3:14). Not concerning that sin does the elder say that one seeing his brother sinning (5:16a) should make a prayerful request to God on his behalf (5:16e). The elder then notes that "all unrighteousness [πᾶσα ἀδικία] is sin [ἁμαρτία], but there is a sin [ἁμαρτία] not resulting in death" (5:17). This recalls that "if we confess our sins [ἁμαρτίας], he is faithful and righteous, so that he will forgive us the sins [ἁμαρτίας] and cleanse us from all unrighteousness [πάσης ἀδικίας]" (1:9). Since there is divine forgiveness for a "sin not resulting in death [οὐ πρὸς θάνατον]" (5:17), anyone seeing a fellow believer sinning a "sin not resulting in death [μὴ πρὸς θάνατον]" (5:16a) should pray for God to forgive this sin so that "those sinning not resulting in death [μὴ πρὸς θάνατον]" (5:16c) may live eternally by loving their fellow believers.[188]

5:18–21 (A'): This One Is the True God and Life Eternal

At this point the audience hear a progression of parallels from the A (5:13–15) to the A' (5:18–21) element of this chiastic unit. "You may know that [εἰδῆτε ὅτι]" (5:13), "you have life eternal [ζωὴν ἔχετε αἰώνιον]" (5:13), "the Son of God [τοῦ υἱοῦ τοῦ θεοῦ]" (5:13), "we know that [οἴδαμεν ὅτι]" (5:15 [2x]), and "from him [ἀπ' αὐτοῦ]" (5:15) occur in the A element. These progress to "we know that [οἴδαμεν ὅτι]" (5:18, 19, 20), "the Son of God [ὁ υἱὸς τοῦ θεοῦ]" (5:20), "life eternal [ζωὴ αἰώνιος]" (5:20), and "from the idols [ἀπὸ τῶν εἰδώλων]" (5:21) in the A' element.

The audience hear the A' element (5:18–21) of this chiastic unit as a chiastic pattern in itself:

a) *We know that* everyone who has been begotten from *God* does not sin, but the one begotten from *God*, he keeps him (5:18a),

    b) and the *evil one* does not touch him (5:18b).

        c) We know that we are from God (5:19a)

    b') but the whole world lies in the *evil one* (5:19b).

a') And *we know that* the Son of *God* has come and has given us understanding so that we might know the true one, and we are in the true one, in his Son Jesus Christ. This one is the true *God* and life eternal. Little children, guard yourselves from the idols (5:20–21).

After the audience hear the unparalleled c) sub-element, "we know that we are from God" (5:19a), at the center of this chiastic sub-unit, they experience a pivot of parallels from the b) to the b') sub-element involving the only occurrences in this sub-unit of the term "evil one." "The evil one [πονηρός] does not touch him" (5:18b) progresses to "the whole world lies in the evil one [πονηρῷ]" (5:19b). The audience then hear a progression of parallels from the a) sub-element (5:18a) to the a') sub-element (5:20–21) involving the initial and final occurrences in this sub-unit of "we know that" and "God." "We know that [οἴδαμεν ὅτι] everyone who has been begotten from God [θεοῦ]" and "the one begotten from God

---

188. Tan, "1 John 5:16–17," 599–609.

[θεοῦ]" (5:18a) progress first to "we know that [οἴδαμεν ὅτι] we are from God [θεοῦ]" (5:19a) and then to "we know that [οἴδαμεν ὅτι] the Son of God [θεοῦ] has come" and "this one is the true God [θεός]" (5:20).

The audience hear the a') sub-element (5:20-21) of this chiastic sub-unit as yet another chiastic pattern in itself:

(a) And we know that the Son of *God* has come and has given us understanding so that we might know the *true one*, and we *are* in the *true one* (5:20a),

(b) in his Son Jesus Christ (5:20b).

(a') This one *is* the *true God* and life eternal. Little children, guard yourselves from the idols (5:20c-21).

After the audience hear the unparalleled (b) sub-element, "in his Son Jesus Christ" (5:20b), at the center of this chiastic sub-unit, they experience a pivot of parallels from the (a) sub-element (5:20a) to the (a') sub-element (5:20c-21) involving the only occurrences in this sub-unit of "God," the verb "to be," and "true." "The Son of God [θεοῦ]," "the true one [ἀληθινόν]," and "we are [ἐσμέν] in the true one [ἀληθινῷ]" (5:20a) progress to "this one is [ἐστιν] the true God [ἀληθινὸς θεός]" (5:20c).

"We know that everyone who has been begotten from God [πᾶς ὁ γεγεννημένος ἐκ τοῦ θεοῦ] does not sin [ἁμαρτάνει], but the one begotten from God [ὁ γεννηθεὶς ἐκ τοῦ θεοῦ], he keeps him, and the evil one does not touch him" (5:18). This resonates with the assertion that "everyone who has been begotten from God [πᾶς ὁ γεγεννημένος ἐκ τοῦ θεοῦ] does not do sin [ἁμαρτίαν], because his seed remains in him, and thus he is not able to sin [ἁμαρτάνειν], because from God he has been begotten [ἐκ τοῦ θεοῦ γεγέννηται]" (3:9). The one begotten from God does not sin because God "keeps" (τηρεῖ) him, and the "evil one" (πονηρός) does not touch him, in appropriate response to the fact that "we keep [τηροῦμεν] his commandments" (3:22) that "we should believe in the name of his Son Jesus Christ and we should love one another" (3:23). Indeed, "the one keeping [τηρῶν] his commandments in him remains and he in him" (3:24; cf. 2:3-5; 5:3). And this recalls Jesus' prayer for his disciples to the Father, "that you keep [τηρήσῃς] them from the evil one [πονηροῦ]" (John 17:15).

That "the evil one [πονηρός] does not touch him" (1 John 5:18) reinforces the assurance to the young men of the audience that "you have conquered the evil one [πονηρόν]" (2:13, 14), that is, the devil, who from the beginning has been sinning (3:8a). But "the Son of God was manifested, so that he might destroy the works of the devil" (3:8b). Consequently, everyone begotten from God does not do the sin (3:9) of not loving his brother (3:10), the sin of failing to love one another (3:11).

"We know that we are from God [ἐκ τοῦ θεοῦ ἐσμεν] but the whole world lies in the evil one" (5:19).[189] This recalls that although the false prophets (4:1) and antichrists (4:3) "are from the world [ἐκ τοῦ κόσμου εἰσίν]" (4:5), "we are from God [ἐκ τοῦ θεοῦ ἐσμεν]" (4:6). Indeed, "we are children of God [τέκνα θεοῦ ἐσμεν]" (3:2) rather than children of the devil/evil one (3:10). Although "the evil one [πονηρός] does not touch" the "one begotten from God [ἐκ τοῦ θεοῦ]" (5:18), "the whole world lies in the evil one [πονηρῷ]," which likens it to Cain, who "was from the evil one [πονηροῦ] and slaughtered his brother" (3:12). Although "the whole world [ὁ κόσμος ὅλος] lies in the evil one," the audience can be encouraged that Jesus Christ "is the expiation for our sins, not for ours only but also for the whole world [ὅλου τοῦ κόσμου]" (2:2).

That "we know that the Son of God [οἴδαμεν δὲ ὅτι ὁ υἱὸς τοῦ θεοῦ] has come" (5:20a) reinforces the elder's assurance to the audience that "you may know that [εἰδῆτε ὅτι] you have life eternal [ζωὴν ἔχετε αἰώνιον], you who believe in the name of the Son of God [τοῦ υἱοῦ τοῦ θεοῦ]" (5:13).[190] The Father "has given us" (δέδωκεν ἡμῖν) love, so that we may be called children of God (3:1). And God "has given us [δέδωκεν ἡμῖν] from his Spirit" (4:13; cf. 3:24), so that we may love one another and thus have our love for God and God's love for us perfected in us (4:12). Indeed, "life eternal [ζωὴν αἰώνιον] God has given us [ἔδωκεν ἡμῖν], and this life [ζωή] is in his Son" (5:11). But the Son of God "has given us [δέδωκεν ἡμῖν] understanding so that we might know the true one, and we are in the true one, in his Son Jesus Christ. This one is the true God and life eternal [ζωὴ αἰώνιος]" (5:20abc).

In Jesus' prayer to the Father at the arrival of his hour of glorification (John 17:1) he stated: "This is eternal life [αἰώνιος ζωή], that they know [γινώσκωσιν] you, the only true God [ἀληθινὸν θεόν], and the one you sent, Jesus Christ" (17:3). And now the elder tells his audience that "the Son of God has come and has given us understanding so that we

---

189. "The choice of 'lies in' instead of 'is in' would make it possible to indicate that it is a very firm relationship indeed" (Olsson, *Letters*, 240).

190. "That he 'has come' is decisive, for only by that intervention into the situation could the victory be won; the tense of the verb (ἥκει, only here in 1 John) puts the emphasis on that coming not as a past event but as something whose effects can neither be reversed nor surpassed" (Lieu, *Commentary*, 232).

might know [γινώσκωμεν] the true one [τὸν ἀληθινόν], and we are in the true one [τῷ ἀληθινῷ], in his Son Jesus Christ. This one is the true God [ἀληθινὸς θεός] and life eternal [ζωὴ αἰώνιος]" (1 John 5:20). This recalls that "in this we know [γινώσκομεν] that we have known [ἐγνώκαμεν] him, if we keep his commandments" (2:3), which include that we should not only believe in him but we should love one another (3:23). And "we are in the true one [ἐσμὲν ἐν τῷ ἀληθινῷ]" as those who keep the word of these commandments, so that "we know [γινώσκομεν] that we are in him [ἐν αὐτῷ ἐσμεν]" (2:5).

That "we are in the true one, in his Son Jesus Christ [υἱῷ αὐτοῦ Ἰησοῦ Χριστῷ]," and that "this one is the true God and life eternal [ζωὴ αἰώνιος]" (5:20) indicates that both the Father and his Son are joined in a dynamic unity as one true God, the source of life eternal.[191] This accords with the communal fellowship of sharing "the life eternal [τὴν ζωὴν τὴν αἰώνιον]" (1:2) "that is ours with the Father and with his Son Jesus Christ [υἱοῦ αὐτοῦ Ἰησοῦ Χριστοῦ]" (1:3).[192] Indeed, "life eternal [ζωὴν αἰώνιον] God has given us, and this life [ζωή] is in his Son [υἱῷ αὐτοῦ]" (5:11). That "we might know the true one [ἀληθινόν], and we are in the true one [ἀληθινῷ], in his Son Jesus Christ," and "this one is the true [ἀληθινός] God and life eternal" (5:20) enables us to become "the true [ἀληθινοί] worshipers" who "will worship the Father in Spirit and truth" (John 4:23). And this means to have life eternal, to begin to live eternally now, by the true worship that consists of loving God as well as one another, our brother believers.[193]

For the final time the elder addresses his audience as "little children" (τεκνία) and closes his letter with the exhortation for them to "guard yourselves from the idols" (1 John 5:21), that is, from the false worship

---

191. "Although the author does not seek to explain the nature of the relationship between God and God's Son in terms of the divine being, he has no doubt that there can be no human experience of God independently of the Son" (Lieu, *Commentary*, 233).

192. "Apart from the postscript of 5:21, 1 John ends with the words 'eternal life.' This serves as a fitting bookend to an epistle whose opening two verses feature three mentions of this life" (Yarbrough, *1–3 John*, 320).

193. "It has, throughout, been at the heart of the letter that life, divine indwelling, and all the other expressions of belonging to the realm of God's light are not primarily individual but are communal (see 2:18; 4:9, 12). That is why love for one another or for the brother has been a repeated theme" (Lieu, *Commentary*, 222). On the adjective "true" (ἀληθινός): "This is the adjective favored by [the Gospel of John] to convey what is real or genuine because divine" (Sloyan, *Walking in the Truth*, 59).

that does not combine the love of God with love for one another.¹⁹⁴ This they have been enabled to do based on the previous addresses of them as "little children." Addressing them as "little children [τεκνία]," the elder exhorted them not to sin (2:1), assured them that their sins have been forgiven (2:12), so that they are to remain in Jesus Christ (2:28); they are not to let anyone deceive them (3:7), but rather to live in the truth of living eternally by loving one another (3:18). He assured them that as "little children" (τεκνία) they are from God and have conquered those in the world (4:4), namely, the false prophets (4:1) and antichrists (4:3), who would deceive them from the true worship of confessing both the Son and the Father to have life eternal (2:18–27). They are thus to guard themselves from such metaphorical "idols" of false worship.¹⁹⁵

The exhortation to "guard yourselves [ἑαυτά] from the idols" (5:21) recalls that we are not to deceive "ourselves" (ἑαυτούς) so that truth is not in us by saying that we do not have sin (1:8), thus denying our need for the blood of Jesus that cleanses us from all sin (1:7). And it recalls the exhortation to "watch yourselves [ἑαυτούς], that you do not lose what we worked for but may obtain a full reward [life eternal]" (2 John 1:8). They are thus to guard themselves from the many deceivers who "have gone out into the world, those not confessing Jesus Christ as coming in flesh. This is the deceiver and the antichrist" (1:7; cf. 1 John 2:18–27). Such deceivers are the metaphorical equivalents of the deceptive "idols" of false worship.

The audience are able to guard themselves "from [ἀπό] the idols" of false worship (5:21) because of "the message which we have heard from him [ἀπ' αὐτοῦ] and announce to you, that God is light and there is no darkness in him at all" (1:5); because "the blood of Jesus his Son cleanses us from [ἀπό] all sin" (1:7) and "from [ἀπό] all unrighteousness" (1:9); because of the anointing they have received "from [ἀπό] the holy one" (2:20), the anointing "from him [ἀπ' αὐτοῦ]" (2:27); and because "whatever we ask we receive from him [ἀπ' αὐτοῦ]" (3:22; 5:15). But the audience are able to guard themselves from the idols of false worship most especially because "this commandment we have from him [ἀπ' αὐτοῦ], that the one loving God should love also his brother" (4:21). This final and

---

194. "The term 'idol' was a standard way in Jewish, and subsequently in Christian, thought of referring to the representations of deities other than the one God whom they worshiped" (Lieu, *Commentary*, 234).

195. According to Brown (*Epistles*, 641), the deceiving false prophets and antichrists who have gone out from the community of believers (2:19) "have themselves become 'idols.'"

climactic negative warning for the audience to guard themselves from the deceptive idols of false worship thus underscores and epitomizes the concerted positive exhortation of 1–3 John for the audience to become true worshipers in Spirit and truth (John 4:23–24), to live eternally by the true worship that consists of loving God and one another.[196]

Summary of 1 John 5:13–21

The elder assured the audience "that you may know that you have life eternal," as among those who believe in the name of the Son of God (5:13). And he further assures them that "if we know that he hears us in regard to whatever we ask, we know that we have the requests which we asked from him" (5:15). This recalls the elder's assurance regarding the possession of life eternal for those who not only believe but also love one another (3:23), when he asserted that "we know that we have moved from death to life, because we love the brothers" (3:14a). Indeed, "the one not loving remains in death" (3:14b). And "that we have the requests which we asked from him" (5:15) further recalls that "whatever we ask we receive from him, because we keep his commandments" (3:22). "And this commandment we have from him, that the one loving God should love also his brother" (4:21).

"There is a sin resulting in death" (5:16d), namely, the sin of not loving one's fellow believer and thus remaining in "death" (3:14). Not concerning that sin does the elder say that one seeing his brother sinning (5:16a) should make a prayerful request to God on his behalf (5:16e). The elder then notes that "all unrighteousness is sin, but there is a sin not resulting in death" (5:17). This recalls that "if we confess our sins, he is faithful and righteous, so that he will forgive us the sins and cleanse us from all unrighteousness" (1:9). Since there is divine forgiveness for a "sin not resulting in death" (5:17), anyone seeing a fellow believer sinning a "sin not resulting in death" (5:16a) should pray for God to forgive

---

196. Merkle, "1 John 5:21," 328–40; McLean, "1 John 5:18–21," 68–78; Watson, "Keep Yourselves from Idols," 281–302; Griffith, *Keep Yourselves from Idols*; Hills, "1 John 5:21 Reconsidered," 285–310. "Positively, 1 John 5:21 clears the ground to implement the message of 1 John in a robust way. . . . Undistracted and unencumbered by the Christ-substitutes that for so long literally bedeviled God's people, believers are now freed to walk in the truth: the light, the faith, the love, and the eternal life won for them by the Son of God" (Yarbrough, *1–3 John*, 325).

this sin so that "those sinning not resulting in death" (5:16c) may live eternally by loving their fellow believers.

"We know that we are from God but the whole world lies in the evil one" (5:19). This recalls that although the false prophets (4:1) and antichrists (4:3) "are from the world" (4:5), "we are from God" (4:6). Indeed, "we are children of God" (3:2) rather than children of the devil/evil one (3:10). Although "the evil one does not touch" the "one begotten from God" (5:18), "the whole world lies in the evil one," which likens it to Cain, who "was from the evil one and slaughtered his brother" (3:12). Although "the whole world lies in the evil one," the audience can be encouraged that Jesus Christ "is the expiation for our sins, not for ours only but also for the whole world" (2:2).

That "we know that the Son of God has come" (5:20a) reinforces the elder's assurance to the audience that "you may know that you have life eternal, you who believe in the name of the Son of God" (5:13). The Father "has given us" love, so that we may be called children of God (3:1). And God "has given us from his Spirit" (4:13; cf. 3:24), so that we may love one another and thus have our love for God and God's love for us perfected in us (4:12). Indeed, "life eternal God has given us, and this life is in his Son" (5:11). But the Son of God "has given us understanding so that we might know the true one, and we are in the true one, in his Son Jesus Christ. This one is the true God and life eternal" (5:20abc).

That "we are in the true one, in his Son Jesus Christ," and that "this one is the true God and life eternal" (5:20) indicates that both the Father and his Son are joined in a dynamic unity as one true God, the source of life eternal. This accords with the communal fellowship of sharing "the life eternal" (1:2) "that is ours with the Father and with his Son Jesus Christ" (1:3). Indeed, "life eternal God has given us, and this life is in his Son" (5:11). That "we might know the true one, and we are in the true one, in his Son Jesus Christ," and "this one is the true God and life eternal" (5:20) enables us to become "the true worshipers" who "will worship the Father in Spirit and truth" (John 4:23). And this means to have life eternal, to begin to live eternally now, by the true worship that consists of loving God as well as one another.

For the final time the elder addresses his audience as "little children" and closes his letter with the exhortation for them to "guard yourselves from the idols" (1 John 5:21), that is, from the false worship that does not combine the love of God with love for one another. This they have been enabled to do based on the previous addresses of them as "little children." Addressing them as "little children," the elder exhorted them not to sin (2:1), assured them that their sins have been forgiven (2:12), so that they are to remain in Jesus Christ (2:28); they are not to let anyone deceive them (3:7), but rather to live in the truth of living eternally by loving one another (3:18). He assured them that as "little children" they are from God and have conquered those in the world (4:4), namely, the false prophets (4:1) and antichrists (4:3) who would deceive them from the true worship of confessing both the Son and the Father to have life eternal (2:18-27). They are thus to guard themselves from such metaphorical "idols" of false worship.

The audience are able to guard themselves "*from* the idols" of false worship (5:21) because of "the message which we have heard *from* him and announce to you, that God is light and there is no darkness in him at all" (1:5); because "the blood of Jesus his Son cleanses us *from* all sin" (1:7) and "*from* all unrighteousness" (1:9); because of the anointing they have received "*from* the holy one" (2:20), the anointing "*from* him" (2:27); and because "whatever we ask we receive *from* him" (3:22; 5:15). But the audience are able to guard themselves from the idols of false worship most especially because "this commandment we have *from* him, that the one loving God should love also his brother" (4:21). This final and climactic negative warning for the audience to guard themselves from the deceptive idols of false worship thus underscores and epitomizes the concerted positive exhortation of 1–3 John for the audience to become true worshipers in Spirit and truth (John 4:23–24), to live eternally by the true worship that consists of loving God and one another.

17

Summary and Conclusion

IN THIS BOOK I treated the three letters of John as a unified epistolary package. I considered 3 John as a letter recommending Demetrius as well as Gaius to the audience of 1–3 John, a sister church to the church of the implied author, "the elder" (3 John 1:1; 2 John 1:1, 13). As an introductory cover letter for 1 John, 2 John places 1 John in an epistolary context. Originally written to be orally performed as a hortatory sermon for the church led by the elder at Ephesus, 1 John, together with 2 and 3 John, was possibly delivered by Demetrius to an outlying sister church. Although the order in which they were authored was most likely 1-2-3 John, the order in which they were to be listened to by the sister church in the context of a communal worship service was most likely 3-2-1 John. The close affinities between the letters and the Gospel of John suggest that the elder authored all four documents. At any rate, the elder seems to presuppose that most of the members of the audience of 1–3 John were familiar with the content in the Gospel of John, especially that true worshipers will worship the Father in Spirit and truth (4:23–24).

And in this book I proposed two new contributions to the study of 1–3 John. First, I presented new comprehensive chiastic structures for each of the three letters of John based on concrete linguistic evidence in the text. These chiastic structures served as the guide for my audience-oriented exegesis of these letters. Secondly, I treated these letters from the point of view of their worship context and themes. Not only were 1–3 John intended to be performed orally as part of liturgical worship, but together these three letters exhort their audience to a distinctive ethical worship. In accord with the subtitle of this book, I proposed that the three letters of John are concerned with giving their audience an experience of living eternally by the worship that consists of loving God and one another.

Although 3 John is sent by the venerable "elder," the leader of the broader Johannine community, to a certain Gaius (1:1), it is not just a personal letter but has a communal dimension. It was meant to be heard in a context of worship by a local church within the Johannine network, a church in which Gaius is a leading member. The chiastic unit (1:1–8) that comprises the first part of 3 John climaxes with an exhortation that the elder, Gaius, and the audience that is his local church, may become coworkers to "the truth" by supporting itinerant believing brothers with hospitality as part of practicing the truth of loving one another (1:8).

The chiastic unit (1:9–15) that comprises the second half of 3 John begins with the elder's announcement that "I have written something to the church" (1:9a), most likely a reference to 1–2 John, which 3 John as a preliminary cover letter is meant to introduce. Although a certain Diotrephes, who refuses to acknowledge the elder and the brothers, may prove to be a threat to a favorable hearing of 1–2 John by the church of Gaius (1:9b–10), the elder recommends to Gaius the well-attested Demetrius (1:12), suggesting that he can assist Gaius in implementing a favorable hearing of 1–2 John by the audience of 3 John. The closing greeting of "peace," a benefit of the risen, eternal life of Jesus, from "friends" and to "friends" as members of the wider Johannine community (1:15) reminds the audience of 3 John that they are the "friends" of Jesus as those who do what he commanded, namely, to love one another as he loved them. This new commandment of love is central to the truth by which they may worship God in Spirit and truth (John 4:23–24), loving God and one another for the peace of already beginning to live eternally.

In 2 John the elder addresses the audience as "an elect lady and her children" (1:1). He prays that the divine benefits of the "grace, mercy, and peace" that accompany eternal life will be with us as those who practice the truth of loving one another (1:3–5). As those who remain in the teaching of the Christ, the teaching that Christ came from God in flesh (1:7) and taught us God's commandment to love one another (1:4–5), the audience may have these divine benefits of eternal life from the Father and the Son (1:9).

As coworkers to the truth of loving one another to live eternally, the elder, Gaius, and the audience, as members of the Johannine community, ought to support with hospitable love those believing brothers who have gone out on behalf of the divine name (3 John 1:7–8). But the many deceivers who have gone out into the world the audience are not to receive with hospitable love, because they do not confess Jesus Christ as coming from God in flesh and they reject the teaching of the Christ to love one another (2 John 1:7–11). Before the elder comes to the audience to speak with them further in person (3 John 1:13–14; 2 John 1:12), they are to listen to 1 John as a substitute for his personal presence. As fellow "children" not only of elect sister churches (2 John 1:1, 13) but of God (John 1:12), the audience, as members of the Johannine community, are to live eternally as fellow "friends" (3 John 1:15) of Jesus who practice the true worship and love of God, the worship in Spirit and truth (John 4:23–24), by loving one another (2 John 1:3–5).

Summaries of each of the thirteen microchiastic units comprising 1 John have been provided above at the conclusion of each of chapters 4 through 16. And so here I present a final summary overview of the dynamics at work for the audience as they experience the macrochiastic structure of 1 John:

> A: 1:1–10: He Will Cleanse Us from *All Unrighteousness*
>
>> B: 2:1–14: If *We Keep His Commandments* the Love of God Has Been Perfected
>>
>>> C: 2:15–17: Do Not Love the Things *in the World*
>>>
>>>> D: 2:18–27: The One Confessing *the Son* Also Has the Father
>>>>
>>>>> E: 2:28–3:6: *You Know* Whoever Does Righteousness Has Been Begotten from Him
>>>>>
>>>>>> F: 3:7–12: *We Should Love One Another*
>>>>>>
>>>>>>> G: 3:13–17: We Ought to Lay Down Our Lives for the Brothers
>>>>>>
>>>>>> F': 3:18–24: We Should Believe and *We Should Love One Another*
>>>>>
>>>>> E': 4:1–6: In This *You Know* the Spirit of God
>>>>
>>>> D': 4:7–12: God Has Sent *His Son* so that We Might Live through Him

C': 4:13–5:2: Just as That One Is so We Are *in This World*

B': 5:3–12: This Is *the Love of God* that *We Keep His Commandments*

A': 5:13:21: *All Unrighteousness* Is Sin

In the G unit (3:13–17) at the center of the macrochiastic structure the elder asserts that we know we have moved from death to life eternal, because we love the brothers (3:14). He then indicates the Christ-like way in which we are to love the brothers, our fellow believers. We ourselves ought for the brothers to lay down our lives, just as Jesus Christ for us laid down his life (3:16). This does not necessarily involve a literal laying down of our lives. We may metaphorically "lay down our lives" by using whatever livelihood we have in the world to help a brother in need, so that the love of God—both God's love for us and our love for God—remains in us (3:17). Jesus' laying down his life for us, an act of sacrificial worship, is not only the model but the means for our own worship. As a result of his sacrificial death, the blood of Jesus cleanses us from all sin (1:9), so that we may live eternally by the worship that consists of loving God and one another.

Having heard in the central G unit (3:13–17) the extent to which we are to love one another by laying down our lives for the brothers (3:16), the audience experience a pivot of chiastic parallels when they hear the F' unit (3:18–24). The exhortation that "we should love one another" (3:11) in the F unit (3:7–12) progresses to the exhortation that "we should believe in the name of his Son Jesus Christ and we should love one another" (3:23). This recalls the stated purpose of the Gospel of John, namely, "that you may believe that Jesus is the Christ, the Son of God, and that, believing, you may have life in his name" (John 20:31). First John emphasizes that not only should we believe in the name of Jesus Christ, but we should also love one another, in order to live eternally.

When the audience hear the E' unit (4:1–6), they hear a progression of chiastic parallels from the E unit (2:28–3:6) involving what they can be assured of knowing. In the E unit the audience are told that "you know" that everyone who does the righteousness of loving his brother (cf. 3:10) has been begotten (2:29) to be among the children of God (3:1–2), those who share the fellowship of divine life eternal with the Father and the Son (1:1–3). In the E' unit the audience are told that "you know" the Spirit of God (4:2), which is the Spirit of truth (4:6), that enables us to become true worshipers who worship in Spirit and truth (John 4:23–24) by loving God and one another to live eternally.

When the audience hear the D' unit (4:7–12), they hear a progression of chiastic parallels from the D unit (2:18–27) involving Jesus Christ as "the Son" of God. In the D unit the audience are told that the antichrist is the one who denies the Father and "the Son" (2:22), and everyone who denies "the Son" does not have the Father, but the one confessing "the Son" also has the Father (2:23). If what the audience heard from the beginning remains in them—that we should love one another—they will remain in the Son and in the Father (2:24), and thus have the promised life eternal (2:25). In the D' unit they are exhorted to love one another (4:7) because God is love (4:8), and the love of God was manifested in his sending "his Son" into the world, so that we might live eternally through him (4:9). Indeed God loved us and sent "his Son" as expiation for our sins (4:10). If God so loved us, we ought to love one another (4:11), so that the love of God—God's love for us and our love for God—is perfected in us (4:12), as we love God and one another to live eternally.

When the audience hear the C' unit (4:13–5:2), they hear a progression of chiastic parallels from the C unit (2:15–17) involving what is "in the world." In the C unit they are exhorted not to love the world or the things "in the world" (2:15), because all that is "in the world" is not from the Father but is from the world (2:16). Although the world is passing away, the one doing the will of God that we should love one another remains forever, living eternally (2:17). In the C' unit they are told that just as Jesus Christ is, so we ourselves are "in this world" (4:17), the world into which God sent the Son as savior of the world (4:14). The commandment that we have from him as savior of the world is "that the one loving God should love also his brother" (4:21), and thus practice the worship that consists of loving God as well as one another in order to live eternally.

When the audience hear the B' unit (5:3–12), they hear a progression of chiastic parallels from the B unit (2:1–14) involving "the love of God" and that "we keep his commandments." In the B unit they are told that if "we keep his commandments" (2:3), especially that we should love one another, then "the love of God"—God's love for us and our love for God—has been perfected in us (2:5). In the B' unit they are told that "the love of God" is that "we keep his commandments" (5:3), in accord with the testimony "that life eternal God has given us, and this life is in his Son" (5:11). This is the testimony of the Spirit of truth (5:6), which enables us to live eternally by the worship that consists of loving God and one another, and thus become true worshipers who worship in Spirit and truth (John 4:23–24).

When the audience hear the A' unit (5:13–21), they hear a progression of chiastic parallels from the A unit (1:1–10) involving "all unrighteousness." In the A unit they are told that if we confess our sins, Jesus Christ will forgive us the sins and cleanse us from "all unrighteousness" (1:9), so that we may share the fellowship of divine life eternal (1:2) "that is ours with the Father and with his Son Jesus Christ" (1:3). In the A' unit they are told that, although "all unrighteousness" is sin, there is a sin not resulting in "death" (5:17), that is, the loss of life eternal by the failure to love one another. They should pray for a brother "sinning a sin not resulting in death" and the Son of God, Jesus Christ, will give him life (5:16), enabling him to live eternally by the worship that consists of loving God and one another, since his Son Jesus Christ "is the true God and life eternal" (5:20).

Finally, the elder exhorts the audience to guard themselves "from the idols" (5:21), that is, from all forms of false worship—any worship that fails to keep the commandment "that we should believe in the name of his Son Jesus Christ and we should love one another" (3:23), in order to have life eternal (John 20:31). Jesus announced that "true worshipers will worship the Father in Spirit and truth" (4:23). Accordingly, the elder in 1–3 John has exhorted his audience, who have been given the Spirit of truth (1 John 3:24; 4:6, 13; 5:6), to continue to live eternally by the true worship that consists of loving God and one another.

Bibliography

Akin, Daniel L. *1, 2, 3 John*. NAC 38. Nashville: B. & H., 2001.
Balz, Horst. "ἁγνίζω." *EDNT* 1.22–23
———, and Gerhard Schneider, eds. *EDNT*. 3 vols. Grand Rapids: Eerdmans, 1990-1993.
Bauer, Walter, Frederick W. Danker, William F. Arndt, and F. Wilbur Gingrich. *Greek-English Lexicon of the New Testament and Other Early Christian Literature*. 3rd ed. Chicago: University of Chicago Press, 2000.
Beale, Gregory K. "The Old Testament Background of the 'Last Hour' in 1 John 2,18." *Bib* 92 (2011) 231–54.
Bigalke, Ron J. "First John Structure Resolved: Exegetical Analysis, Part 2." *HTS Teologiese Studies* 69 (2013) 1–7. http://dx.doi.org/10.4102/hts.v691.2053.
———. "Unravelling the Structure of First John: Exegetical Analysis, Part 1." *HTS Teologiese Studies* 69 (2013) 1–10. http://dx.doi.org/10.4102/hts.v691.2023.
Blass, Friedrich, Albert Debrunner, and Robert W. Funk. *A Greek Grammar of the New Testament and Other Early Christian Literature*. Chicago: University of Chicago Press, 1961.
Brickle, Jeffrey E. *Aural Design and Coherence in the Prologue of First John*. LNTS 465. London: T. & T. Clark, 2012.
Brown, Raymond E. *The Epistles of John: Translated with Introduction, Notes, and Commentary*. AB 30. Garden City, NY: Doubleday, 1982.
Byron, J. "Slaughter, Fratricide and Sacrilege: Cain and Abel Traditions in 1 John 3." *Bib* 88 (2007) 526–35.
Campbell, B. L. "Honor, Hospitality and Haughtiness: The Contention for Leadership in 3 John." *EvQ* 77 (2005) 321–41.
Carnazzo, Sebastian A. *Seeing Blood and Water: A Narrative-Critical Study of John 19:34*. Eugene, OR: Pickwick, 2012.
Carson, D. A. "God Is Love." *BSac* 156 (1999) 131–42.
Clark, D. J. "Discourse Structure in 3 John." *BT* 57 (2006) 109–15.
Combs, W. W. "The Meaning of Fellowship in 1 John." *Detroit Baptist Seminary Journal* 13 (2008) 3–16.
Connell, M. F. "On 'Chrism' and 'Anti-Christs' in 1 John 2:18–27: A Hypothesis." *Worship* 83 (2009) 212–34.

Culy, Martin M. *1, 2, 3 John: A Handbook on the Greek Text*. Waco, TX: Baylor University Press, 2004.

De Waal Dryden, J. "The Sense of σπέρμα in 1 John 3:9: In Light of Lexical Evidence." *Filología Neotestamentaria* 11 (1998) 85–100.

Do, J. T. "Does περὶ ὅλου τοῦ κόσμου Imply 'the Sins of the Whole World' in 1 John 2,2?" *Bib* 94 (2013) 415–35.

———. "'That You May Not Sin.' On the Reading of 1 John 2,1b." *ZNW* 102 (2011) 77–95.

Edwards, Ruth B. *The Johannine Epistles*. New Testament Guides. Sheffield, UK: Sheffield Academic, 1996.

Frick, P. "Johannine Soteriology and Aristotelian Philosophy. A Hermeneutical Suggestion on Reading John 3:16 and 1 John 4:9." *Bib* 88 (2007) 415–21.

Glasscock, E. "Forgiveness and Cleansing according to 1 John 1:9." *BSac* 166 (2009) 217–31.

Griffith, Terry. *Keep Yourselves from Idols: A New Look at 1 John*. JSNTSup 233. London: Sheffield Academic, 2002.

Heckel, T. K. "Die Historisierung der johanneischen Theologie im Ersten Johannesbrief." *NTS* 50 (2004) 425–43.

Heil, John Paul. *Blood and Water: The Death and Resurrection of Jesus in John 18–21*. CBQMS 27. Washington: Catholic Biblical Association, 1995.

———. *The Book of Revelation: Worship for Life in the Spirit of Prophecy*. Eugene, OR: Cascade, 2014.

———. "The Chiastic Structure and Meaning of Paul's Letter to Philemon." *Bib* 82 (2001) 178–206.

———. *Colossians: Encouragement to Walk in All Wisdom as Holy Ones in Christ*. SBLECL 4. Atlanta: Society of Biblical Literature, 2010.

———. *Ephesians: Empowerment to Walk in Love for the Unity of All in Christ*. Studies in Biblical Literature 13. Atlanta: Society of Biblical Literature, 2007.

———. *Hebrews: Chiastic Structures and Audience Response*. CBQMS 46. Washington: Catholic Biblical Association, 2010.

———. *The Letter of James: Worship to Live By*. Eugene, OR: Cascade, 2012.

———. *The Letters of Paul as Rituals of Worship*. Eugene, OR: Cascade, 2011.

———. *1 Peter, 2 Peter, and Jude: Worship Matters*. Eugene, OR: Cascade, 2013.

———. *Philippians: Let Us Rejoice in Being Conformed to Christ*. SBLECL 3. Atlanta: Society of Biblical Literature, 2010.

———. *Worship in the Letter to the Hebrews*. Eugene, OR: Cascade, 2011.

Hengel, Martin. *The Johannine Question*. London: SCM, 1990.

Hills, Julian. "'Little Children, Keep Yourselves from Idols': 1 John 5:21 Reconsidered." *CBQ* 51 (1989) 285–310.

Hofius, Otfried. "ὁμολογέω." *EDNT* 2.514–17.

Horsley, Richard A. *Text and Tradition in Performance and Writing*. Eugene, OR: Cascade, 2013.

Houlden, J. L. *A Commentary on the Johannine Epistles*. BNTC. New York: Harper & Row, 1973.

Jensen, Matthew D. *Affirming the Resurrection of the Incarnate Christ: A Reading of 1 John*. SNTSMS 153. Cambridge: Cambridge University Press, 2012.

———. "The Structure and Argument of 1 John." *JSNT* 35 (2012) 54–73.

Jobes, Karen H. *1, 2, & 3 John*. ZECNT 19. Grand Rapids: Zondervan, 2014.

Johnson, Luke Timothy. *The Writings of the New Testament.* 3rd ed. Minneapolis: Fortress, 2010.
Jung, C. W. "Main Thrust of the Sentence(s) in 1 John 3:19–20: Encouragement or Warning?" *Neot* 41 (2007) 97–111.
Keener, Craig S. "Transformation through Divine Vision in 1 John 3:2–6." *Faith & Mission* 23 (2005) 13–22.
Köstenberger, Andreas J. *A Theology of John's Gospel and Letters.* Grand Rapids: Zondervan, 2009.
Kruse, Colin G. *The Letters of John.* The Pillar New Testament Commentary. Grand Rapids: Eerdmans, 2000.
Lee, Dorothy. "Friendship, Love and Abiding in the Gospel of John." In *Transcending Boundaries: Contemporary Readings of the New Testament*, edited by Rekha M. Chennattu and Mary L. Coloe, 57–74. Biblioteca di Scienze Religiose 187. Rome: Libreria Ateneo Salesiano, 2005.
Lieu, Judith M. *I, II, & III John: A Commentary.* NTL. Louisville: Westminster John Knox, 2008.
Lorencin, I. "Hospitality versus Patronage: An Investigation of Social Dynamics in the Third Epistle of John." *AUSS* 46 (2008) 165–74.
Marshall, I. Howard. *The Epistles of John.* NICNT. Grand Rapids: Eerdmans, 1978.
Marulli, L. "A Letter of Recommendation? A Closer Look at Third John's 'Rhetorical' Argumentation." *Bib* 90 (2009) 203–23.
McLean, J. A. "An Exegetical Study of 1 John 5:18–21." *BSac* 169 (2012) 68–78.
Merkle, Benjamin L. "What Is the Meaning of 'Idols' in 1 John 5:21?" *BSac* 169 (2012) 328–40.
Michaels, J. Ramsey. "By Water and Blood: Sin and Purification in John and First John." In *Dimensions of Baptism: Biblical and Theological Studies*, edited by Stanley E. Porter and Anthony R. Cross, 149–62. London: Sheffield Academic, 2002.
Mitchell, Margaret M. "'Diotrephes Does Not Receive Us': The Lexicographical and Social Context of 3 John 9–10." *JBL* 117 (1998) 299–320.
Moberly, R. W. L. "'Test the Spirits': God, Love, and Critical Discernment in 1 John 4." In *The Holy Spirit and Christian Origins: Essays in Honor of James D. G. Dunn*, edited by Graham Stanton, Bruce Longenecker, and Stephen Barton, 296–307. Grand Rapids: Eerdmans, 2004.
Moloney, Francis J. *Love in the Gospel of John: An Exegetical, Theological, and Literary Study.* Grand Rapids: Baker, 2013.
Morgan-Wynne, John. *The Cross in the Johannine Writings.* Eugene, OR: Pickwick, 2011.
Morgen, Michèle. "Le (Fils) *monogène* dans les écrits johanniques: Évolution des traditions et elaboration rédactionnelle." *NTS* 53 (2007) 165–83.
———. "Le prologue de la première épître de Jean: sa structure et sa visée." *RevScRel* 79 (2005) 55–75.
Neufeld, Dietmar. *Reconceiving Texts as Speech Acts: An Analysis of 1 John.* BIS 7. Leiden: Brill, 1994.
Olsson, Birger. *A Commentary on the Letters of John: An Intra-Jewish Approach.* Translated by Richard J. Erickson. Eugene, OR: Pickwick, 2013.
Painter, John. *1, 2, and 3 John.* SP 18. Collegeville, MN: Liturgical, 2002.
Roitto, Rikard. "Practices of Confession, Intercession, and Forgiveness in 1 John 1.9; 5.16." *NTS* 58 (2012) 235–53.

Schnackenburg, Rudolf. *The Johannine Epistles: Introduction and Commentary*. New York: Crossroad, 1992.

Schnelle, Udo. *Die Johannesbriefe*. THKNT 17. Leipzig: Evangelische Verlagsanstalt, 2010.

Schuchard, Bruce G. *1-3 John*. Concordia Commentary. St. Louis: Concordia, 2012.

Shelfer, L. "The Legal Precision of the Term 'παράκλητος.'" *JSNT* 32 (2009) 131-50.

Sloyan, Gerard S. *Walking in the Truth: Perseverers and Deserters: The First, Second, and Third Letters of John*. Valley Forge, PA: Trinity, 1995.

Smalley, Stephen S. *1, 2, 3 John*. WBC 51 (Revised Edition). Nashville: Nelson, 2007.

Tan, Randall K. J. "Should We Pray for Straying Brethren? John's Confidence in 1 John 5:16-17." *JETS* 45 (2002) 599-609.

Thatcher, Thomas. "'Water and Blood' in AntiChrist Christianity (1 John 5:6)." *Stone-Campbell Journal* 4 (2001) 235-48.

Thettayil, Benny. *In Spirit and Truth: An Exegetical Study of John 4:19-26 and a Theological Investigation of the Replacement Theme in the Fourth Gospel*. CBET 46. Leuven: Peeters, 2007.

Thomas, John Christopher. "The Literary Structure of 1 John." *NovT* 40 (1998) 369-81.

Trebilco, Paul. *The Early Christians in Ephesus from Paul to Ignatius*. Grand Rapids: Eerdmans, 2007.

———. *Self-Designations and Group Identity in the New Testament*. Cambridge: Cambridge University Press, 2012.

Voelz, James W. *Fundamental Greek Grammar*. 3rd ed. St. Louis: Concordia, 2007.

Von Wahlde, Urban C. *The Gospel and Letters of John: Volume 3: Commentary on the Three Johannine Letters*. Eerdmans Critical Commentary. Grand Rapids: Eerdmans, 2010.

Wallace, Daniel B. *Greek Grammar Beyond the Basics: An Exegetical Syntax of the New Testament*. Grand Rapids: Zondervan, 1996.

Watson, Duane F. "'Keep Yourselves from Idols': A Socio-Rhetorical Analysis of the *Exordium* and *Peroratio* of 1 John." In *Fabrics of Discourse: Essays in Honor of Vernon K. Robbins*, edited by David B. Gowler et al, 281-302. Harrisburg, PA: Trinity Press International, 2003.

Wendland, E. R. "What Is Truth? Semantic Density and the Language of the Johannine Epistles (with Special Reference to 2 John)." *Neot* 24 (1990) 301-33.

Witherington, Ben. *Letters and Homilies for Hellenized Christians. Volume I: A Socio-Rhetorical Commentary on Titus, 1-2 Timothy and 1-3 John*. Downers Grove, IL: InterVarsity, 2006.

Yarbrough, Robert W. *1-3 John*. BECNT. Grand Rapids: Baker, 2008.

Scripture Index

Old Testament

Genesis

4:8   121, 122

Isaiah

6:10   62

New Testament

John

1:1-4	60	1:31	176n171
1:1-2	63, 74, 85	1:33	176n171
1:1	61, 66	2:7	176n171
1:2-4	84	2:9	176n171
1:3-4	61, 74	3:11	62, 63
1:4	28, 34, 39, 48, 56, 63, 77, 81, 90, 107	3:12	62
		3:15-16	61
1:5	81	3:15	77
1:9	81	3:16-17	84n84
1:10	108	3:16	28, 40, 56, 76, 87, 152, 153, 154, 156, 160, 168
1:12-13	48		
1:12	34, 39, 56, 107, 108, 112, 188, 202	3:17	152, 153, 156, 160, 168
1:13	34, 39, 107		
1:14	28, 51, 52, 62, 152	3:18	152, 188
1:17	28, 48, 60	3:21	66
1:18	40, 52, 66, 84, 152, 154, 156	3:23	176n171
		3:35	49
1:26	176n171	3:36	49, 56, 61
1:29	68, 75	4:7-15	176n171

John (cont.)

4:14	49	8:40	117, 118
4:23-24	28, 33, 36, 43, 44, 51, 56, 65, 68, 70, 76, 87, 103, 104, 109, 112, 113, 137, 138, 147, 148, 160, 168, 171, 178, 182, 184, 185, 197, 199, 200, 201, 202, 204, 205	8:41	118
		8:42	52
		8:44	60n56, 69, 85, 117, 118, 125, 128
		8:47	39
		8:51-52	49
		8:55	69, 75
		9:5	66, 77, 81
4:23	195, 198, 205	10:3	42
4:34	92	10:18	50
4:36	65	10:28	49, 62
4:41	61	11:25-26	62
4:42	61, 160, 168	11:25	56, 61
5:7	176n171	11:26	49
5:24	56, 61, 125	11:52	34
5:26	64	12:34	92
5:30	92	12:35	77, 82, 88
5:36	181	12:39	62, 82, 88
5:37	181	12:40	62, 82, 88
5:38	86, 88	12:46	66, 81
6:27	51	12:48-50	61
6:38	92	12:49	50, 136, 137, 138
6:40	56, 61	12:50	28, 40, 75, 78, 87, 92, 136, 137, 138, 160, 168, 171
6:46	40		
6:47	56, 61		
6:51	49	13:1	74
6:53-56	176n171	13:5	176n171
6:54	180, 184	13:14	36, 78, 127, 129
6:58	49	13:18	48n40
6:63	180, 184	13:33	73
6:68	75, 161, 169	13:34	28, 29, 33, 36, 39, 40, 48, 50, 61, 75, 78, 87, 92, 127, 129, 136, 138, 160, 168, 171
6:69	75, 161, 169		
6:70	48n40		
7:16	52		
7:17	39, 52	14:6	28, 48, 60, 61, 68, 81, 92
7:18	69		
7:37-38	176n171	14:7	85, 86, 88
7:38	180, 185	14:9	40, 52
7:39	180, 185	14:12	74
8:12	66, 77, 81	14:13-14	188n184
8:21	68	14:13	134
8:24	68	14:14	134
8:29	134, 137	14:15	75
8:32	48	14:16	28, 49, 74, 137, 138, 160, 168
8:35	92		

14:17	28, 29, 33, 48, 49, 68, 103, 137, 138, 146, 148, 168, 171, 177, 184	16:14-15	65
		16:17	74
		16:23-24	188n184
		16:23	65, 134
14:21	75	16:24	55, 65, 133
14:23	76	16:25	63
14:26	28, 74, 97, 103	16:26	134
14:28	74	16:28	74
15:4-7	78	16:33	85, 176, 183
		17:1	194
15:4	78, 136	17:2	62
15:5	136	17:3	28, 77, 86, 88, 194
15:7	134, 188n184	17:11-12	35, 84, 84n84
15:9	78, 163	17:13	55, 65
15:10	55, 65, 76, 78, 163	17:14	91
15:11	55, 65	17:15	85, 193
15:12-13	29	17:16	91
15:12	28, 29, 33, 39, 40, 48, 50, 55, 56, 61, 65, 76, 77, 78, 92, 126	17:23	77
		17:26	49
		19:34	176, 180, 184, 185
15:13-15	43	19:35	42
15:13	28, 33, 50, 126	20:17	74
15:14	56	20:19	42, 49
15:16	48n40, 134, 188n184	20:21	42, 49
15:17	29, 33, 39, 40, 48, 78	20:22	97, 137, 138
15:19	48n40	20:23	69, 84
15:21	84n84	20:25	62
15:26	28, 29, 33, 74, 137, 138, 146, 148, 168, 171, 177, 178, 184	20:26	42, 49
		20:27	62, 69
		20:28	66
16:3	86, 88	20:29	40
16:7	28, 74	20:31	35, 56, 61, 62, 64, 136, 138, 188, 203, 205
16:10	74		
16:13	28, 29, 33, 48, 65, 137, 138, 147, 148, 160, 168, 171, 177, 184	21:1	62
		21:14	62
		21:24	42

1 John

1:1-10	7, 9, 23, 25, 57-70, 74, 187, 202, 205	1:1	7, 57, 58, 59, 60, 60n56, 61, 62, 63, 65, 67, 69, 84, 87, 88, 91, 112, 113, 160, 168
1:1-5	8, 58-65, 67		
1:1-3	58, 59, 203		
1:1-2	27, 29, 59, 70, 146, 148, 156		

1 John (cont.)

1:2	7, 57, 58, 59, 62, 63, 74, 97, 102, 107, 111, 112, 113, 125, 128, 144, 147, 151, 152, 160, 168, 177, 182, 184, 195, 198, 205		111, 112, 113, 116, 120, 122, 131, 133, 137, 143, 196, 199
		2:2-3	73
		2:2	8, 71, 73, 75, 76, 82, 87, 111, 153, 156, 163, 169, 194, 198
1:3	7, 28, 57, 58, 59, 63, 64, 65, 66, 67, 70, 97, 98, 99, 102, 103, 104, 112, 113, 117, 177, 184, 195, 198, 205	2:3-5	193
		2:3-4	27
		2:3	8, 9, 23, 71, 72, 73, 75, 77, 82, 86, 87, 96, 97, 108, 112, 113, 126, 132, 134, 173, 175, 183, 195, 204
1:4-5	58, 59		
1:4	7, 57, 64, 70, 73		
1:5-6	8, 66, 70		
1:5	7, 8, 57, 59, 65, 66, 67, 120, 122, 196, 199	2:4-5	72, 73, 86, 88
		2:4	8, 9, 29, 71, 72, 73, 74, 76, 79, 81, 82, 84, 87, 98, 104, 112, 113, 131, 134, 136, 166, 175, 178, 183, 184
1:6	7, 8, 29, 57, 66, 67, 76, 77, 131, 178, 184		
1:7-10	8, 67-69, 70		
1:7-9	67, 68	2:5	8, 9, 23, 71, 73, 74, 76, 77, 78, 79, 82, 86, 87, 88, 90, 96, 108, 112, 126, 128, 129, 132, 136, 137, 138, 155, 156, 162, 169, 173, 174, 175, 182, 183, 195, 204
1:7	7, 8, 58, 66-67, 68, 69, 70, 75, 77, 111, 176, 176n171, 181, 184, 185, 196, 199		
1:8	7, 29, 58, 68, 69, 75, 76, 84, 109, 178, 184, 196		
1:9-10	67, 68	2:6	8, 9, 71, 77-78, 79, 81, 82, 87, 97, 107, 109, 111, 112, 113, 116, 126, 129, 136, 138, 163
1:9	7, 23, 58, 67, 68, 69, 75, 84, 107, 110, 111, 116, 120, 122, 187, 191, 196, 197, 199, 203, 205		
		2:7-8	27, 109, 111, 113, 117, 126, 129, 136, 138
1:10	7, 9, 58, 67, 68, 69, 74, 76, 86, 88, 111, 113, 181, 185	2:7	8, 9, 71, 78-79, 85, 86, 88, 96, 108, 113, 133, 137, 141, 150, 160, 169
2:1-14	8-9, 10, 23, 25, 71-88, 90, 173, 202, 204	2:8-11	9, 79-82
2:1-5	9, 72-77, 82	2:8-9	80
2:1-3	72, 73	2:8	8, 9, 71-72, 79, 81, 82, 85, 87, 88, 91, 96, 103, 144, 147
2:1-2	84, 126		
2:1	8, 9, 71, 73, 75, 78, 84, 85, 87, 97, 98, 107,		

SCRIPTURE INDEX

2:9	8-9, 72, 80, 81, 87, 88, 125, 128, 166, 170	2:20	11, 93, 95, 97, 98, 99, 103, 104, 196, 199
2:10-11	80	2:21	11, 12, 29, 93, 95, 96, 98, 99, 100, 103, 104, 107, 111, 132, 178, 184
2:10	9, 29, 72, 80, 81, 86, 87, 90, 92, 97, 120, 122, 125, 166, 170		
2:11	9, 72, 79, 81, 82, 87, 88, 91, 98, 125, 128	2:22-23	12, 99
		2:22	11, 12, 24, 93, 98, 99, 104, 147, 150, 166, 204
2:12-14	9, 82-87		
2:12-13	82, 83		
2:12	9, 72, 82, 83, 84, 84n84, 85, 107, 111, 112, 116, 131, 143, 196, 199	2:23	11, 24, 93, 99, 104, 150, 160, 168-69, 204
		2:24-27	11, 99-103
		2:24	11, 93, 99, 100-101, 102, 107, 112, 117, 121, 144, 147, 160, 169, 204
2:13	9, 72, 82, 83, 84, 85, 86, 88, 108, 143, 176, 183, 193		
2:14	9, 10, 72, 82, 83, 85, 86, 88, 90, 96, 98, 104, 118, 121, 143, 144, 147, 176, 183, 193	2:25	11, 29, 93-94, 100, 102, 103, 104, 125, 128, 144, 146, 147, 148, 152, 156, 160, 169, 178, 182, 184, 188, 204
2:15-17	10, 11, 23, 25, 89-92, 94, 158, 202, 204		
2:15-16	10, 89-91	2:26-27	100, 101
2:15	10, 23, 89, 90, 91, 92, 108, 112, 125, 128, 129, 142, 143, 158, 163, 169, 204	2:26	11, 94, 99-100, 102, 116, 188
		2:27	11, 12, 94, 99, 100, 101, 102, 103, 104, 107, 111, 112, 113, 117, 121, 127, 129, 144, 147, 196, 199
2:16-17	10, 91-92		
2:16	10, 23, 89, 90, 91, 92, 127, 129, 142, 143, 146, 158, 163, 169, 204		
		2:28–3:6	12, 13, 14, 24, 25, 105-13, 115, 140, 202, 203
2:17	10, 11, 89, 91, 92, 94, 96, 97, 107, 110, 142, 189, 204	2:28–3:2	13, 106-8, 109
		2:28-29	106
		2:28	12, 13, 105, 107, 108, 109, 111, 112, 113, 116, 131, 133, 137, 143, 162, 196, 199
2:18-27	10-11, 13, 24, 25, 93-104, 107, 149, 196, 199, 202, 204		
2:18-21	11, 94-98, 99	2:29	12, 13, 24, 105, 107, 108, 109, 110, 111, 112, 113, 116, 117, 120, 122, 140, 151, 155, 175, 183, 188, 203
2:18	10-11, 93, 94, 96, 97, 98, 99, 104, 142, 143, 147		
2:19-21	94		
2:19	11, 93, 94, 95, 96, 97, 99, 102, 107, 112, 142, 162, 169	3:1-2	116, 203

1 John (cont.)

3:1	12, 13, 105, 106, 108, 109, 110, 112, 113, 124-25, 128, 133, 142, 143, 146, 148, 151, 155, 175, 183, 194, 198		141, 143, 151, 155, 166, 167, 175, 183, 194, 198, 203
		3:11-12	119
		3:11	13, 14, 24, 114, 119, 120, 121, 122, 125, 126, 129, 131, 136, 137, 138, 144, 146, 147, 148, 151, 155, 156, 162, 166, 169, 174, 175, 178, 182, 183, 184, 194, 203
3:2	12, 13, 105, 106, 107, 108, 109, 110, 112, 113, 116, 118, 125, 133, 137, 142, 143, 150, 194, 198		
3:3	12, 13, 105, 108-9, 110, 111, 116, 126, 163	3:12	13-14, 15, 114, 119, 120-21, 122, 124, 125, 128, 194, 198
3:4-6	13, 109-12		
3:4	12, 13, 14, 105, 110, 111, 112, 113, 115, 117	3:13-17	14-15, 16, 24, 25, 29, 30, 123-29, 131, 202, 203
3:5-6	110	3:13-15	15, 124-26, 127
3:5	12, 13, 105, 109, 110, 111, 112, 113, 117, 126, 163	3:13-14	124
		3:13	14, 15, 123, 124, 127, 128, 129, 142
3:6	12, 13, 105-6, 109, 110, 111, 112, 113, 117, 166	3:14-15	29, 146, 148, 178, 184
		3:14	14, 24, 29, 123, 124, 125-26, 127, 128, 129, 131, 151, 152, 155, 156, 163, 165, 166, 170, 189, 190, 191, 197, 203
3:7-12	13-14, 15, 24, 25, 114-22, 124, 131, 202, 203		
3:7-9	14, 115-18, 119		
3:7-8	115	3:15	14, 123, 124, 125, 127, 128, 129, 144, 147, 151, 152, 155, 156, 166, 170, 182, 185, 190
3:7	13, 14, 114, 116, 119, 120, 121, 122, 126, 131, 143, 163, 175, 183, 196, 199		
3:8	13, 14, 114, 115, 117, 118, 119, 120, 121-22, 193-94	3:16	14, 15, 24, 29, 123, 126-27, 128, 129, 131, 154, 161, 163, 169, 182, 185, 203
3:9	13, 14, 114, 115-16, 117, 118, 119, 120, 121, 122, 141, 151, 155, 166, 175, 183, 193, 194	3:17	14-15, 16, 123, 127-28, 129, 131, 161, 167, 169, 170, 173n168, 174, 182, 203
3:10-12	14, 119-21	3:18-24	15-16, 17, 24, 25, 130-38, 140, 202, 203
3:10-11	29		
3:10	13, 14, 114, 118, 119, 120, 121, 122, 125,	3:18-19	16, 131-32, 134

3:18	15, 16, 29, 130, 131, 132, 133, 134, 137, 143, 178, 184, 196, 199	4:2	16-17, 24, 139, 140, 141, 142, 143, 144, 146, 147, 148, 177, 184, 203
3:19-20	132, 133	4:3	17, 139, 140, 142-43, 144, 146, 147, 148, 158n159, 163, 169, 176, 183, 194, 196, 198, 199
3:19	15, 16, 29, 130, 132, 132n133, 133, 134, 137, 138, 146, 148, 178, 184		
3:20	15, 16, 130, 132, 132n133, 133, 137, 144, 147, 151, 155, 181	4:4	17, 139, 143-44, 146, 147, 151, 158n159, 163, 169, 176, 181, 183, 196, 199
3:21-22	16, 133-34	4:5-6	17, 144-47
3:21	15, 16, 130, 133, 137, 141, 150, 162, 188	4:5	17, 139, 144, 145, 146, 147, 194, 198
3:22-24	27	4:6	17, 29, 139, 144-45, 146, 147, 148, 150, 151, 159, 168, 177, 184, 189, 194, 198, 203, 205
3:22	15-16, 130, 133, 134, 137, 175, 183, 188, 189, 193, 196, 197, 199		
3:23-24	16, 134-37	4:7-12	18, 20, 24, 25, 149-56, 158, 202, 204
3:23	16, 24, 29, 130, 131, 134, 135, 136, 137, 138, 141, 144, 146, 147, 148, 151, 155, 156, 161, 162, 166, 167, 169, 170, 174, 175, 176, 178, 181, 182, 183, 184, 185, 188, 189, 193, 195, 197, 203, 205		
		4:7-8	18, 150-51, 153
		4:7	18, 29, 149, 150, 151, 153, 154, 155, 156, 161, 167, 170, 174, 175, 182, 183, 204
		4:8	18, 149, 150, 151, 153, 155, 156, 161, 166, 204
3:24	16, 17, 130-31, 134, 135, 136, 137, 138, 140, 141, 146, 148, 155, 156, 159, 161, 168, 175, 177, 181, 183, 185, 193, 194, 198, 205	4:9	18, 19, 24, 149, 150, 151-52, 153, 154, 155, 156, 160, 168, 173n168, 174, 175, 176, 176n171, 182, 183, 184, 204
		4:10	18, 24, 149, 150, 153, 156, 160, 166, 168, 170, 176, 184, 204
4:1-6	16-17, 18, 24, 25, 139-48, 150, 202, 203	4:11-12	18, 29, 153-55
4:1-3	17, 140-43, 144	4:11	18, 149, 153, 154, 156, 166, 170, 204
4:1-2	140, 141		
4:1	16, 17, 139, 140, 141, 142, 144, 146, 147, 150, 152, 176, 183, 194, 196, 198, 199	4:12	18, 20, 149, 153, 154, 155, 156, 158, 160, 162, 168, 169, 194, 198, 204

1 John (cont.)

4:13–5:2	19, 20, 23, 25, 157-71, 173, 203, 204	5:3	20, 21, 23, 172, 173, 174, 175, 178, 183, 193, 204
4:13-16	20, 158-61		
4:13	19, 20, 157, 158, 159, 160, 161, 168, 171, 177, 194, 198, 205	5:4-5	175-76, 183
		5:4	20, 21, 172, 173, 174, 175, 176, 178, 183
4:14	19, 157, 158, 159, 160, 168, 169, 176, 177, 184, 204	5:5-6	173, 174, 178
		5:5	20, 21, 172, 173, 174, 176, 178, 180, 181, 182, 183, 184, 185
4:15	19, 20, 157, 158, 159, 160, 161, 168		
4:16	19, 20, 157, 158, 159, 161, 162, 167, 169, 170	5:6	20, 21, 29, 172, 176, 177-78, 180, 181, 182, 184, 185, 204, 205
		5:7-12	21, 178-82
4:17-18	20, 161-63, 164		
4:17	19, 20, 24, 157, 158, 161, 162, 163, 164, 169, 170, 204	5:7-9	178, 179
		5:7-8	179
		5:7	20, 172, 179, 180, 181, 184
4:18	19, 20, 157, 162, 163, 164, 169, 170	5:8	20, 21, 172, 178, 180, 181, 184, 185
4:19–5:2	20, 21, 164-68		
4:19-21	29	5:9	20-21, 172, 178, 179, 180, 181, 185
4:19-20	164, 165		
4:19	19, 157, 165, 170	5:10	21, 172-73, 178, 179, 181, 182, 185
4:20-5:2	178, 184		
4:20	19, 20, 157-58, 164, 165, 166, 167, 170	5:11-13	29
		5:11-12	179, 180
4:21-5:2	164, 165	5:11	21, 173, 178, 179, 180, 181, 182, 185, 190, 194, 195, 198, 204
4:21	19, 20, 27, 158, 165, 166, 167, 170, 189, 196, 197, 199, 204		
		5:12	21, 22, 173, 178, 182, 185, 187
5:1-2	29	5:13-21	21-22, 23, 25, 186-99, 203, 205
5:1	19, 20, 158, 165, 167, 170, 175, 176, 183, 184		
		5:13-15	22, 187-89, 192
5:2-3	27	5:13-14	187
5:2	19, 20, 21, 158, 165, 167, 171, 173, 175, 183	5:13	21, 22, 186, 187, 188, 189, 192, 194, 197, 198
5:3-12	20-21, 22, 23, 25, 172-85, 187, 203, 204	5:14	21-22, 186, 187, 188, 190
		5:15	22, 186, 187, 188, 189, 190, 192, 196, 197, 199
5:3-6	21, 173-77		
5:3-4	173, 174	5:16-17	22, 191-92

5:16	22, 29, 186, 189-90, 191, 192, 197, 198, 205	5:19	22, 186, 192, 193, 194, 198
		5:20-21	192, 193
5:17	22, 23, 186, 187, 191, 197, 205	5:20	22, 29, 186-87, 192, 193, 194, 195, 198, 205
5:18-21	22, 192-97		
5:18	22, 186, 192-93, 194, 198	5:21	22, 28, 187, 192, 195, 197, 198, 199, 205

2 John

1:1-13	5, 45-56		120, 122, 131, 136, 138, 178, 184
1:1-8	6, 46-51, 53	1:6	5, 45, 46, 47, 48, 50, 51n45, 61, 66, 78-79, 96, 102, 136, 138
1:1-5	68, 70, 76, 87		
1:1-3	46, 47		
1:1-2	47	1:7-11	56, 202
1:1	1, 5, 6, 27, 29, 45, 47, 48, 49, 50, 51, 51n45, 53, 55, 56, 59, 63, 200, 201, 202	1:7-8	46, 47
		1:7	5, 6, 45, 47, 51, 52, 53, 54, 56, 68, 69, 96-97, 98, 99, 102, 104, 116, 141-42, 143, 147, 196, 201
1:2	5, 29, 45, 47, 49, 51, 52, 68, 97		
1:3-5	56, 201, 202	1:8	5, 6, 45, 48, 51, 53, 55, 196
1:3	5, 27, 29, 45, 47, 49, 51, 53, 55, 60, 64, 97, 98	1:9	5, 6, 45, 52-53, 54, 56, 63, 99, 102, 103, 104, 143, 147, 201
1:4-6	27		
1:4-5	46, 56, 201	1:10-13	6, 53-56
1:4	5, 6, 29, 45, 47, 50, 51, 53, 54, 55, 64, 66, 136, 138, 178, 184	1:10-11	55
		1:10	5, 6, 27, 46, 48, 53, 54, 55, 96
1:5-7	75, 87	1:11	5, 6, 46, 53, 54, 63
1:5-6	160, 169	1:12-13	53, 54
1:5	5, 29, 45, 46, 47, 50, 51, 51n45, 53, 54, 55, 56, 63, 64, 66, 67, 75, 78, 81, 87, 96, 102,	1:12	5, 6, 46, 48, 53, 54, 55, 56, 64, 184, 202
		1:13	1, 5, 6, 27, 46, 53, 55, 56, 59, 63, 200, 202

3 John

1:1-8	2-3, 31, 43, 201	1:1	1, 2, 3, 26, 29, 31, 32, 33, 35, 43, 47, 48, 56, 59, 78, 200, 201
1:1-3	3, 32-34		

3 John (cont.)

1:2	2, 3, 27, 31, 32, 33, 34, 35, 39, 78	1:9-15	4, 36, 43, 201
1:5-8	34-36	1:9-10	4, 36-39, 40, 43, 201
1:3-8	26	1:9	4, 26, 36, 37, 38, 40, 41, 42, 43, 56, 59, 64, 201
1:3-6	26		
1:3-4	50		
1:3	3-4, 29, 31, 32, 33, 34, 35, 37, 41, 64, 81, 87	1:10	4-5, 26, 36, 37, 38, 39, 40, 42, 81, 87
1:4	3, 29, 31, 34, 48, 55, 64, 66	1:11	4, 36, 39-40, 52, 78
1:5-8	3	1:12-15	4, 40-43
1:5	3, 31, 35, 38, 39, 78, 81, 87	1:12	4, 29, 36, 40, 41, 42, 43, 59, 98, 201
1:6	3, 31, 35, 37, 38, 41	1:13-14	54, 56, 202
1:7-8	56, 202	1:13	4, 36, 40-41, 42
1:7	3, 31, 35, 51, 54	1:14	4, 36, 41, 42
1:8	3, 26, 29, 31, 35, 36, 38, 39, 41, 43, 51, 54, 131, 201	1:15	4, 27, 36, 40, 41, 42, 43, 44, 49, 55, 56, 201, 202

Author Index

Akin, Daniel L., 48n42, 49n43
Balz, Horst, 109n107
Beale, Gregory K., 96n98
Bigalke, Ron J., 2n5
Brickle, Jeffrey E, 64n63
Brown, Raymond E., 2n5, 35n24, 36n25, 69n67, 74n71, 118n116, 124n121, 134n137, 161n160, 177n174, 196n195
Byron, J., 121n119
Campbell, B. L., 26n13
Carnazzo, Sebastian A., 176n171
Carson, D. A., 161n161
Clark, D. J., 2n 5, 42n34
Combs, W. W., 64n60
Connell, M. F., 97n101
Culy, Martin M., 85n86, 111n111
De Waal Dryden, J., 118n116
Do, J. T., 74n72, 75n74
Edwards, Ruth B., 1n3
Frick, P., 152n152
Glasscock, E., 69n68
Griffith, Terry, 197n196
Heckel, T. K., 65n64
Heil, John Paul, 2n6, 26n10, 176n171, 177n173
Hengel, Martin, 1n3
Hills, Julian, 197n196
Hofius, Otfried, 69n67
Horsley, Richard A., 1n3
Houlden, J. L., 61n57
Jensen, Matthew D., 2n5

Jobes, Karen H., 1n1, 118n116, 118-19n117, 125n123, 127n126, 128n128, 133n135, 134n136, 143n144, 143n145, 152n151, 155n157, 176n170, 181n178, 190n186
Johnson, Luke Timothy, 1n1, 26n12, 37n28
Jung, C. W., 132n134
Keener, Craig S., 112n112
Köstenberger, Andreas J., 28n15
Kruse, Colin G., 2n5, 52n49
Lee, Dorothy, 28n15
Lieu, Judith M., 2n5, 60n54, 77n76, 82n83, 85n87, 87n90, 90n93, 96n98, 97-98n102, 103n103, 111n110, 118n116, 120n118, 121n119, 126n124, 127n125, 131n130, 131n131, 142n143, 144n146, 152n153, 166n164, 167n165, 177n172, 182n181, 194n190, 195n191, 195n193, 196n194
Lorencin, I., 26n11
Marshall, I . Howard, 2n5, 79n79, 86n89, 132n132
Marulli, L., 26n13, 38n31
McLean, J. A., 197n196
Merkle, Benjamin L., 197n196
Michaels, J. Ramsey, 181n179
Mitchell, Margaret M., 38n29
Moberly, R. W. L., 141n141

Moloney, Francis J., 29n16
Morgan-Wynne, John, 29n16
Morgen, Michèle, 65n63, 152n151
Neufeld, Dietmar, 38n32
Olsson, Birger, 35n23, 42n36, 48n40,
    54n50, 60n55, 62n59, 64n62,
    81n81, 84n84, 90n94, 91n95,
    97n102, 109n108, 110n109,
    111n111, 117n114, 117n115,
    121n119, 137n138, 142n142,
    153n155, 161n160, 180n176,
    182n180, 194n189
Painter, John, 34n22, 37n28, 51n45,
    54n51, 67n65, 91n95, 110n109
Roitto, Rikard, 69n68
Schnackenburg, Rudolf, 2n5, 69n67
Schnelle, Udo, 27n14
Schuchard, Bruce G., 1n1, 36n25,
    37n27, 37n28, 38n30, 42n34,
    48n39, 48n41, 52n48, 54n50,
    61n58, 65n63, 65n64, 78n77,
    78n78, 84n85, 85n86, 85n87,
    96n99, 97n102, 107n106,
    109n107, 117n114, 118n116,
    118n117, 127n127, 141n140,
    146n147, 146n148, 153-55,
    163n163, 178n175, 180n177,
    190n187
Shelfer, L., 74n73

Sloyan, Gerard S., 195n193
Smalley, Stephen S., 27n14, 33n20,
    42n35, 48n42, 49n43, 55n52,
    62n59, 64n61, 68n66, 90n92,
    92n96, 97n101, 125n123,
    141n141, 167n166, 175n169
Tan, Randall K. J., 192n188
Thatcher, Thomas, 176n171
Thettayil, Benny, 28n15
Thomas, John Christopher, 2n5
Trebilco, Paul, 1n2, 2n4, 33n20
Voelz, James W., 78n78
Von Wahlde, Urban C., 2n5, 107n105
Wallace, Daniel B., 111n111
Watson, Duane F., 65n63, 197n196
Wendland, E. R., 52n49
Witherington, Ben, 37n28, 51n47,
    54n50
Yarbrough, Robert W., 1n1, 2n 5, 35n23,
    37n28, 43n37, 51n46, 55n52,
    64n62, 69n69, 74n73, 75n74,
    75n75, 77n76, 81n80, 84n85,
    85n87, 85n88, 97n100, 103n103,
    109n107, 117n114, 125n122,
    142n143, 151n150, 153n154,
    155n156, 162n162, 181n178,
    188n183, 189n185, 190n187,
    195n192, 197n196

www.ingramcontent.com/pod-product-compliance
Lightning Source LLC
Chambersburg PA
CBHW022015220426
43663CB00007B/1086